MARGARET ATWOOD AND THE LABOUR OF LITERARY CELEBRITY

For every famous author there are many individuals working behind the scene to promote and maintain celebrity status. This timely and thoughtful book considers the particular case of internationally renowned writer Margaret Atwood and the active agents working in concert with her, including her assistants and office staff, her publicists, her literary agents, and her editors. Lorraine York explores the ways in which the careers of such writers are managed and maintained and the extent to which literary celebrity spawns a constant tension between their need for solitude for creative purposes and the give-and-take of the business of being a writer of significant public stature.

Making extensive use of unpublished material in the Margaret Atwood Papers at the University of Toronto, York demonstrates the extent to which celebrity writers must embrace, *and* at the same time protect themselves from, the demands of the literary world, including by participating in – or even inventing – new forms of technology that facilitate communication from a slight remove. This informative study points to the ways in which literary celebrity is the result not only of creativity and hard work, but also of an ongoing collaborative effort among professionals to help maintain the writer's place in the public eye.

LORRAINE YORK is the Senator William McMaster Chair in Canadian Literature and Culture and a professor in the Department of English and Cultural Studies at McMaster University.

Margaret Atwood and the Labour of Literary Celebrity

LORRAINE YORK

UNIVERSITY OF TORONTO PRESS
Toronto Buffalo London

Toronto Buffalo London
www.utppublishing.com
Printed in Canada

ISBN 978-1-4426-4613-1 (cloth)
ISBN 978-1-4426-1423-9 (paper)

Printed on acid-free, 100% post-consumer
recycled paper with vegetable-based inks.

Library and Archives Canada Cataloguing in Publication

York, Lorraine M. (Lorraine Mary), 1958–
Margaret Atwood and the labour of literary celebrity / Lorraine York.

Includes bibliographical references and index.
ISBN 978-1-4426-4613-1 (bound)   ISBN 978-1-4426-1423-9 (pbk.)

1. Atwood, Margaret, 1939–. 2. Authors, Canadian (English) – 20th century – Biography. 3. Celebrities – Canada – Biography. I. Title.

PS8501.T86Z634 2013   C818'.54   C2013-900425-4

University of Toronto Press acknowledges the financial assistance to its publishing program of the Canada Council for the Arts and the Ontario Arts Council.

This book has been published with the help of a grant from the Canadian Federation for the Humanities and Social Sciences, through the Awards to Scholarly Publications Program, using funds provided by the Social Sciences and Humanities Research Council of Canada.

University of Toronto Press acknowledges the financial support of the Government of Canada through the Canada Book Fund for its publishing activities.

Contents

Acknowledgments

This study of a collaborative industry owes many thanks to a little collaborative collective of my own: fewer in number and complexity than the Atwood collective, but deserving of my warmest gratitude. First and foremost, I thank Siobhan McMenemy, acquisitions editor at the University of Toronto Press, for in the spirit of this book that foregrounds the contributions of editors and other cultural agents, I think she must be thanked first and not last. Her critical perceptiveness and amazing skills of organization and communication brought me back again to the University of Toronto Press, and her generous sharing of her expertise as an editor and her knowledge of the publishing world have meant a great deal to me in this project. I also thank Matthew Kudelka for his incisive and witty copy-editing, and Frances Mundy for seeing the book through production with a steady hand.

I am very grateful to Margaret Atwood for permission to quote from her archive at the Thomas Fisher Rare Book Library, University of Toronto, and for her generous reminder about members of her editorial team who should be included in my account. Thanks to the Margaret Atwood archivists at the Fisher Library, who were, as always, models of organization and helpfulness. I have received assistance over and above the call of duty from assistants at O.W. Toad, particularly Laura Stenberg and Sarah Webster. Many thanks to Sarah Cooper, for showing such enthusiasm for the project.

For their contributions to a book that is, in many ways, about unsung labour, I thank the Press's anonymous readers; this is work that is often unrecognized and simply added to the increasingly heavy workloads of academics. This book is better for their suggestions. I benefited, too from the suggestions of audiences at the Association for Canadian College and University Teachers of English's annual meeting in 2009, where I presented work on Atwood and literary agents; the MLA Margaret Atwood Society session in 2009, where I spoke on Atwood and digital media; and the 2012 MLA session on social media, where I shared work derived from chapter 4 on Atwood and Twitter.

Speaking of cultural agents, this book would not be here without the extensive labour and support of several brilliant research assistants: Erin Aspenlieder, Paul Huebener, Katja Lee, Sharlee Reimer, and Pamela Ingleton. I am honoured to have worked with you, and your wisdom and labour are everywhere apparent in this work.

A special thank you to Professor Reingard Nischik, who generously spoke with me while I was on a research trip in Germany in 2009, and who extended warm hospitality in Konstanz.

At McMaster, I have benefited from a supportive community in the Department of English and Cultural Studies. Thanks to Peter Walmsley, our chair, who does so much to support our intellectual lives every day. Grateful thanks to colleague-friends Daniel Coleman, Sarah Brophy, Katja Lee, Ron Granofsky, Chandrima Chakraborty, Roger Hyman, and Grace Kehler, and to friend extraordinaire Lynn Shakinovsky.

My gratitude to the Faculty of Humanities at McMaster, and its Dean, Suzanne Crosta, for a Senator William McMaster Chair in Canadian Literature and Culture. Thanks to this support, I was able to complete this book ahead of schedule.

I received support for this project, in the form of a Standard Research Grant, from the Social Sciences and Humanities Research Council of Canada. My thanks.

My family has been a source of support and cheer. Many thanks to Anna Ross for the dedicated photographic sleuthing and Twitter expertise, and to Michael Ross, for reading all, commenting, critiquing, encouraging, and cracking me up.

MARGARET ATWOOD AND THE LABOUR OF LITERARY CELEBRITY

Introduction: The Dead Moose and the Publishing Pie

When we conceptualise celebrity as something to be professionally managed, rather than discursively deconstructed, we think about it differently.

Graeme Turner, *Understanding Celebrity*

In the summer of 2011, Margaret Atwood's visibility as a Canadian literary celebrity came under sustained and energetic public scrutiny. It all began on 21 July, when she marshalled her considerable ranks of followers – 225,302 strong (Samson) – on Twitter to fight proposed cuts to Toronto's library system. The city had just received a report from its hired consultants KPMG (whose corporate motto is, ominously, "Cutting Through Complexity" [kpmg.com]), which recommended that the system be privatized, that cuts be made to library outreach services and programs, and that some branches possibly be closed. Atwood retweeted in response: "Toronto's libraries are under threat of privatization. Tell city council to keep them public now. ourpubliclibrary.to." This was enough to crash the server of the Toronto Public Library Workers Union CUPE 4948, whose petition, "Project Rescue," was linked to the tweet (Rider). CUPE 4948 managed to remount its petition after a thirty-minute repair, and by the next day, 22 July, 17,300 people had already signed (Rider). By the following Tuesday, 26 July, that number had risen to over 24,000.

This instance of Atwood's online activism (a phenomenon I will consider in some detail in chapter 4) brought her into direct conflict with Toronto's fiscally and socially conservative mayor Rob Ford, and especially with his brother, Toronto city councillor and close adviser Doug Ford. In defending the report, Doug Ford had opined that Toronto had too many library branches, pointing to his own ward of Etobicoke, which boasted more libraries, he claimed, than Tim Hortons donut shops (that iconically "Canadian" business that trades heavily on its connections with other national emblems such as hockey ... and the military ("Tim Hortons & Canadian Forces Announce Opening in Afghanistan"). Of course, he was wrong. His ward contains a grand total of thirty-nine Tim Hortons outlets and thirteen branches of the Toronto Public Library, placing the libraries at a 3:1 numerical disadvantage. Tongue planted firmly in cheek, Maureen O'Reilly, chair of local 4948, placed the visibility of Canada's premier literary celebrity up against that of the donut and coffee chain:

> It's a huge plus for our campaign to be recognized by such a prominent writer in Canada. We have other initiatives reaching out to the writer community, so her recognition of this will help us there, and the cause we're fighting for. She may not be as big an icon, to some, as Tim Hortons, but she's a huge literary hero and her support is amazing. (Rider)

This passage balances various levels of social visibility: as a "prominent writer," Atwood is cast as possessing a considerable amount of cultural capital. This capital is, in turn, set beside the national iconicity of Tim Hortons, which is positioned as a more broadly recognized popular brand. O'Reilly nods to the broader demographic sweep of Tim Hortons's fame and implicitly critiques its popular origins ("to some") but then rhetorically pumps up Atwood's cultural capital in order to suggest that, within the field of literary production, Atwood is a star: "a huge literary hero." Pierre Bourdieu's concepts of cultural capital (prestige, respect) and economic capital (money) are fairly dancing around each other in this passage, as they do in the literary celebrity of Margaret Atwood. Atwood, for her part, did a classic job of deconstructing the very opposition that Ford had divisively set up: "Twin Fordmayer [Atwood's satirical name for the Ford brothers] seems to think that those who eat Timbits (like me) don't read, can't count, & are stupid, eh?" ("Margaret Atwood Tweets to Save Toronto Libraries").

The debate over Atwood's public visibility, however, was just getting warmed up. In reaction to the massive response to Atwood's online appeals, Doug Ford made a singularly rash public comment: "Well good luck to Margaret Atwood. I don't even know her. If she walked by me, I wouldn't have a clue who she is. She's not down here, she's not dealing with the problem. Tell her to go run in the next election and get democratically elected and we'd be more than happy to sit down and listen to Margaret Atwood" (Daubs). And with that ill-advised salvo, an international news story was born: newspapers and radio stations from Montreal to New York to the UK picked up and reported the tale. The large book chain Chapters-Indigo sided with Atwood, tweeting the link to Atwood's call for petition signatures: "Know this woman? http://ow.ly/50W6K Indigo loves Canada's libraries! Thru Jul. 31 show your library card in-store for 30% off @MargaretAtwood." Canadian filmmaker Norman Jewison brought his considerable international celebrity to the cause in a CBC radio interview, wondering aloud about Doug Ford – "Where does he live – in a hole?" – and making a larger connection between this verbal contretemps and Conservative arts policy: "I felt that all Canadian artists were betrayed by a statement like that" (Rider). Even the *Toronto Sun*, known for its consistent support of Ford-ist policies, admitted that "it's probably best not to take on literary giant Margaret Atwood in a war of words" (Peat). "With a single tweet," wrote the *Globe and Mail*'s John Barber, "she rocked city hall" ("Should Writers Run for Office …?"). Faced with such overwhelmingly bad press, Doug Ford retracted his statement while retaining its divisive pitting of cultural elites against the metropolitan Everyman: "Everyone knows who Margaret

Atwood is. But if she were to come up to 98 per cent of the people, they wouldn't know who she was. But I think she's a great writer and I look forward to her input" (Rider). Ford, for all his apparent contrition, held tight to the harmful distinction between artists or consumers of art and "real" people that Atwood had handily demolished. As Atwood reiterated to Linda Nguyen of the *Ottawa Citizen*, "all this babble about being intelligentsia and elitist, that's crap. [Library users] are not people with humongously rich incomes. To start off by trying to drive a wedge between people who drink Tim Hortons and people who use the library – well it's the same people" (Nguyen).

I narrate this Canadian- and even Toronto-centric story in such detail because it sets the stage for the competing ideas about writing, celebrity, economy, labour, and visibility that are at the heart of this book. In claiming not to recognize, not to "see" Atwood, Doug Ford was, in effect, attempting to delegitimize the social power and labour of a literary celebrity. If celebrities are, as many theorists have mused, primarily involved in an economy of visibility (Rein et al.), then the most invalidating charge that can be turned against the celebrity is that of invisibility: "If she walked by me, I wouldn't have a clue who she is." And it is not only Atwood's face that Councillor Ford would not discern; he couples his non-recognition of Atwood's person with a non-recognition of her labour: "Tell her to go run in the next election and get democratically elected and we'd be more than happy to sit down and listen to Margaret Atwood." Implicit in Ford's intemperate rant is this question: What does she do that is of importance anyway, this Margaret Atwood, this artist?

In my previous book, *Literary Celebrity in Canada*, I examined the preoccupations, themes, and tensions attending the experience of literary fame as it was experienced by earlier generations of Canadian writers such as Stephen Leacock, Pauline Johnson, Mazo de la Roche, and L.M. Montgomery, as well as by three more recent writers: Michael Ondaatje, Carol Shields, and Atwood. When I turned my attention to Atwood, I readily perceived a contest between privacy and publicity, between national and international celebrity status, but I also noted how very early in her career, she was recognized and endlessly reproduced as a visual spectacle. As early as 1973, William French wrote that "she has become something of a celebrity, a visible public figure" (28). Years later, in 1999, Roy MacSkimming, researching his valuable book on the Canadian publishing industry, *The Perilous Trade,* sat down to speak with Atwood and her partner Graeme Gibson about those very days. Recalling the publication in 1972 of her handbook to Canadian literature, MacSkimming asked Atwood what impact its publication had on her. Without blinking an eye, Atwood spoke of her celebrity: "It made me extremely well known very suddenly." "Almost more than you could manage at that point?," MacSkimming probed, to which Atwood replied "No doubt more" ("The Perilous Trade Conversations" 22). By the end of that decade, in 1979, Atwood would recount to Roslyn Nudell of the *Winnipeg Free Press* that "I've been recognized, even in places like India and Afghanistan" (35). But not in 2011, by a councillor in her own city.

Besides Atwood's swift absorption into a visual economy of celebrity, the other characteristic of her literary celebrity that I took note of was her remarkable degree of professionalization, at a time when many writers in Canada had little idea about what professionalization entailed. I was aware of earlier writers, like Leacock, adopting professional strategies and associations, but Atwood's degree of professional organization was of a greater – indeed, industrial – order: in 1976, she became the first Canadian writer, to my knowledge, to incorporate herself as a company, O.W. Toad. The implications of this move, and the expansion of Atwood's global career in the years since 1976, call out, I feel, for special study, since the growth of what Graham Huggan calls "Atwood, Inc." poses some new and intriguing questions about literary celebrity considered as an amalgamation of the visual economy of fame and industrial labour relationships. So although Atwood's career is indeed exceptional in its degree of industrial organization, at least in Canada, the complicated exchanges between art and commerce that I discern in her career are fairly typical of the field of literary publishing in general.

Many considerations of celebrity, whether academic or popular, focus intently on the individual, or on celebrity as the public performance of subjectivities. My analysis of Atwood, by contrast, offers an occasion to shift the theoretical paradigm more towards celebrity as the product of the labour of many other agents in dialogue with a celebrated individual: in the literary field, this means editors, agents, office staff, publishers, publicists, and the like. I find that this focus on the industrial relations that enable and reproduce literary celebrity, rather than diffusing or erasing the labour of the artist, highlights that labour precisely because we witness its articulation in dialogue.

To be fair, in the midst of all of its intense – not to say obsessive – scrutiny of the individual, celebrity theory has, at moments, been attentive to collective labour. There are suggestive moments in the critical literature, threads that may usefully be pulled out and examined, the better to understand celebrity in its broader dimensions, as a phenomenon that happens not only to individuals but to a whole web of cultural workers. Richard Dyer's volumes *Stars* (1979) and *Heavenly Bodies* (1986) were fundamental to the formation of a more systemic analysis of celebrity, and while Dyer's focus on the range of meanings connected to a star text was salutary and welcome, it did tend to direct future work to a semiotic reading of particular stars (of a sort that Dyer himself performed brilliantly in the cases of Judy Garland, Paul Robeson, and Marilyn Monroe in *Heavenly Bodies*). As Su Holmes and Sean Redmond put it in their introduction to *Framing Celebrity*, Dyer's work focused on celebrity as a discourse of the self (9). If one returns to *Stars* and to *Heavenly Bodies*, though, there is also plentiful evidence that Dyer gave thought to stars as a (contested) site of labour. In the former study, commenting on a magazine spread showing the "awful factories" in which screen stars toil – that is, handsomely appointed dressing rooms – Dyer shows how the labour of stars is consistently denied, rendered as its opposite: leisure. And in *Heavenly Bodies*, he astutely observes that (cinematic) "stars are involved in making themselves into commodities; they are both labour and the thing that labour produces" (5). Out of that duplicity, for Dyer, emerges both contradiction and tension: an alienation between labour and product. More recent critics have imported this formulation into the field of literary celebrity. Thus, Tom Mole, writing of that ultimate in literary celebrities, Lord Byron, echoes Dyer's insight: "The celebrity experiences the subjective trauma of commodity capitalism in a particularly acute fashion. He is both a producer of commodities and himself, in a sense, a commodity" (4) – a powerful internalization of the classic Marxist notion of alienated labour.

It is interesting, from my perspective, that these discussions of labour and celebrity, too, circle back to the self as the primary theatre of action. In P. David Marshall's brilliant book *Celebrity and Power*, as well, the social relations and ideological struggles endemic to celebrity play out on the battlefield of the subjective: "The term celebrity has come to embody the ambiguity of the public forms of subjectivity under capitalism" (4). And while these discussions are both crucial and perceptive, there is room for considering other types of labour involved in the social transactions that constitute celebrity: labour supplied by other agents in the social production of art. When Paul MacDonald contributed his supplementary chapter for the second edition of Richard Dyer's *Stars*, one of the main subjects that he signalled, implicitly, as supplementary to Dyer's theories was labour, but he tended to assume that the labour at issue was still that of the celebrity individual. Melding Dyer's theories with film historian Richard DeCordova's description of how, in early-twentieth-century Hollywood, a discourse of creative "acting" took over from a more passive language of "posing" for pictures, MacDonald observes how "differences in the ways work is represented will produce professional inequalities between performers; generally the work of stars enters discourse while the work of 'unknown' performers goes unrecognised" (195). I would argue that a far more glaring instance of professional inequality and silenced labour in the field of cinema involves not the supporting actors but the editors, sound technicians, set designers, script supervisors, prop masters, and carpenters. Although these jobs are at least named and distinguished in great detail in the field of film, and although some are accorded a measure of celebrity visibility in the Hollywood system in the form of Technical Achievement Oscars, the names of their practitioners skim by our eyes rapidly at the end of a film, and the public recognition of some of them on Oscar night provokes many a yawn and complaint on the part of a bored home viewing audience waiting up late to see who wins the major acting honours.[1] In this study, located not in cinema but in the literary field, the "unknown performers" whose labour rarely enters discourse are not the fellow artists who inhabit the differentiated labour market that MacDonald describes; they are, like the cinema's technical workers, agents in allied industries – publishing, publicity, marketing.

Another way that labour has been implicated in accounts of celebrity is as an economic factor affecting the production of stars. In "Articulating Stardom," Barry King argues that the overabundance of actors on the market at any one time results in idiosyncratic personal qualities being overvalued in hiring decisions – overvalued, that is, in relation to thespian abilities. This preference for the actor as a personality over what the actor can do, King suggests, produces celebrity (178). Again, the primary assumption seems to be that the only relevant labour involved in the production of celebrity belongs, if even in an alienated form, to the celebrity.

Revisiting Dyer's work, Graeme Turner begins to pry open previous ideas about the labour of celebrity to envision additional actors; he builds upon Dyer's perception that celebrities are both "cultural workers" who "are paid for their labour" (34) and also "property" (*Heavenly Bodies* 5): "a financial asset to those who stand to gain from their commercialization

1 The current tendency to shrink credit screens at the end of television broadcasts, rendering them nearly illegible in order to accommodate longer commercial breaks, is another case in point.

– networks, radio companies, producers, agents, managers" (34–5). It is this fuller consideration of the diversity of celebrity labour that I examine in relation to the literary field: the literary celebrity labours to write; labours further to perform socially both by publishing and by appearing publicly as a celebrity writer; and, in fulfilling both roles, enlists the labour of others in turn. The complexities of these three degrees of labour, and their interactions, absorb me in the career of Margaret Atwood and, by extension, in the literary field at large.

This extended labour of celebrity is implicit in many basic definitions of the phenomenon. Richard Dyer, for instance, defines celebrity as "everything that is publicly available about stars" (*Heavenly Bodies* 2). And Tom Mole, assessing the literary celebrity phenomenon of the nineteenth century, renders some of this implicit industry – the labour of making "everything … available" – explicit; he defines celebrity as "a cultural apparatus consisting of three elements: an individual, an industry, and an audience" (1). In my study of Atwood's twentieth- and twenty-first-century literary celebrity, I focus especially on the second of these, the industry, as it acts in concert with the first and the third of Mole's elements: the individual celebrity and the audience.

It is rare to see that second element of the celebrity apparatus – industry – treated in a sustained or focused way in academic studies of celebrity. When Graeme Turner, Frances Bonner, and P. David Marshall introduced their chapter on "Producing Celebrity" in their 2000 study of Australian *Fame Games*, they hoped to mitigate this critical paucity, "to make these activities" of publicists, agents, and managers "more visible" (60). Four years later, when Graeme Turner offered a brief analysis of Hollywood film and television agents and managers in his critical guide, *Understanding Celebrity*, he could still claim that he was supplying "information that rarely finds its way into analysis of the production of celebrity, or of the wealth of texts this production process employs" (41). The significance of this inclusion goes far beyond the filling in of an informational gap, however; as Turner goes on to suggest, thinking about the operations of publicity and promotions industries alters the ways in which we theorize about the celebrity phenomenon itself; we can potentially see "both the ambiguities and the power of celebrity as a component of our public culture … a little clearer" (136). In this study of the many industries that circulate and participate in the literary celebrity of Margaret Atwood, I do perceive many an ambiguity – particularly involving the interlaced relationship between art and the market – but I also find, as Turner promises, many a sign of the agency of celebrity, especially the agency of *this* celebrity.

The major reason why relatively little attention has been paid to the workings of the celebrity culture industries is their own complicity in silenced labour. Su Holmes and Sean Redmond, in 2007, suggest as much in their introductory comments to their *Stardom and Celebrity* reader's section on "Producing Fame": "there remains a larger drive toward concealing the labour that produces the phenomenon, and for some time, academic work seemed to replicate this structure, rendering the work of producing fame invisible" (189). A possible objection to this claim is the prevalence, from 2000 on, of representations of star-making processes, most frequently in the form of reality television shows such as *The Apprentice* and *Pop Idol* and their numerous spinoffs. After all, in their introduction to *Framing Celebrity*, Holmes and Redmond seem, initially, to contradict their own claims about the concealment of celebrity industrial labour: they observe that reality television and similar vehicles prioritize "the 'authorship' of the apparatus over the celebrities it produces, reflecting the argument that the publicity machine has become a highly visible player in the cultural fabrication of celebrity" (12). But such representations are skewed in many ways, and their representations of the labour of supporting workers in the celebrity industries are grossly overshadowed by representations of the celebrity aspirants as having particular personal qualities that qualify – or disqualify – them for star status, so it seems very doubtful to me that the "'authorship' of the apparatus" has overwhelmed the celebrity subject being produced.

Slowly, though, considerations of the celebrity industry have started to enter academic analysis, laying the groundwork for a potential theory of celebrity industrial labour. Rosemary Coombe, working from the philosopher of intellectual property, E.C. Hettinger, who warns that "simply identifying the value a laborer's labor adds to the world with the market value of the resulting product ignores the vast contributions of others," makes the parallel argument about celebrity authorship: "The star image," she concludes, "is authored by multitudes of persons engaged in diverse activities" (95).

Not always is the mention of these multitudes so value-neutral; in fact, a marked tendency is to follow in the long-standing tradition of seeing all celebrity production as the false manufacture of hollow goods – a tradition that reaches back to Horkheimer and Adorno in the mid-1940s and to historian Daniel Boorstin's book *The Image* (1962).[2] More recently, Chris Rojek, in his 2001 book *Celebrity*, has pointeds out that celebrities are mediated through "chains of attraction … cultural intermediaries who operate to stage-manage celebrity" – the agents, marketing personnel, promoters, and assistants whom Turner acknowledges. But Rojek's tone is unremittingly critical; these people "concoct the public presentation of celebrity personalities" and are therefore engaged in "cultural fabrication" (10). In some cases, of course, this is surely true, yet as an analytical observation meant to apply to "celebrity" in general, it is lacking in complexity and rigour.

As David Marshall acknowledges, celebrity is a system: "The concept of the celebrity is best defined as a system for valorizing meaning and communication" (*Celebrity and Power* x). And although the systematic emphasis here would seem to call for an industrial analysis, it is left to Graeme Turner and, especially, Joshua Gamson to supply it. Turner engages in such an

---

2 Technically, it reaches much further back, to the first recorded usage of the word celebrity as a noun referring to a person: "Did you see any of those 'celebrities' as you call them?" (1849) OED.

analysis, briefly, in *Understanding Celebrity*, emphasizing, first of all, that what we are dealing with here is undoubtedly an industry: "The sum of these processes," he writes of promotion, publicity, and advertising, "constitutes a celebrity industry, and it is important that cultural studies' accounts of celebrity deal with its production" (4). Dealing primarily with the entertainment industries, Turner takes note of "especially close patterns of economic interdependencies that bind the celebrity and their representatives (agents, managers, publicists, PR people), to the entertainment industries and to the entertainment and news media" (45). Like other analysts, Turner admits that these close bonds are methodologically difficult to study, since they are "deliberately mystified so that the processes through which they work ... are not visible" (45). In my study of such interdependencies in the literary field, and in particular in the public career of Margaret Atwood, I find less a bond between the celebrity and her agents and the media, and more of a pattern of interdependencies within the circle of cultural agents: between, that is, Atwood and those to whom she has entrusted the labour of managing her literary career. There is, of course, some measure of interdependency between "Atwood, Inc." and the media; outlets have been quick, for instance, to seize upon the story of Atwood's clash with Rob and Doug Ford, and they are certainly dependent, to some degree, on the labour of Atwood's interviews, statements, and online commentaries on the cause célèbre; but this dependency does not operate as intensively as it does between entertainment celebrities and media outlets, each of whom desperately needs the other. While Atwood may need media for purposes of promoting her books, she is not as consistently or deeply dependent on general and frequent media "coverage" as an entertainment celebrity aspirant is.

One area in which Turner's observations about celebrity systems ring truer for literary celebrities is that of new and integrated media. Writing of the effects of media convergence (the delivery of content from various media platforms) on celebrity production, Turner observes that "the celebrity ... is a very useful way of connecting these cross-media processes" (33) and that as a result, the commodification of the celebrity is occurring at an ever-quicker pace (34). He draws particular attention to the related phenomenon of content streaming – that is, the alteration of content to suit these various media platforms. Turner is among the first to grasp, fully, the significance of technological developments in media to the production of celebrity. In my chapter on Atwood as an increasingly enthusiastic user of 2.0 or interactive social media such as Twitter and blogs, I argue that these new media platforms constitute every bit as much of an agent of literary celebrity as editors, publishers, and assistants.

The major influence on my study of Atwood's celebrity labour is the American sociologist Joshua Gamson's examination of celebrity as an industry in his book *Claims to Fame: Celebrity in Contemporary America*. Acknowledged by Turner as a pioneer in this field, Gamson has signalled a turn towards a dynamic, systemic approach to celebrity. That is, agents who produce and reproduce celebrity within an industry have variable relations of dependency and independence with one another: their networks of allegiance and competition are complex ones. He studies, for instance, the ways in which publicists and journalists do battle over information about the celebrity, with the publicist restricting access and the journalist persistently seeking new tidbits or scoops (89). Presumably, some of this competitive dependency exists in the management of public relations for literary celebrities, but the main contribution of Gamson's approach to celebrity to my own work on Margaret Atwood's career is his basic conviction that celebrity production is "a commercial industry much like other commodity-production systems" (58), and his canny sense of the tug of war between celebrity as labourer and celebrity as spectacle: "there is a good deal of commercial pressure to simply allow the actor as worker to be subsumed by the celebrity as celebrity" (58). Much of Margaret Atwood's management of her public star "text" has to do with reasserting the primacy of the writer as worker in the face of a similar pressure. In Dyer's terms, Atwood as writer is "both labour and the thing that labour produces," and in order to retain her cultural legitimacy and capital, she constantly needs to sever the connection between the two, reminding her audience that her global celebrity is inauthentic compared to the labour of writing. "Pay no attention to the facsimiles of the writer that appear on talk shows, in newspaper interviews, and the like," Atwood advises her readers in *Negotiating with the Dead*: " – they ought not to have anything to do with what goes on between you, the reader, and the page you are reading, where an invisible hand has left some marks for you to decipher" (125–6). Of course, this separation is shot through with contradiction, since the writing is the ground and inspiration for the subsequent gaining of fame, in the field of literary celebrity. Still, the pressure to sever, even momentarily, these intertwined processes is keenly felt in the literary field of production.

Though I maintain that the celebrity industry in the literary field is full of contradictions and tensions between artistic and economic capital, one remarkable aspect of the group of agents with whom Atwood surrounds herself in order to manage her career is its degree of integration and functionality. Gamson's portrait of duelling cultural agents pitted against those on whom they depend has validity in the literary field in terms of the diversity of objectives that publishers, editors, and publicity people can often have. For a humorous fictional portrait of some of these industrial clashes, I examine Atwood's *Lady Oracle* in chapter 5. But what is extraordinary about Atwood's close working circle of agents, editors, and assistants is its relative harmony, though it is, I suggest, a harmony that has been cultivated and carefully constructed, with Atwood at the centre as the coordinating force.

Theorists of literary celebrity have started to engage with an industrial perspective; Joe Moran, for example, in *Star Authors*, examines the effects of the industrial concentration of publishing on authorship in the United States. For the most part, his perspective on this phenomenon, like Gamson's on the entertainment industries, is deeply critical. Moran describes, for example, the rise of author-centric modes of promotion, the economic decisions of publishers to devote large portions of their promotional budgets to a very few likely bestsellers, and the use of large author advances as a species of author publicity (35–9). The title of the chapter in which these trends are described speaks volumes about his theoretical approach to the literature industry: "The Reign of Hype." In this study of Atwood, however, I hold fire on such automatically negative cultural critique, though the concentration of publishing houses in fewer hands and the inauguration of large-author-advance "buzz" are developments that I, too, find unfortunate and counterproductive. My estimate of the professional exchanges that take place among the various agents of literary production recognizes both their productive aspects and their problematic ones. And I am especially committed to troubling assumptions about which literary production agents are primarily associated with economic capital (agents) and which are romanticized as devotees and defenders of literary quality (editors).

In studies of Canadian literary production, much more needs to be done to account, in sophisticated ways, for the crucial role of cultural intermediaries. In many ways, the groundwork has already been laid by several books and articles that document the industry and its history. Roy MacSkimming's *The Perilous Trade* is a goldmine of information on the history of Canadian publishing, though its aims seem mainly documentary and anecdotal. Eli MacLaren's book *Dominion and Agency* surveys copyright policy and the state of publishing in Canada between Confederation and the end of the First World War, arguing that the location of publishing industries outside the new nation during these years seriously delayed the development of a national literary culture. In many ways, his book is a natural follow-up to Nick Mount's *When Canadian Literature Moved to New York*, in which Mount documents the prevalence of writerly exile to the United States in the last decades of the nineteenth century, largely as a result of the industrial conditions that MacLaren describes. Janet B. Friskney and Carole Gerson's entry on "Writers and the Market for Fiction and Literature" in volume 3 of the *History of the Book in Canada* offers similarly valuable historical context, as does George Fetherling's entry on "Literary Agents" in the *Encyclopedia of Literature in Canada*.

Inspired by this growth of a lively, critical book history scholarship in Canada, literary critics have begun to offer case studies of more recent Canadian writers' interactions with publishing intermediaries, such as Linda Morra's engaging essay "Vexed by the Crassness of Commerce: Jane Rule's Struggle for Literary Integrity and Freedom of Expression" (2010) and JoAnn McCaig's *Reading In: Alice Munro's Archives*, both of which I discuss in further detail in chapter 1. These works tend to reinscribe a narrative of the writer devoted to aesthetic criteria beset by the forces of commercialism.[3] In this study of Atwood's literary dealings, I try to shake this automatic alignment of industrial workers with crass commercialism, since the literary field and all agents working within it disclose more varied combinations of cultural and economic imperatives and motives.

The growing study of literary prizes offers a wealth of insights about this intermingling of the cultural and the economic. Though in this book I tend to focus on the labour that attends the formation of the literary work on the part of authors, agents, editors, researchers, and publishers, the post-production phase – particularly the promotional culture involved in marketing books – offers another rich site where the previously

3 In the case of Jane Rule, such a perspective is understandable, given the unauthorized editing and censorship of her work. Still, beyond those issues, there remains the question of whether Rule's other expectations of her publishers and agents were consistently reasonable. An interesting exception to the tendency to champion authors and criticize publishers is Ruth Panofsky's even-handed analyses of Jalna novels author Mazo de la Roche and her stranglehold on her publishers, whose occasional aesthetic concerns about the later novels in the series were derailed by de la Roche's repeated threats to take her extremely lucrative business elsewhere ("Don't Let Me Do It").

silenced workings of the literary machine can be made explicit. Gillian Roberts's *Prizing Literature: The Celebration and Circulation of National Culture* takes a close look at Canada's literary prize culture and the ways in which it is, in her words, "tied to national projects" (6). This is markedly true, as Roberts demonstrates, of immigrant writers, whose prize-winning works tie them ever more closely to national culture, as a "host" rather than a "guest," to invoke Jacques Derrida's suggestive work on hospitality (6–7).[4]

Several of these recent contributions to the field feature archival research, as does this project, and the implications of this research methodology are worth pondering. The first three chapters of this book, in particular – on literary agents, editors, and the Atwood office – are deeply reliant on materials from the Margaret Atwood Archive at the University of Toronto's Thomas Fisher Rare Book Library. I am aware that in forming conclusions about the management of Atwood's career based on this voluminous archive, I am operating within distinct parameters. Foremost among these is the fact that the archive, like all others, is arranged and selective; as Robert McGill writes, "the content of the [Atwood] archive, as well as the classification of that content, bespeaks an attempt to circumscribe the orientation of academic inquiry, even as the archive ostensibly encourages and engenders critical interest in Atwood" (96). In Atwood's case, that circumscription takes the form of a focus on the professional rather than the personal, and that choice suits my own academic objectives perfectly well. Still, inevitably, some of my estimations of the workings of this small literary industry surrounding Atwood – such as my observations on the relative harmony among the agents of Atwood's fame – are based on an archive that is necessarily incomplete. However, a good deal of evidence about the nature of these working

4 See also Owen Percy's work in this important field of inquiry: "GGs and Gillers and Griffins, Oh My!" as well as his forthcoming book, *Prize Possession*.

relationships is available, and I observe what I can, out of the materials I have available to me, remarking on those occasions when the archive is admirably frank in its account of the challenges of living a remorselessly public life. As I point out in chapter 1 on Atwood's literary agents, it is noteworthy that, in shaping the archive, Atwood has sometimes allowed evidence not only of harmony and joy in the workplace, but also of disagreements and even of her occasional frustration with the continual round of public commitments that come between her and her writing privacy.

A second methodological consideration has to do with the validity of applying insights gained from celebrity theory to the literary field, since the former area has been long dominated by analyses of entertainment culture, especially film and television. This is a methodological choice that I made, as well, in *Literary Celebrity in Canada*, and I remain convinced that the potential advantages of working across fields of cultural production far outweigh the hazards. At the same time, I acknowledge when the distinctive differences of the literary field render theory derived from empirical observation of entertainment cultures inadequate or in need of elaboration or revision. As Su Holmes and Sean Redmond point out in their introduction to *Framing Celebrity*, this need to retain the specificity of celebrity in various areas of study is a matter of balancing the discourse of celebrity with the locality of that discourse's performance (13). Indeed, keeping these locations of celebrity hermetically sealed off from each other would prevent the valuable work that some celebrity theorists are doing on the migration of celebrity phenomena across various cultural sites (to name but one example: P. David Marshall's study of celebrity discourses in contemporary American politics in *Celebrity and Power* 203–40). I continue, however, to be guided by Graeme Turner's sage advice: "Tempting though these big connections are, they tend to obscure the fact that what constitutes celebrity in one cultural domain may be quite different in another" (17). To me, though, this very fact makes cross-field comparisons all the more inviting and revealing; the possible insights gained from these comparisons are well worth the responsibility of being attentive to generic contexts.

One critic of literary celebrity who has answered this invitation is Wenche Ommundsen, whose article "From the Altar to the Market-Place and Back Again: Understanding Literary Celebrity" makes the valuable point that the comparison between celebrity at sites of entertainment media (such as television and film) and within the literary field is exactly what literary celebrity is made of: "The notion of an author as a cultural hero unsullied by the manipulations of commercial or popular culture, though seemingly in stark opposition to common ideas of celebrity, in fact works in conjunction with them to produce a distinct brand of fame" (245). She argues that one oversight of Pierre Bourdieu's articulation of cultural and economic capital is that the marketplace has the potential "to capitalize on the distinction itself, to incorporate it into its commercial practices" (245). Actually, Bourdieu very much foresaw this kind of trading on the economic advantages of artistic high-mindedness; it was this that he was referring to when he wrote that "the literary and artistic world is so ordered that those who enter it have an interest in disinterestedness" (40). But whatever the source, the importance of the insight is this: only by comparing how various forms of capital operate at different cultural sites can we discern that complicated balancing act of defending one's interest in disinterestedness. It happens in a host of quotidian ways – in interviews, for example, when an internationally celebrated writer like Atwood feels the need to place her literary celebrity in the context of entertainment divas: "book writers have never been rock stars or movie stars" (E. Wagner "Margaret Atwood"). Meanwhile, though, news of Atwood's impending publication of *The Year of the Flood* hit the "Breaking Entertainment News" segment of the *Globe and Mail* in early January of 2008, underneath a photograph of Ringo Starr visiting Liverpool. The integrated headline ran: "Starr Power; Atwood Novel on the Way."

So the management of literary celebrity on the part of the writer and sometimes those who assist her frequently consists of the strategic disentangling of the intertwined fields of economics and art. My own work as a critic of this phenomenon is to re-member their intertwined nature. As Ommundsen describes this inevitable entanglement,

> Once imbricated in the discourse of celebrity, writers become cultural functions, subjected to (or subjecting themselves to – they're not all innocent bystanders) practices, meanings, and manipulations acted out in the public life of literature (the media, the internet, prize ceremonies, festivals, the publishing and marketing industries) and manifesting as figures of intense scrutiny, projections of various forms of desire. (249)

I laud Ommundsen's wise parenthetical remark about not all writers entering the public realm of authorship unwillingly, but I would add that, within an individual writer, one discerns the complexities and multiple allegiances of this imbrication. It is more complicated by far than writers either opting to subject themselves or being subjected to public authorship. Indeed, those who attempt to repudiate this involvement in the public side of authorship – the Salingers, the Pynchons – are still implicated in the publicity machines that Ommundsen describes. Indeed, their very seclusion stokes the fires of public speculation and literary celebrity.

Ommundsen maintains that the current moves towards global cultural marketplaces make it ever more difficult to disarticulate literary culture from celebrity (253), and while developments like the buying up, concentration, and collapsing of publishing houses would certainly suggest that this is so, we should not lose sight of a historical approach to literary celebrity that reminds us, time and again, that it was ever thus. Joe Moran, in his study of American twentieth- and twenty-first-century writers like Updike, DeLillo, Roth, and Acker, agrees that celebrity has been a major part of what it is to be an author for some time and that, in particular, one cannot simply blame increasing publicity for literary stardom; as he points out, people have been making complaints about the market-driven nature of publishing for decades, even centuries. His conclusion intertwines art and commerce – "celebrity authors continue to ply their trade in the middle ground between cultural kudos and commercial success" (42) – though he tends to value the first and be suspicious of the second.

More recent scholars of modern literatures have continued to read modernism through celebrity systems, going beyond the notion of celebrity as an external condition that authors must contend with to explore the ways in which modernism and celebrity are closely related cultural phenomena. Aaron Jaffe's scrupulously researched book *Modernism and the Culture of Celebrity* shows us just how fully complicit the canonical modernists – Eliot, Joyce, Pound, Lewis – were with the concerns of the marketplace, notwithstanding their many public pronouncements on the alienation of art from commerce. Indeed, this claim for the entanglement of modernism and celebrity is recently gaining ground in modernist studies; the title of Jonathan Goldman's 2011 book *Modernism Is the Literature of Celebrity* succinctly sums up his argument that modernism and celebrity are far from the antagonists they were once assumed to be; indeed, he points out, "these two supposedly separate aspects of culture are, in truth, mutually constitutive, two sides of the same cultural coin" (2). Writing together in the introduction to their co-edited collection *Modernist Star Maps*, Jaffe and Goldman refine this point; "celebrity," they claim, "names the form that fame takes under conditions of modernity" (9) and once "we view modernism's model of the author alongside the production of popular celebrity, we can conceptualize the relationship between these supposedly divergent spheres of culture as more of a collaboration than a parting of the ways of cultural production" (10).

A similar objective informs Joel Deshaye's forthcoming study of celebrity in later Canadian modern poetry, between the years 1955 and 1980. Like Goldman, Deshaye draws together modernist aesthetics and celebrity culture, arguing that for poets of this period – Layton, Cohen, Ondaatje – celebrity became a metaphorical crisis – that is, a crisis *of* metaphor – in which the making of the private public in both metaphor and celebrity produced tension, challenge, and risk. The metaphor of celebrity that writers in this period experienced and struggled with, according to Deshaye, was "privacy is publicity": an insight closely allied to Goldman's conviction that modernism *is* celebrity culture.[5]

My own approach to this question accords much more strongly with this recent, integrative trend in modernist celebrity studies, whose assumptions are nicely captured by James F. English and John Frow, writing on "Literary Authorship and Celebrity Culture" in contemporary British fiction:

> It is necessary, rather, to accept from the start a more multidimensional model of the literary field, and to propose that both the individual and the institutional agents involved in literary production … have come to act more strategically … The intense celebrity culture of contemporary British literature … is a symptom not of homogenization and simplification ("it's all about money now") but rather of increasing complexity in the way that literary value is produced and circulated. (45)

A careful study of Margaret Atwood's archives, her interactions with social media, and her writing, betrays exactly this nuanced and strategic approach to literary production – and the consequent production of literary celebrity.

A new consideration of literary celebrity needs to suspend, at moments, the understandable suspicion of economic processes that cultural studies theory and practice have inculcated in us. We must not let the undeniably myriad ways in which commercial regimes are constraining freedoms and constricting avenues of artistic and political expression around the world keep us from acknowledging those instances when the commercial intertwines productively with the artistic. Acknowledging the

---

5 See earlier versions of his arguments in his articles, "Celebrity and the Poetic Dialogue of Irving Layton and Leonard Cohen" and "Celebrity and Passing in Gwendolyn MacEwen's *The T.E. Lawrence Poems*."

labour of writing surely demands that we allow these two fields to become mutually implicated. In her landmark study *The Social Production of Art*, published in 1981, Janet Wolff offered up a plea that we open our minds to this intertwining, in all its complexities and implications, and her arguments are as trenchant today as they were thirty years ago. Arguing against the sequestering of the notion of the artist outside of the commercial, either as a Romantic secluded outcast or as an enemy of the social order, Wolff argues that such a view "ignores new forms of patronage and employment for artists, many of whom are indeed integrated, as artists, into various branches of capitalist production and social organization" (11). So she urges us to turn our attention to graphic artists, to designers, to advertising creatives, in much the same way that this book asks us to turn our attention to literary agents, editors, publishers, researchers, online platforms and communities, assistants and office staff.

A recent and notable contribution to Canadian publishing studies that answers Wolff's call for a thoroughgoing understanding of artistic production as a social act is Darcy Cullen's collection of essays *Editors, Scholars, and the Social Text*. Though Cullen and her contributors focus mainly on scholarly and academic rather than trade production, the foundational understanding that the book is a "social text" is one that applies equally to the sorts of trade publishing that I examine in relation to Atwood's career. This notion of the "social text," Cullen explains, is based on "the premise that a text is no longer exclusively within the purview of the author but produced, rather, through meaningful collaborations between heterogeneous communities of readers and writers" (4). Editors, for Cullen, are firmly located within the parameters of this "social text."

In a similar spirit, chapter 1, "'You Are a Necessity of Life': Atwood and Literary Agency," examines Atwood's history of working with literary agents, particularly with her long-standing agent Phoebe Larmore, proposing that the agent, considered from the earliest days of the profession as an unwelcome commercial eruption into the realm of disinterested art, be considered as a worker of a significantly more variegated nature. Chapter 2, "'Who's the Very Best at Spellin'?': Editing Margaret Atwood," performs a similar cultural studies–inflected archival task, but takes up the inverse case: editors, often romanticized as Maxwell Perkins–like champions of creativity, are implicated in economic concerns too, and their job involves a challenging act of balancing the two in their quest to deliver books from authors to readers. Chapter 3, which knits together such artificially separated positions as agent and editor, analyses the workings of Atwood's Toronto office, O.W. Toad, bringing to visibility the labour that supports her writing, as well as coordinates the various international agents involved in its promotion and publication. Chapter 4, "@MargaretAtwood: Interactive Media and the Management of Literary Celebrity," critically engages with Atwood's growing reputation as "Canada's national tweeting treasure" (Nestruck) as well as her invention of the remote signing device the Long Pen, while pointing to the larger theoretical questions that these raise about the links between celebrity and embodiment. Finally, the study would not be complete, to my mind, without a critical examination of the kinds of representations of celebrity industries – editing, publishing, promotion, social media – that Atwood's writing places in circulation. These representations are not simplistic, transparent versions of Atwood's opinion or any objective view of publishing in Canada, though they may reflect and refract both those things. As with my analysis of the archival evidence of Atwood's business, in chapter 5, "'The Cloak of Visibility': Art and Industry in the Works of Margaret Atwood," I look to the writing (mainly fiction) for strategic positionings and debates over the jostling of art and commerce. Devoting chapters to the office, to social media, and to literary texts, as well as to the personified agents and editors, is a way of underlining that the agents of literary celebrity go far beyond the individual and personal.

As I was in the latter stages of writing this book, in February 2011, Margaret Atwood gave a keynote speech at the Tools of Change publishing conference in New York City called "The

Publishing Pie." Typically, she managed to find a creative, richly metaphorical way of explaining the nexus of industrial relationships that constitute literary celebrity, though she did not phrase her subject in terms of celebrity. Atwood began her illustrated lecture by likening her drawing of an enormous filled pie to "the entire business that surrounds books." Her understanding of the capaciousness of this business accords with my own; as she glossed her image of the pie, "we are all part of that, whether we are idealistic tech people or whether we are scribblers." And she pointed out that in the digital age, writers' shares of this publishing pie are getting smaller; she cited the smaller income accorded writers by e-book publication. At the same time, however, the demands made upon writers in the digital age are greater because online platforms have provided additional venues for the promotion of books. So, Atwood asked, why should writers continue to supply this labour if their benefits are being reduced? She observed that 10 per cent of writers support themselves through their writing activities, but her concern was mainly for those who were struggling, unlike herself, to realize economic returns from their writing. And in two slides that together summed up much of the vision of literary celebrity as labour that I develop in this study, she warned her audience that the author is a primary source that must be protected. Her metaphor of the primary source, as she explained, was borrowed from biology, and in her talk it was demonstrated by her drawing of a dead moose (See figure 1). Every moose carcass, she pointed out, supports at least thirty other life forms and, as such, it was comparable to her next case scenario: the dead author. "Helpful industry hint," Atwood paused to advise: "Never eliminate your Primary Source." Atwood's next illustration, featuring a feet-in-the-air, blotto Shakespeare surrounded by a halo of industrial agents – bookseller, agent, school, printer, reviewer, college, publisher, editor, librarian (see figure 2) – could well serve as an emblem for my study of the Atwood industry – except in one particular. The author need not be depicted as dead or, metaphorically, as powerless in the transaction. I think

1 "When a moose dies, it feeds over 3 dozen other species. It is a primary source." By Margaret Atwood, from her lecture presented at the 2011 Tools of Change Conference in New York Feb 15, 2011 and later published on the Margaret Atwood: Year of the Flood blog (marg09wordpress.com). Reprinted by permission of the artist. ©Margaret Atwood 2011.

of Ommundsen's reminder that not all authors are victims of the forces of commodification, by any means. Accordingly, Atwood, in speaking of this slide at the Tools of Change conference, admitted, to the amusement of her audience, that "they don't have to be dead, although dead ones have been very lucrative." My own emblematic drawing would feature a living, breathing model: Atwood herself.

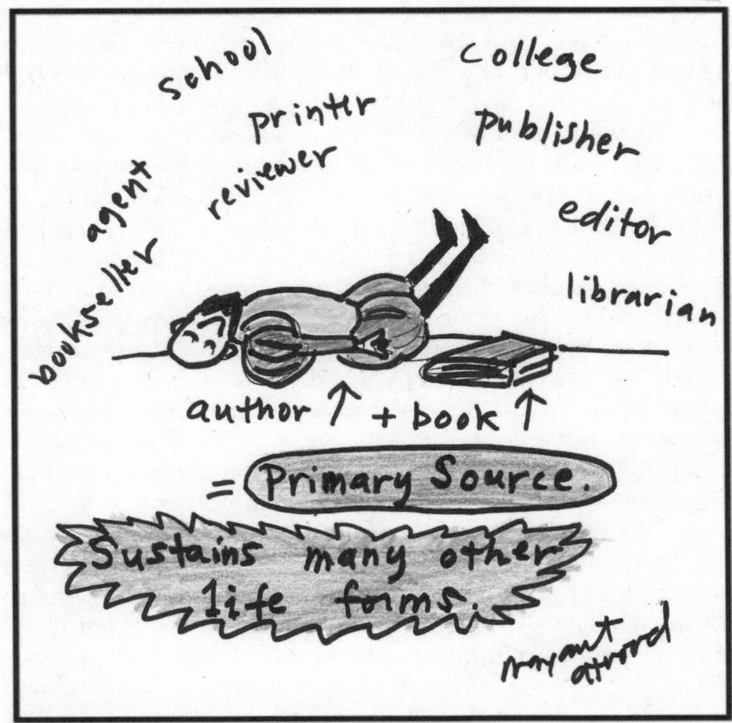

2 "The Dead Author sustains many other life forms". By Margaret Atwood, from her lecture presented at the 2011 Tools of Change Conference in New York Feb 15, 2011 and later published on the Margaret Atwood: Year of the Flood blog (marg09wordpress.com). Reprinted by permission of the artist. ©Margaret Atwood 2011.

In her presentation to the Tools of Change conference, Atwood also sketched the changes in the "publishing pie" over the last century, particularly the diminishment of the pie that has attended the industrialization of the publishing industry since the nineteenth century. She referenced the growth of new professions such as that of the literary agent, positioning such developments in the context of the increasing burden of dependents that the "primary source," the author, needs to support and feed. But amidst the serious critique of the crowding out of the author's claims in an increasingly specialized industry, Atwood saved space for her characteristic reflexive irony. At the bottom of one of her slides, on which she asked how authors buy the time to do their writing, Atwood added in caps, "N.B. ROCK CONCERTS AND T-SHIRTS ARE NOT AN OPTION." She explained that some younger people had asked her, on previous occasions, why writers did not respond to the economic pressures of their industry by doing what musicians have, in some cases, done in the face of digital downloading of their artistic property: shift the emphasis to live performance and to cross-merchandising. Atwood had no room for any such option, but even as she was speaking at the Tools of Change conference, her website for *The Year of the Flood* was still operative, offering details of Atwood's and local artists' live performances to launch her novel, and to support environmental causes – a negotiation of the artistic and the economic that I will turn my attention to in chapter 4. And at present, on Atwood's blog, T-shirts containing several of her slides from her talk are available. On the blog, Atwood claimed that her resistance to the idea of authors making their living from diversified marketing – the selling of T-shirts – had spawned this idea. Such a tongue-in-cheek, self-reflexive practice reminds me of Ommundsen's account of a 2004 talk she attended by Jeanette Winterson, at which Winterson satirically skewered the fetishizing of authors, with a performative verve that made the talk itself an example of such fetishizing – "demonstrating," in Ommundsen's words, "that it is possible for the author to have it both ways: to court the audience's veneration and to mock it too" (250).

Atwood's T-shirts do some of this work of mock-veneration too, and as such they are evidence of her self-conscious awareness of her position smack in the filling of the publishing pie. But this primary source is alive and kicking, articulately aware of the ways in which, as a primary source, she feeds an entire industry.

So in response to the controversy that erupted in the summer of 2011, when the Toronto mayor's brother, Councillor Doug Ford, took measures to deny Margaret Atwood's legitimacy, both as a visible celebrity and as a labourer, this study, *Margaret Atwood and the Labour of Literary Celebrity*, envisions a reply to the myriad ways in which the arts are invalidated by current neoliberal regimes: the author is a primary source in an industry that feeds many others – agents, editors, researchers, librarians, book designers, publishers, critics like me, and yes, Councillor Ford, you and your city too.

1
"You Are a Necessity of Life": Atwood and Literary Agency

On 25 October 1965, a still unknown young Canadian poet and novelist mailed a copy of her novel manuscript to S.J. Totten, an editor with McClelland and Stewart. Before signing off, she thought it advisable to add the following postscript: "P.S. It may not be pertinent, but perhaps I should tell you that I have acquired an agent, in London. I'm not sure what it's supposed to do, but Jane DESERT OF THE HEART Rule said I ought to have one and kindly supplied me with hers" (Atwood MS COLL 200.92:1). The offhand tone is understandable, under the circumstances; the professionalization of the writing life was a relatively slow and belated process in Canada, and aspiring young writers were not routinely confronted with the advice to "get yourself an agent" with the regularity that they are today. For that matter, the rate of publication of non-agented books in Canada remains much higher today than it is in the United States[1], mainly for reasons of the size of the domestic literary market. As a result, debates as to the necessity of obtaining a literary agent circulate here in a way that they do not tend to do south of the border. However, this young writer, a Canadian doing graduate work at Harvard, was quick to acknowledge the professional dimensions of the writing that she hoped to

1 Recent figures suggest that 80 per cent of writers in Canada currently do not have an agent (Medley, "Licence to Deal.")

make her life's work; just over a month later, she wrote to her new agent that she was "pleased … that I allowed Jane Rule to convince me that you are a necessity of life, rather than a mere luxury, as I had always held agents to be" (MS COLL 200.92:1). Today, as "Margaret Atwood," she is Canada's most celebrated writer, and her career offers an example of one of the most enduring and productive of author–agent relationships.

In my study of that relationship, I want to avoid the tendency to diminish or mask the labour and efficacy of the author as a cultural agent that I have noticed in some treatments of agent–author relations. An extensive study of the working relationship between Atwood and her long-time agent Phoebe Larmore, as reflected in the papers collected in the Atwood archive at the University of Toronto's Fisher Rare Book Library, has impressed upon me how these industrial relationships that I have described as being at the heart of celebrity sharpen rather than blunt our perceptions of the celebrity in question. Out of all the negotiations and relationships that make up a successful literary partnership like this one, emerges a marked understanding of the interventions of the author into crucial decisions about how her writing enters and circulates in the marketplace. The flurry of correspondence that attends the running of any extremely successful international literary career – the back-and-forth of letters, faxes, e-mails –cannot obscure that agency. In this spirit, my subtitle for this chapter, "Atwood and Literary Agency," punningly plays on that coexistence of the business of the literary agent with the marked nature of Atwood's authorial interventions into the shaping of her own career.

One drawback of some treatments of this subject in the past has been an insufficient understanding of what, exactly, literary agents do; another has been a poor appreciation of the short but revealing history of their profession. This inadequate contextualization of literary agency has tended to produce a certain amount of scepticism or hostility towards the agent on the part of academics who either are firmly invested in concepts of the disinterestedness of art or, on the other hand, are so deeply critical of commodity capitalism that they see the literary agent as an embodiment of its fetishizing evils. Both approaches underestimate the complex positionings of literary agency in its relations with both cultural and economic forms of capital.

Greater understanding of these positionings has been delayed by the paucity of analytical studies of the literary agent. Before 2007, when Mary Ann Gillies published her valuable book, *The Professional Literary Agent in Britain, 1880–1920,* there had been only one other book-length critical study of the agent, James Hepburn's *The Author's Empty Purse and the Rise of the Literary Agent,* published in 1968. (There were, previously, memoirs by literary agents such as Curtis Brown's *Contacts*, published in 1935, but they tended to be largely anecdotal accounts of their dealings with literary greats.) As its title suggests, Hepburn's book is a study of how the literary agent emerged in the 1870s and 1880s, as well as a description of the backlash against that emergence – among publishers in particular. Gillies traces the rise of the agent in more detail and, through minutely researched analyses of early British agents such as A.P. Watt and J.B. Pinker, argues that two models of literary agency took shape during that time: some agents promoted already successful, popular, "establishment" writers (as represented by Watt), while others championed newer, unknown, riskier modernist writers. Among the latter agents was Pinker, whose role she compares to that of a patron (99). Other, scattered articles on the subject have tended to focus on debates about the precise timing of the emergence of this cultural figure (McHaney), and which historical figure might qualify as the first genuine literary agent (Barnes and Barnes), discussions that easily become embroiled in questions of definition and semantics.

As my sketch of the meagre previous work in the field suggests, the research is largely focused on Britain and the United States and on the transatlantic literary exchange between the two countries that helped drive the emergence of the literary agent, since writers in America, in particular, came to require a literary representative to protect their interests – especially copyrights – abroad (McHaney). When we consider the Canadian literary field, the scholarship on this question is even sparser. George Parker's *The Beginnings of the Book Trade in Canada* offers no treatment of this figure, unsurprisingly, given that it leaves off in 1900; and Roy MacSkimming's portrait of the publishing industry in Canada from the Second World War to 2003, *The Perilous Trade*, devotes only two pages to the growth of literary agencies in Canada. According to MacSkimming, by the late 1970s, one Toronto agent, Matie Molinaro, was representing Canadian writers, but not young apprentices; her company, the Canadian Speakers' and Writers' Service, Canada's first literary agency, established in 1950, represented writers who had already established a considerable public presence, including Marshall McLuhan and Adrienne Clarkson (366). And as its title suggests, the agency worked with a large number of Canadian media celebrities generally, such as National Ballet founder Celia Franca and humorist Ben Wicks.

During the 1970s, MacSkimming notes, other agents such as Beverley Slopen and Bella Pomer joined her. But the major growth came in the latter half of that decade, when Lucinda Vardey established her agency and Stanley and Nancy Colbert came to Canada from the United States and founded The Colbert Agency. Eventually, the latter became McNight Gosewich Associates; it and the Vardey Agency were then bought by Bruce Westwood, forming what remains the largest Canadian literary agency, Westwood Creative Artists. In the early 1970s, though, when Atwood's career was becoming established, the picture was quite different; as Atwood told Roy MacSkimming, authors would often agree to disadvantageous publishing contracts, sometimes accepting as little as 5 per cent royalties on a hardcover book: "Nobody knew. The publisher would say to the writer, 'Well, this is standard for the industry.' Of course nobody had any way of checking what writers were accepting, because there was no repository of contracts. There were practically no literary agents in Canada then" ("The Perilous Trade Conversations" 16). Currently, by contrast, there are more than thirty literary agencies in Canada (Medley, "Licence to Deal").

This consolidation and growth of literary agencies in Canada took place long after the novice writer Margaret E. Atwood took her first tentative step in hiring a British agent; clearly, in 1965, there were few other options. In *The Red Shoes: Margaret Atwood Starting Out,* Rosemary Sullivan comments briefly on Atwood's decision; it was, for her, "a relief to hand over the confusing business of selling her work to an agent. At the time, of course, there were no Canadian agents looking to take up young writers" (148). That is technically true, given that the few agents who existed in Canada at the time, like Matie Molinaro, dealt mainly with established, celebrity writers. Still, the story of Canadian writers' dealings with agents outside of Canada remains an absorbing, important, but as yet largely untold story.

There are a few exceptions to that statement. Linda Morra's essay on Jane Rule's professional relationship with her agents, "Vexed by the Crassness of Commerce," is a carefully researched, archivally rich study of the sometimes fiery business relations between Rule and her agents; but as the title suggests, it tends to see Rule as consistently at the mercy of the publishing machine. To a large degree, this reading is understandable, since Rule faced not only irritating and irresponsible editing of her work, especially in magazine formats, but also heavy censorship for its lesbian content. Still, some of the archival evidence suggests that Rule could be an extremely demanding and even obsessive protector of every comma and clause: not the easiest author to edit. Morra's larger project on Canadian women's agency in their relations with the publishing industry, in progress at this time, should be a welcome and much-needed contribution to the study of mid-twentieth-century Canadian writers and their non-Canadian agents.

The other major contribution to the field amounts to something of a cautionary tale. One of the first extended studies of a Canadian writer's relationship with her agent was JoAnn McCaig's article and subsequent book on Alice Munro's long-standing arrangement with Virginia Barber, her New York agent. McCaig researched this successful professional relationship in the University of Calgary's Alice Munro archives and published her initial results in a special issue of *Essays on Canadian*

Writing devoted to Munro in 1998. In that article, "Alice Munro's Agency: The Virginia Barber Correspondence, 1976–83," McCaig argued that the professional arrangement between the two women allowed a species of division to take place between the economic sphere, represented by Barber, and the realm of art as a disinterested calling, represented by Munro. In a sense, McCaig sees Barber as inhabiting what Pierre Bourdieu would describe as the displaced and repressed realm of economic capital, the better to allow Munro, as an artist, to distance herself from that realm. According to McCaig, the friendship that developed between the two women both managed and complicated that tension between art and the marketplace. Not surprisingly, Barber and Munro, when applied to for permission to quote from their correspondence, were not enormously pleased or convinced by this reading of their relationship, so they only grudgingly granted their permission, while making it clear that they, in the words of their letter to Robert Thacker, the special issue's editor, "neither endorse nor dispute the opinions or analysis of Ms. McCaig" (McCaig *Reading In* x). When McCaig expanded her analysis and incorporated a revised version of this essay in a book manuscript, Munro and Barber revoked permission entirely, leaving McCaig to reformulate her argument without direct recourse to their letters or those of Ann Close, Munro's editor at Knopf, who also denied permission to quote from her correspondence with the author.

Looking back at this conflict just over a decade later, several productive cautionary lessons about analysing the relationship between authors and agents emerge. First of all, the tendency to see individuals as separate embodiments of cultural forces in tension should be resisted and queried. For instance, for McCaig to refer in her book to Barber as Munro's "cultural banker" (*Reading In* 63) is disrespectful to Barber and, furthermore, drastically simplifies the manifold ways in which the literary agent's job straddles considerations of economy and art. She even suggests that in doing her job to ensure profitable publication agreements for Munro, Barber was a dupe to "patriarchal literary culture" ("Alice Munro's Agency" 10).

Correspondingly, we need to question the tendency, not only in McCaig's study but also in studies of literary celebrity generally, to see the celebrity author as in full or even hypocritical denial of his or her role in commodity capitalism. Denial and, indeed, hypocrisy have been constant motifs in these studies. We need a new model of the modern and contemporary author as a participant in the business of writing books, a model that does not necessarily erase his or her agency and awareness.

At the same time, academic scandals like the one that attended the publication of McCaig's book have had the unfortunate effect of polarizing the field, with writers and academics jumping onto one side or the other of the debate. For this reason, in spite of what I see as its missteps in bringing together the worlds of publication archives and cultural theory, it is worthwhile to consider the positive contributions that McCaig's project made to the nascent study of the literary agent in contemporary Canada. Foremost among those, to my mind, is her defence of the need for cultural studies scholars of literature to look to literary archives for inspiration: "It is my conviction that literary archives are an under-utilized source of useful information about culture, authorship, and literary process" (*Reading In* 13). "There is an untapped potential in literary archives, and … cultural studies theory can be usefully applied to all types of texts, published or not" (17). I heartily agree, and the present study is a response to this need and invitation.

What this study of Atwood and her agent has to offer is a more rounded, historically informed examination of the work of the literary agent, greatly assisted by more recent scholarship such as Gillies's, as well as by many interviews on record with literary agents. Rather than seeing the agent as the iron fist of commodity capitalism striking at the innocent sacrificial lamb of art, I try to enter into the full exchange between art and commerce that takes place within the agent's job itself, and within the job of the professional writer, who faces the challenge of protecting time and privacy to create while levelheadedly acknowledging that she or he participates in a business within a larger commodity culture.

First of all, a history of the literary agent shows that the suspicion of the agent as a corrupting economic force – a suspicion I have discerned in recent treatments – was a condition of the emergence of the profession. From the very beginning, the new profession attracted hostility and distrust, mostly from publishers, who felt that agents would drive up production costs by forcing them to make more generous deals with authors. Many studies cite William Heinemann's 1893 denunciation of the agent as a "parasite" "middleman" (Hepburn 1; Gillies *Professional Literary Agent* 3). "What a battle I fought with that fine old gentleman of the publishing world, Henry Holt!," recalled Curtis Brown in 1935, though he mischievously added that the *Fortnightly Review* article that he penned in response to Holt's attacks, circulated as a pamphlet, ultimately attracted more authors to his agency (239). As James Hepburn astutely notes, though, those publishers who went on the offensive against the newly professionalized agents "did not mention that they themselves were but recently middlemen, coming between author and printer-bookseller" (2–3). It can hardly be said that the rise of agents disrupted an Arcadian peace between publishers and authors; indeed, disputes between the two were partly responsible for that rise.

Outside the Anglo-American setting, hostility against literary agencies continues apace today in countries such as France. As William Cloonan and Jean-Philippe Postel point out in their review of novels published in France in 1996 for *The French Review*, the literary agent is growing in importance in that country. Originally trained to handle the translation rights for American authors, they are beginning to attract French writers to their agencies; in doing so, they are also attracting exactly the same sorts of hostility and arguments against their very existence that publishers advanced in England and the United States in the 1890s and early 1900s. Cloonan and Postel argue in apocalyptic mode that agents are "altering or destroying what had previously been a sacrosanct relation between artist and editor" (796). In her study of the literary agent, Mary Ann Gillies writes that agents "destabilized the author–publisher dyad, thereby causing changes in the interactions between authors and publishers" (*The Professional Literary Agent* 26). Her language, unlike Cloonan and Postel's, is determinedly neutral; "destroying" is, of course, an entirely different – and, I would argue, dubious – charge. Cloonan and Postel interview French editors on this question and find not only hostility but also "indifference." As an editor for Éditions de Minuit explains to them, their market is an elite niche, so, he claims, they have use neither for agents nor for publicity, for that matter (798). Such positions of economic disinterestedness, as Bourdieu would maintain, are themselves founded on the workings of capital (40), for the greater role of government funding for cultural groups that one finds in many European nations allows smaller publishing ventures to take up this appearance of indifference towards the market.

Another aspect of the French hostility towards literary agencies is directly tied to the subject of this study: celebrity. Éditions P.O.L. adopts the position that "le texte est la vedette" (Cloonan and Postel 802) and therefore refuses to deal with agents at all, apart from translation agents who are marketing French texts abroad. The notion that literary agency turns writers from ideologically pure servants of Art into royalty-greedy spoilt stars is a distortion of literary history, for the cultural visibility of writers has long predated the relatively recent establishment of literary agents. Still, this attitude persists not only in France and in other countries where literary agencies are a recent arrival, but also in countries where literary agency has been established for more than a century.

At the end of their survey, Cloonan and Postel note the rare exception to their findings: the occasional French editor who believes that the literary agent is not the handmaiden of crass economic determinism. This position, as represented by Olivier Nora, a director-general at Éditions Calmann-Lévy, is very much in keeping with my own wish to complicate any easy dichotomy between economics and literature. Nora argues that the hostility of most French publishers towards agents is short-sighted because many of those agents were originally editors, who bring to their job impressive critical reading skills. As a businessperson, Nora is quick to appreciate that agents who are thus skilled in editorial work could save presses a great deal of money that they would otherwise spend on external readers of manuscripts. Though I am sceptical as to whether the editing skills of agents can – or should – render in-house editing redundant, I agree with the fundamental assumption that most literary agents – and all of the very successful ones – are "literary" as well as "business" people, to draw for a moment on that dichotomy.

Because the short history of literary agency has been filled with hostility and scepticism from the beginning, the recurring debate that has surrounded the profession has been over the very need for them. The relative belatedness of the profession's emergence in Britain in the late 1870s, according to Mary Ann Gillies, raises the question, "What was it about this time that prompted [A.P.] Watt, and others who followed his lead, to embark on a business that until then had not been thought of as necessary?" (*The Professional Literary Agent* 12). A mere forty years later, according to Gillies, "by 1910, the usefulness of agents was still hotly debated, but there was a noticeable shift" away from the question of whether agents ought to be used at all, to when and how best to benefit from the services of an agent (*The Professional Literary Agent* 109, 110). By the time of Watt's death in 1914, she claims, "the agent was a prime player in the publishing world" ("A.P. Watt" 2).

Although this may have been the state of affairs in Britain at the outbreak of the Great War, the fact remains that "prime player" or not, the agent has remained a questionable necessity in the eyes of many. Even contemporary American guides to literary agencies, such as Debbie Mayer's much-consulted *Literary Agents: The Essential Guide for Writers*, offer a surprisingly unsympathetic assessment of the profession: "All agents, even the most effective, are at best a necessary evil. In the best of all possible worlds, writers and publishers would work in concert, with no need for a middleman" (6). This may be the ideology of the free market speaking; and indeed, such comments resemble early and continuing denunciations of labour unions; but it also signals the degree to which the "necessity" issue still attaches itself to literary agency, even in America at the beginning of the twenty-first century.

For these reasons, the young Margaret Atwood's somewhat diffident admission to McClelland and Stewart that, on the advice of an older, successful colleague, she had obtained an agent, and her own pleased recognition that this agent is "a necessity of life, and not a mere luxury," need to be read in the context of the history of literary agency. That "necessity" has been a fraught question since the inception of literary agency; yet Atwood, even as a young and relatively inexperienced writer, was able to grasp that the literary agent did not dilute or threaten her role – this, at a time when, in Canada, writing was seen as a cottage-style, restricted-production industry. As Atwood recalls of the Canadian arts scene just a few years earlier, in the late 1950s, "the artsy group [in Toronto] was small, just like the artsy group in Canada itself, and everyone connected with it usually fiddled around in more than one field of activity" (*Negotiating with the Dead* 20).

Why was Atwood, at such a tender stage in her career, able to grasp the utility of but not be threatened by the literary agent, that perennial focal point for hostility and dismissal? The answer lies in the archival evidence from the early years of her career. As she pointed out, she was advised to get an agent by the novelist Jane Rule, with whom she had become friendly when she took up a sessional teaching post at the University of British Columbia in 1964–5, the year she completed the novel that she so optimistically sent off to McClelland and Stewart in the autumn of 1965, *The Edible Woman*. As she later recalled, Rule and her partner, the artist Helen Sonthoff, "were the first people I met. They helped me rent an apartment, they lent me a card table – I wrote *The Edible Woman* on it – they lent me plates, they invited me to parties" (Martin, "B.C. Novelist"). Rule, an American who had taught in England before settling in Vancouver, was a crucial female mentor, an older colleague whose professional writing experience was wide-ranging. Her persistence in bringing the fruits of her writing into distribution was especially impressive; her breakthrough lesbian novel, *Desert of the Heart,* had been published the year Atwood began teaching at UBC, after having been rejected twenty-two times by publishers. In her detailed and valuable account of Rule's professional relationships with her agents, Morra observes that Rule was so intent on ensuring that her short fiction would not be cut, rewritten, or condensed by magazine editors without her express consent that she was willing to sever relationships with agents and insist upon a contract clause protecting her against unauthorized editing. Indeed, Morra points out, "she consistently put freedom of expression ahead of financial reward in her interactions with publishing figures and especially with her own editors" (102). So here was a mentor who combined fierce dedication to her writerly, political vision with a determined and knowledgeable navigation of the publishing business.

But there is also evidence in the archives that from the outset, Atwood, while she valued Rule's advice and mentorship, and was quietly willing to follow her own sharpening professional instincts. She continued to have recourse to Rule's valuable advice in dealings with her new agent; in one of her first letters to Hope Leresche of Hope Leresche and Steele in London, she broached the subject of North American publication of her work: "Jane DESERT Rule said that it would be all right for me to peddle the ms. on this side of the ocean, but that you would get a % and handle things if anyone decided to take it. Is that correct?" (This was a lesson that Rule herself had learned, according to Linda Morra, a few years earlier, in 1957, when her agent at the time, Willis Kingsley Wing of A.P. Watt and Son, warned her that his agency would be entitled to commission payments on stories that Rule submitted directly to Canadian magazines; 96–97). But Leresche encouraged Atwood to look beyond Canadian houses, and demurred somewhat at Atwood's list of possible publishers. Atwood diplomatically responded to her, "I have a provincial partiality for Canadian publishers, but as J. Rule is so fond of saying, Business is business, I suppose" (MS. COLL 200.92:1). As the next few years would establish, however, Atwood was very much keeping her own counsel as to the importance of publishing her work in Canada. As Rosemary Sullivan describes in *The Red Shoes*, Atwood's decision to go against the conventional sorts of advice handed Canadian writers at that time – to publish with an American or British publisher first and then, only if the subject matter required, arrange afterwards for a Canadian edition – was a ground-breaking one. As Sullivan rightly says, many wise heads in publishing at the time would have considered this, in Leresche's terms, "putting the cart before the horse," and we know from the studies of earlier writers' publishing conditions that Canadian writers in the nineteenth and early twentieth centuries had to relocate outside Canada to produce and promote their works (Mount, MacLaren). So when McClelland and Stewart eventually did publish *The Edible Woman* first, purchasing world rights and placing it with publishers abroad, "the cart had been put before the horse, and it worked" (Sullivan 208).

Unlike many of her contemporaries, Atwood saw the need to organize her professional life through the services of a literary agent. This was, I suspect, for several reasons. First of all, as the archival materials make clear, in the early to mid-1960s in Canada, anyone contemplating writing as a profession needed to devote a great deal of time to the business of securing individual writing jobs, since those assignments, taken singly, were anything but remunerative. One had to orchestrate quite a number of them in order to bring in even a slender income. Atwood's correspondence with journal and magazine editors dating back to these years offers a compelling portrait of this piecemeal existence: offers of $10 or $25 per poem were common; and all too common, too, was the sort of arrangement that Henry Beissel proposed in a letter to her of 8 May 1964, offering to publish three poems in *Edge: An Independent Periodical* but shamefacedly admitting that "unfortunately we have not yet found a way to pay our contributors – other than by sending them two complimentary copies of the issue in which their work appears" (MS COLL 200.1:13). When Barbara Kilvert, Executive Assistant of Public Relations of the Hudson's Bay Company, wrote to Atwood to see if she might be interested in selling them a poem for their new advertising initiative for a sum of $50 per poem, a rather cash-strapped Atwood wrote back from her graduate student digs in Cambridge and sent several poems for consideration, all within ten days (MS COLL 200.1.43).

During the first years that she worked with Hope Leresche, Atwood was generous in sharing her experiences with other writers who were, like her, struggling to construct a professional life out of their writing. She wrote to the poet Daryl Hine in January 1967 that "my agent was obtained through Jane Rule, who'll tell you all about that too: suggest you inquire." She then provided the full address of Hope Leresche's agency. "Jane says she is good but slow," she observed, but then in fairness was quick to add, "But do ask – J. may have changed her mind since I last talked to her about it" (MS COLL 200.1:38). Several years later, when she was working with Phoebe Larmore's agency, Atwood put friend and fellow writer Matt Cohen in touch with them, though he did not end up working with Larmore (MS COLL 200.2:3). Clearly, having benefited herself from Jane Rule's professional advice, Atwood extended the same mentorship to others.

By the late 1960s, there was evidence that Atwood, her career growing after she had won the Governor General's Award for Poetry for 1966, needed to consider professional representation closer to home. By 1968 she had published her second collection, *The Animals in That Country*, and was in discussions with editor Peter Davison of The Atlantic Monthly Press about publishing an American edition. In a letter to Bill Toye, her editor at Oxford, she noted of Davison that "he seemed a jolly, well-wishing type; told me I needed a New York agent" (13 March 1968 MS COLL 200.92:4). The seemingly offhand tone should not obscure the fact that Atwood was willing to take the advice of a seasoned editor very seriously. As it turned out, it was Davison who brought Atwood into contact with the woman who would remain her agent for almost four decades. Phoebe Larmore had found a copy of *The Edible Woman* while on a holiday in Montreal in 1969. On her first day back at work, she picked up the phone to Davison and left him a message: Did this talented young writer Margaret Atwood have an agent? As Larmore recounts the story, she had no sooner put down the telephone than her other line lit up; Davison was on the line to ask her if she would be willing to represent Atwood (Nischik 293).

In analysing the long, productive professional relationship between these two women, I find that their exchanges closely reflect not only what agents today tell us about their profession but also numerous aspects of the history of that profession. Indeed, in carrying out research on literary agents, I was surprised at how much continuity there is between what literary agents do today and what they did a century ago, notwithstanding the tremendous changes in the communications technologies they rely on to conduct their day-to-day business. For the sake of clarity, those duties include the following:

- Finding a good match between the author's manuscript and an editor and publishing house, based on the agent's intimate knowledge of both, and proposing the manuscript to them.
- Negotiating a beneficial contract.
- Collecting royalty statements and payments due to the author, deducting the agent's fee, and then forwarding payment to the author; keeping accurate records as they do so.
- Supervising the process of publication of the manuscript, particularly as regards following the letter of the contract.
- Looking ahead and taking the "long view" of the writer's career; providing advice on the wise management of that career.
- Handling foreign publication rights, should this be an option. (Mayer, 7, 11)

Those are the "bare bones" of an agent's job; on closer inspection, however, there are many additional roles. As the

American agent Joe Regal once put it, "an agent is one-third lawyer, one-third editor, and one-third schmoozer, with a little bit of psychologist thrown in" (Mayer 78). This business position, therefore, comes laden with a fair degree of both artistic and affective responsibility, and one can discern the combination of these realms in the way Phoebe Larmore describes her role in Margaret Atwood's writing life:

> Year by year, title by title, I have dedicated myself to shepherding and championing her work within the publishing community, to laboring to expand her reading audience throughout the world, and to obtaining for her as much financial recompense as possible, so that she could be not only financially secure but also well rewarded for her creations. (Nischik 293–4)

Looking back over some of the historical studies of literary agency, the basic responsibilities are much the same; James J. Barnes and Patience P. Barnes, writing about Thomas Aspinwall (1786–1876), whom they argue was the first transatlantic literary agent, observe that "Aspinwall performed a variety of services for his clients in addition to negotiating their copyrights … Keeping track of receipts and disbursements was particularly important" (324). Indeed, from the nineteenth century to the present, the only role of the agent that has significantly fallen off has been the financial assessment of publishing businesses that are to be sold. The loss of that task reflects the fact that the earliest agents would readily take assignments from publishers (to find them an author or a piece for publication) as well as authors. As time went on, agents tended to work mainly on behalf of authors, though clearly that work remained valuable to editors and publishers in bringing likely literary talents to their notice. Otherwise, as Gillies observes in her study of A.P. Watt, the two other major duties were the "sales of serial, translation, and foreign rights for editors and publishers, and sales of literary property" generally ("A.P. Watt, Literary Agent" 2). These form the backbone of the literary agent's business today.

In the Atwood archives, they are also the backbone of the literary agent's job, though as time goes on, and Atwood's career becomes a truly international one, a certain degree of specialization takes place. In a letter of 19 June 1996 to Roberta Mazzanti of the Giunti Gruppo Editoriale publishers in Florence, who was inquiring about publishing *Alias Grace* in Italian, Atwood's assistant Sarah Cooper explains that "Phoebe Larmore is the Agent of Record, but only deals directly with North American contracts," whereas Diana Mackay, of the venerable Curtis Brown agency in London, is "our translation agent" (MS COLL 335.9:8). In publication discussions, Phoebe Larmore is the authoritative source of advice on contractual obligations; in one exchange among Atwood, her American publisher Nan Talese, and Larmore about the constitution of the American combined edition of *Murder in the Dark* and *Good Bones*, entitled *Good Bones and Simple Murders*, Larmore intervenes to remind the other two that they cannot use as many selections as they originally had wished to from *Murder in the Dark* because they do not have the rights to reproduce that many (MS COLL 200.164:1). She offered a similar intervention during discussions of the publication of *Writing with Intent* in the United States, pointing out that the title was the same as the subtitle used by Anansi for *Moving Targets* and advising that it had best be cleared first with them. Furthermore, she adds, no essays from *Second Words* can be included in *Writing with Intent* "because the U.S. distribution rights belong to Anansi" (MS COLL 335.127.1:19).

Such matters seem dryly legalistic and commercial in nature, yet they are intimately connected with those other, affective, forms of advocacy that literary agents offer and that Larmore, in particular, has offered to Atwood over the years. In a letter to Atwood dated 24 August 1993, she looks forward to meeting Atwood in New York during the promotion of *The Robber Bride* so that they can talk about contract negotiations for the *next* novel; as she explains, "it is always my policy to negotiate for the next work with the American publishers at the high point of publishing the immediate work" (MS COLL 335.2:1). Again, this sounds like – and is – sound business practice, but it is also part of the "shepherding and championing" roles that

Larmore sees for herself. By thinking forward to the next novel (no matter how difficult that must be for the writer who has not yet written it), the literary agent attends to the shape and trajectory of the writer's career, sometimes mentoring that writer over several decades.

That concern for the shape of the career easily shades into aesthetic response to the work; indeed, it is intriguing to see how, from the beginning of their professional relationship, Larmore responds to Atwood's work in much more than a market-oriented way. In a letter of 29 September 1980, in sharing her opinion of what poems might be included in *True Stories*, Larmore suggests that either "Bluejays" or "Down" should be included, because they "parched the same empty desperate feeling in me upon reading" (MS COLL 200.15:9). Fourteen years later, Larmore responds to the manuscript of *Morning in the Burned House* by describing how particular poems will alter the way she experiences specific events or even looks at individual objects around her. (MS COLL 335.6:1, 16 Mar. 1994).

This is the dimension of the literary agent's work that is missed when one tries to see him or her as simply a "cultural banker." As I mentioned earlier, many agents began their professional lives as editors, and some of the agent's work continues to intersect with that of the editor, complicating any simple dichotomy between commercial and aesthetic labour. For instance, when the collective of editors and publishers who have formed a long and loyal working relationship with Atwood over the years – such as Nan Talese of Doubleday, Liz Calder, her British publisher at Bloomsbury, and Ellen Seligman from McClelland and Stewart – meets in a Toronto hotel to read over the manuscript of the next Atwood novel, Larmore is part of that working collective, offering Atwood crucial initial feedback on a work that she has, up till that point, kept secret, as many writers do. This practical overlap reflects a larger trend within the industry: the growing editorial role of agents. As Debby Mayer explains, "publishers are less and less likely these days to accept material that they feel will require substantial revision" (12), so agents often step in to offer editorial advice, in order to ensure that the manuscript is in the best possible form to impress the editors who will be considering it for publication. One of the most respected agents in the United States, Lynn Nesbit, has commented in an interview that younger agents today tend to do more editorial work than she and her contemporaries did when they entered the profession. She attributes this to the "pressure on editors to come in with something that's almost ready to go"; as a result, "the agents are assuming part of what the editors used to do" (Ferrari-Adler, "Agents & Editors: A Q&A with Agent Lynn Nesbit" 73). In other interviews I read with agents, this was a common theme, and in some cases, the combination creates a certain amount of role conflict. Agent Molly Friedrich notes that agents may run into trouble if they first woo an author by expressing unqualified admiration for their manuscript and then, once they have signed the author, "begin the hard work of getting the book into shape" (Ferrari-Adler, "Agents & Editors: A Q&A with Agent Molly Friedrich" 11). This may suggest to the author that the agent has been disingenuous or has lost some amount of commitment to the work. She makes it a point to be honest about what she feels the strengths and weaknesses of the manuscript are, but she admits that she has "lost authors because of it." The most searching discussion of this shift in agenting responsibilities comes from Nat Sobel, long-time agent with Sobel Weber Associates in New York, who notes that agents today need to be "first line editors" for their authors – and much else besides, for they find themselves involved in jacket design as well as copy for the jacket and the catalogue. When he entered the profession, he recalls, "you made the deal, you negotiated the contract, and that was it – the publisher took over" (Ferrari-Adler, "Agents & Editors: A Q&A with Agent Nat Sobel"). Asked why he thinks this seepage of roles has taken place, Sobel singles out the overworking and underfunding of publishing companies. This sounds very likely, yet there has always been seepage between the roles of business agent and editor, both because of the historic tendency I have mentioned of agents entering the profession from editing and because the effective marketing of literature proceeds from an intelligent understanding of what, exactly, one is marketing and what makes it exciting and worthwhile to bring to a reading public's attention.

Because this business arrangement between agent and author straddles artistic mentorship and commercial service, a major part of the agent's duties involves protection: and it is indeed a catch-all term. In the Atwood archives, that protection takes on many dimensions, and at certain moments it is not at all possible to separate commercial from artistic objectives. In July 1999, for example, Larmore wrote to Atwood to advise her on an offer from filmmakers Francine Zuckerman and Lori Spring to adapt six of her short stories, a project that resulted in "Atwood Stories," released in 2002. In that letter, she vets their qualifications: "As you will see [from their résumés], they have considerable experience as film makers. You will also be interested to know that Ellen Seligman thinks very highly of Francine Zuckerman" (MS COLL 335.137.11:4). Here, the opinions of agent and editor (Atwood's long-time editor with McClelland and Stewart) dovetail, and one has a sense of a collaborating team of professionals working together to protect Atwood's interests along this broad spectrum from the economic to the cultural; clearly, Seligman's high opinion of one of the filmmakers would be expected to resonate with Atwood, for it acts as a guarantee of quality from an editor whose aesthetic judgments are notoriously keen. In the next breath, Larmore makes sure that the economic protection is in place as well: "Were we to proceed with granting rights to six of your stories, I recommend that it should not happen unless a television network were already involved and of course, that the purchase price was acceptable" (MS COLL 335.137.11:4). Cultural and economic capital go hand in hand, and both must be vigilantly protected.

In attempting to place shorter fictional works with magazines, the agent can provide a vital link between the author and the first-line editorial response to the writing. In a 1983 letter to Atwood, Larmore keeps her author posted on which of the short stories that will eventually be collected in *Bluebeard's*

Egg have been sent where, but she also encloses "several of the recent letters of return which reflects the general reaction thus far to the stories" (MS COLL 200.65:1; 11 July 1983). This is potentially very valuable to the writer as she ruminates over shaping a possible collection. Serving as middle person between magazine and journal editors and the author can be a delicate business, requiring diplomatic skills, but it is a crucial task; earlier in their association, in 1975, Larmore returned to Atwood a story that was originally aired on radio, "The Porcupine Murders," enclosing a note from Barry Callaghan, who had recently (1972) founded the journal *Exile*. The note is painfully frank: "I do want to publish Atwood, but at her best. I heard this story when it was broadcast, and didn't like it much. I like it even less now that I read it. I hope that there are other stories, or poems, and that you will let me have a look at them" (MS COLL 200.2:5; 24 Sept. 1975). Larmore reread the story and, on consideration, advised Atwood to leave it as a radio story, though the ultimate decision, of course, was the author's: "How do you feel?" (MS COLL 200.2:5; 26 Sept. 1975). This is professionally direct and helpful, if a bit difficult; it also reveals some of the negotiations that attend representing an author whose work, by 1975, had received national acclaim. Callaghan's letter makes it clear that publishing Atwood (which he did; she appeared in the very first issue of *Exile*) would be a coup for the journal, but he also is determined, as an editor, to be in the running for more recent work that might represent even more of a coup. Larmore, in all of this, is not simply seeking to sell a work; her protection extends to ensuring that only the best material circulates to editors. This is protection of reputation, and it is a major part of the job of representing already successful authors.

In the case of a long-standing professional relationship between an author and an agent, one that spans decades of a successful literary career, that role as protector can potentially extend to the daunting task of advising a late-career writer when to stop publishing. As Atwood told the television interviewer Charlie Rose, the spectre of diminished literary powers at the end of a career "is a fear of mine … So I said to my agent, if I get to that point, you know, if things are really slipping, you have to tell me." Though she added, with her characteristically acerbic wit, that Larmore "said, I won't be able to tell you, because I'll be that way myself" (Atwood, Interview with Charlie Rose).

Guides to literary agents emphasize the great care they take to protect the reputations of successful authors by looking to the future. Another way in which agents manifest that concern is by looking to the past, to how earlier works have been marketed in the light of that success. (A case in point was the decision, in Carol Shields's career, to reissue her earlier, often overlooked novels in an attractive Random House edition after she won the Governor General's Award and the Pulitzer Prize for *The Stone Diaries*.) Clearly, Phoebe Larmore felt that something similar should be done outside of North America for Atwood: "As I have been saying for some time, it once again was evident that your foreign backlist has not been as aggressively marketed as I believe a writer of your status warrants" (MS COLL 335.137.11:4; 19 March 1999).

Managing the timing of publication is another way in which agents protect the reputation and economic returns of writers – particularly prolific authors like Atwood. In a faxed letter to Atwood on 9 August 1994, Larmore passes on Nan Talese's opinion that "time-wise … this collection [*Morning in the Burned House*] should not come out too soon after GOOD BONES AND LITTLE MURDERS, so her first thinking would be for some time in 1996" (MS COLL 335.6:2). With publication dates of editions in various countries falling at different times, this can be a demanding schedule to manage. And there are other considerations affecting the timing of publication; Larmore, along with Seligman, Talese, and Atwood's London publisher Lennie Goodings of Virago, conferred with Atwood on alternative publication dates for *The Year of the Flood*. Their concern was that a publication date of September 2008 would fall too close to the much-anticipated American presidential election in November of that same year (Adams, "Release of Atwood Novel Postponed" R4).

At times, questions of timing and reputation need to take into account specific requirements and conditions of the writer's life. Years earlier, in March 1976, Larmore provided advice for Atwood about the possibility of writing a book in the "Canada's Illustrated Heritage" series. (This book, which Atwood did go on to write, was *Days of the Rebels*, a history book detailing the years 1815 to 1840, covering the uprisings in Upper and Lower Canada.) "To repeat my accessment [*sic*] of this book foryou [*sic*]," she wrote, "writing this book will in no way tarnish your reputation. However, it is unlikely that it will contribute to it either. What it will provide will be a comfortable income and a comfortable writing assignment, at a time when that combination is a prime requirement" (MS COLL 335.137.11:3; 11 March 1976). That "time" was no doubt Atwood's pregnancy (she gave birth to her daughter two months later, in May 1976).

One of the most important ways in which the agent provides protection is by shielding the writer, for as long as possible, when the writer is deeply engaged in a project, from the very exigencies of the marketplace that the literary agent is hired to manage. In 1981, Larmore forwarded a postcard reminder that she had received about an overdue contribution that Atwood had promised for an anthology of contemporary fairy tales, but she had already written back to the editor to say that Atwood was busy completing a novel. Still, to emphasize that she wished to protect that precious writing time, she ended her note to Atwood, "I remind you not to feel pressured by this deadline, for no actual publication date has been set" (MS COLL 200.2:13; 13 Feb. 1981). (For the record, Atwood, a conscientious respecter of deadlines, got the story to the editor the very next month.) In the summer of 1998, part-way through the composition of *The Blind Assassin*, Atwood seriously needed time and space to write and was finding it increasingly difficult to do so, given the myriad ways her time was being taken up both by public commitments and by the sizeable task of running the day-to-day business of being Margaret Atwood. In this instance, Larmore was once again a supportive buffer, reminding Atwood that she and other intermediaries like her office assistants were there precisely to protect her from having her time consumed by these quotidian affairs. "I applaud the fact that you are not going to deal with other issues until you've reached the 200 page point," she wrote to Atwood on 12 August. "There is no need for you to do so. Sarah [Cooper] and I have things well in hand so don't be concerned about any business affairs – just continue as Writer Supreme, as of course you are!" (MS COLL 335.137.11:4). Easier said than done, unfortunately. The pressures exerted on Atwood of a public and business sort were, and continue to be, gargantuan, and it is hardly surprising that she should express frustration at the lack of privacy, though in all of the archives that I consulted in the Thomas Fisher Rare Book Library, I only found one – entirely understandable – instance of her losing her characteristic sangfroid at the various incursions on her time. A month later, in September 1998, she wrote to Phoebe Larmore,

> What does this all boil down to? That when I'm in Toronto, people get after me to do stuff. That my fall has become more chopped up and attached to other folks' agendas than I'd like; that I need time to write; that it is not yet time in the writing process for me to feel the dread hand of Publication Stress on my shoulder. I would write a lot more happily if I felt I wouldn't ever have to actually PUBLISH anything! It's becoming more & more of a meat market. Thinking about it, or about any of the related business stuff (contracts etc.) is a certain and sure path to Writers' Block and/or "I don't have to be doing this." (MS COLL 335.137.11:4; 13 Sept 1998)

The balance is a precarious one; given the very real threat to privacy and productivity that literary celebrity means for Atwood, it is surprising that there are not more instances in the archival record of her frustration.

This capacity of literary agents to mediate among various needs – the need of the writer for privacy; the need of the publisher for copy – means they must be particularly adept at balancing and negotiating relationships among the various cultural players in the literary field. This has always been at the heart of literary agency, and the titles of two memoirs by celebrated agents say as much: Curtis Brown's *Contacts* (1935) and Paul R. Reynolds's *The Middle Man* (1971). Relationships are so fundamental to the profession that they have become a mantra in interviews with agents. Molly Friedrich flatly states that "the business of being an agent is the business of forming relationships, and everything is a seedling" (Ferrari-Adler, "Agents & Editors: A Q&A with Agent Molly Friedrich."). Attending writers' conferences, generating word of mouth, being remembered: all of these things are, in Friedrich's terms, "seedlings" that can be harbingers of future working partnerships. At the same time, however, these relationships – in particular, the condition of being the "middle man" or woman between the publisher and the author – can be challenging and fraught. As Friedrich also points out: "My job is to do the best job I can for my author without ever being in collusion with the publisher. That's a very tricky business." Tricky indeed, when one takes into account that agents must cultivate those "relationships" with publishers and editors too, so as to win their respect and a hearing for the authors being represented. In terms of literary agency, 'twas ever thus; as Thomas McHaney shows in his historical analysis of James Lawson, whom he maintains qualified, in the early nineteenth century, as a bona fide literary agent, "like the modern agent, whose stable of established writers is a weapon to encourage acceptance of newcomers or of the less popular, Lawson could make it easier for his writer friends to reach print because publishers and editors were in his debt or sought his influence. He could help his editor friends to attract work and authors they wanted simply by the range of his acquaintances" (180). In her portrait of A.P. Watt, Mary Ann Gillies basically agrees with this scenario; in the late nineteenth century, she argued, the literary agent walked "a narrow line attempting to be fair to both publisher and author," for "in any given transaction, the agent would be negotiating with a publisher with whom he wished to work in the future" (5, 4). She does recognize, however, that any agent who was perceived to give clear preference to publishers "could not hope to stay in business for long" (4). It remains the case that agents, unlike editors, make their living by negotiating with authors and publishers, whereas editors are hired and paid by publishers. Though, as I have maintained, agents now are closer to advocates for their writers and more distanced from publishers than their very early predecessors simply by virtue of no longer being actually hired, on occasion, as financial assessors of publishing firms, the need to maintain productive working relationships with both parties is still a pressing and challenging concern – as, indeed, it is for editors, who also balance advocacy for the author with the needs of the business.

In the case of Atwood and Larmore, the ability to forge that kind of balance has been a major factor in the success of their working relationship. It is clear from the archives that the labour involved in supporting Margaret Atwood's international literary career has required collaboration among various cultural workers. In fact, in separating out the strand of archival documents that specifically concern Atwood and Larmore, I have somewhat artificially disentangled them from a complex network of labour involving editors, office assistants at Atwood's company O.W. Toad, agents, and publicists. And over all of this, Larmore has established warm but utterly professional working relationships, never forgetting that her prime objective is to enable the writing to happen by making a writing life possible and rewarding – in all senses – for Margaret Atwood.

As this description intimates, such a long-standing professional association may evolve into friendship; and in the case of Atwood and Larmore, and of other long-standing writer–agent pairings such as Alice Munro and Virginia Barber, it certainly has. Like the other aspects of literary agency that have attracted my attention, this one, too – friendship – has been much discussed in studies of the agent. I also maintain that it has been much misunderstood. The suspicion that has always attached itself to the literary agent has also, I believe, attached itself specifically to the element of friendship in many of these working relationships. In McCaig's take on the Munro–Barber association, friendship seems suspect; on one hand, she suggests that the friendship that the two women developed sustained them when they faced "harder issues" relating to the exigencies of the marketplace ("Alice Munro's Agency"), which seems likely. Yet McCaig also expresses surprise at the combination of the commercial and the personal in their correspondence, noting that Barber's first letter to Munro explored a personal response to one of her short stories, but that the second got right down to the business of her roles and fee: "Whereas in Barber's first letter the connection is personal, and Barber addresses Munro as one who understands and supports her work, her second letter unmasks the underlying economics of the author–agent relationship" ("Alice Munro's Agency"). Problematically, this formulation reproduces a simple economic determinism, wherein capital is always the substructure that is masked by affect and other superstructural forces.

Instead, I believe that this coexistence of commerce and friendship is productively read in the context of the history and nature of literary agency as an interlocking rather than a masking. Because "protection" and the mentoring and shaping of individual careers are, as I have shown, at the heart of what agents do, friendship has been a constant presence in literary agency. Historically, the agent's profession grew out of what was, in earlier years, essentially an act of friendship. Thomas McHaney writes that more than fifty years before professional agencies were established, American writers would enlist the assistance of "an energetic relative, or a friend, or a willing diplomatic officer" to run errands abroad relating to their publishing affairs (179). When James J. Barnes and Patience P. Barnes assembled their arguments for considering Thomas Aspinwall to be the first transatlantic literary agent, they did so by distinguishing him "from the traditional 'friend of the author'" in pointing out that he did receive a set fee (322). Even so, as they note later in their article, he became close friends with James Fenimore Cooper, for whom he occasionally acted as an agent abroad (326–327). Friendship is a recurring motif in Gillies's definitive study of agency; she titles one section of her chapter on A.P. Watt "Friends," pointing out that many of the writers he represented subsequently became friends (74), and she includes a corresponding section in her chapter on J.B. Pinker, mainly dealing with that agent's long-standing friendship with the notoriously difficult Joseph Conrad (155). From the very beginning, agency, like editing, has meant, to some degree or other, an amalgamation of friendly advocacy and promotion of business interests, no matter how successful or disastrous those amalgamations have turned out to be.

One result of this historical amalgamation of the texts of friendship and business has been that an agent must convince a prospective writer, from the very beginning, that in addition to negotiating the most favourable contracts, he or she will advocate for the work in a broader sense of representing it as culturally valuable and worth attending to. For that reason, it is entirely reasonable that a letter of introduction, like the one that Virginia Barber wrote many years ago to Alice Munro, would seek to demonstrate an affective response to that work. And this is what keeps many established writers loyal to their agents; as Rosellen Brown, another of Virginia Barber's longtime authors, explained, "because she takes such good care of my work and my psyche, I am still with Virginia Barber" (Mayer vii). It is possible to try to write this off, of course, as an opportunistic mimicry of "friendship" on the part of the agent, but there are compelling reasons not to: to begin, it is not the way that agents interact with all of their authors; and, more important, if the friendship or commitment is assumed rather than felt, it is far more likely to crack under the strains of negotiation and editing. There are cases, of course, where this does happen, but they are misalliances rather than the effective working relationships of which I write here.

Reading through the archives, it is easy to discern how the letters between Larmore and Atwood become more reflective and personal over time as both friendship and professional relations deepen: "It is such a pleasure reading your poetic voice again," she warmly writes in response to the manuscript of

Morning in the Burned House in 1994 (MS COLL 335.6:1; 16 Mar. 1994). It is revealing, I think, that when Larmore came to pay tribute to her long association with Atwood in a rare published commentary for Reingard Nischik's *Margaret Atwood: Works and Impact*, published on the occasion of Atwood's sixtieth birthday, she did not subsume the friendship to the business relationship or vice versa. Describing herself as a fortunate member of Atwood's "inner circle of family, friends and colleagues," Larmore writes about her efforts to obtain proper financial compensation for Atwood's labour, and ends with a description of herself as "her literary agent and her friend" (293, 294).

Business is never, in these documents, subsumed under the banner of friendship, even when friendship has developed between a literary agent and her client. Rather than being incompatible – or hypocritically inauthentic – force fields, as some treatments of literary agency would suggest, the two operate in tandem in the Atwood archives. One factor for the strong intermingling of the two in Atwood's career has been, I would suggest, the fact that Atwood had a firm business sense from the very beginning of her career, so any friendship that might develop out of her business dealings would need to be integrated with the already existing foundation of professionalism. The archives are impressive in showing just how astute Atwood has been from the beginning; this was so even at a time in Canada when, as she has said on many occasions, publishing was a distinctly small-production affair: "the usual sales of poetry books [in the early 1960s] numbered in the hundreds, and a novel was doing well if it hit a thousand copies" ("Survival, Then and Now" 54). Even at the beginning of the next decade, when she wrote *Survival* for the struggling Anansi Press, she considered what she was doing the work of "a kind of bake-sale muffin lady, doing a little cottage-industry fundraising in a worthy cause" (55). Still, eight years before, as a graduate student, she had vigorously applied herself, in spite of her many other commitments, to sending out poems and stories. From the beginning, as biographers Rosemary Sullivan and

Nathalie Cooke have shown, she had a firm sense of her artistic decisions; though willing to listen, always, to the informed feedback of readers and editors, she would not be railroaded into artistic decisions she felt were not amenable to the work at hand. An early example of this is a fascinating exchange that she had in May 1965 with Alan Bevan, who was editing *Evidence: A Periodical of Literature and Art*. Atwood had sent him a short story "Going to Bed," and he earnestly tried to talk her out of a relatively muted ending of the story, though he said he would publish in any case. A copy of Atwood's response is not in the Fisher archives, but in his next letter, he thanked her for her "interesting and provocative" response and assured her that "the story will, as you request, be published without emendation" (MS COLL 200.1:13; 25 May 1965).

Reading through the archives, I am struck by the sheer amount of labour involved here, at a time when fax machines were undreamt of, not to mention e-mail. Atwood managed her correspondence promptly and met her deadlines, all while pursuing her PhD studies. When Barbara Kilvert of the HBC approached her with the proposal for ads featuring poetry by up-and-coming Canadian poets in journals and magazines like *Queen's Quarterly*, Atwood was clearly excited by the venture. In Kilvert's letter acknowledging receipt of the poems, which Atwood had submitted a mere ten days after her letter – with New Year's holidays intervening – she sounded surprised and gratified by Atwood's response: "It's a delight to encounter such an enthusiastic response" (MS COLL 200 1:43, 10 Jan. 1966).

When Atwood published her first full collection of poetry, *The Circle Game*, she cleverly realized that this event could assist her in two goals: of making writing her profession and, more immediately, of temporarily relieving the poverty of a graduate student-poet. In November 1966, the year *Circle Game* was published, on the advice of the poet John Newlove, she wrote a letter of inquiry to Laurie Lerew in Montreal with regard to possibly selling her the manuscripts of the collection, along with those of her first pamphlet publication of poems,

Double Persephone, and some Charles Pachter materials, which she would sell "partly on ... behalf" of her artist friend. Again, we see Atwood listening to the advice of an experienced writer and trying, as a struggling graduate student, to realize some source of income from her writing. This proved challenging, for Lerew asked her to place a value on the manuscripts, and that must have been difficult, not to say strange for the young poet to do. She struggled with this question of value, preferring in the end to turn that question over, as it should be, to readers; as she wittily suggested to Laurie Lerew,

> as for my status as "one of Canada's coming young poets" – well, I can't really sing a cantata in praise of myself; guess I'll have to wait till conviction strikes you, in the form of reviews or a bolt from the blue. Meanwhile, I would prefer to "file" the material with you rather than cart it around myself; perhaps you can stash it in a cellar somewhere and wait till it matures – like cheese." (MS COLL 200.92:2; 6 Jan. 1967)

Grateful for a much-needed advance on the price of the manuscript, Atwood wrote back to thank Lerew for "your prompt reply and your beautiful blue cheque" (MS COLL 200.92.2; 11 Jan. 1967), a witticism that recalls Dorothy Parker's observation about the financial exigencies of the literary life: "The two most beautiful words in the English language are: check enclosed" (Frewin 108). Two months later, she received a call in Cambridge telling her that she had won the Governor General's Award for poetry. As bolts from the blue go, this one was well timed; the cheese in the cellar was ripening.

As the years progressed, and Atwood's dealings with agents and editors and all the apparatus of a successful international career became more time-consuming, her business acumen remained impressive. It was certainly not the case that business concerns were handed holus-bolus over to these intermediaries in a blunt division of art and commerce. What the archives show is that Atwood would always step in when necessary or when productive, to make the crucial decisions or to formulate an initiative. One such idea was the combination edition of

Murder in the Dark and *Good Bones* in the United States. Atwood got the idea while she was working on *Good Bones*; in August 1991, she faxed a letter to Larmore proposing this rather ingenious idea: "It strikes me that if Nan [Talese] is still into it, she could do a combination of the best of 'Murder' and 'Good Bones' and do it in the States. We gave coach House [*sic*] US right [*sic*] on Murder and they were distributing it through some small clearing house, but I'm sure they'd cancel that for a weeny percent of US sales of the 2 books combined. Eh? Whatya think?" (MS COLL 335.1:1; 7 Aug. 1991). The apparatus supporting Atwood's business concerns is far-flung and diverse, yet it is clear that she has a firm handle on all aspects of her concerns. More important, the formation of this network of cultural agents clearly highlights rather than obscures or compromises the agency that Atwood possesses over her career.

One example of this agency is Atwood's intervention, when necessary, in such matters as publicity and the effective marketing of her books. She is at all times aware of these decisions, but when necessary, she can suggest alternatives, as she did with the publishing format of *Good Bones and Little Murders* in the United States. Another is that when print ads were being devised for *The Robber Bride*, in 1993, Atwood gathered, from her assistant Sarah Cooper, that there was some discussion and controversy about the proposed ads being too redolent of romance fiction. In a fax to Marly Rusoff, her publicist at Doubleday, Atwood intervened with good humour and a clever suggestion: though she felt the ads were fine, "an objection I could see is that it might sound a little too much like a Danielle Steele or something. How about:

> Header: The Robber Bride. She takes no prisoners
> Banner. Women are her targets. Men are her loot.
> Or something of the sort? Tones down the black-lace-underwear totality of it all just a bit." (MS COLL 335.2:4;29 Oct 1993)

She seems here to be having a good deal of fun with the promotional task facing them; what is more, when dealing with the objections voiced (I am assuming in the publishers' offices) that the copy might be too déclassé or popular, she cannily suggests copy that is parodic of that genre – that uses and at the same time distances itself from it in a way that recalls Linda Hutcheon's understanding of parody: "It is rather like saying something whilst at the same time putting inverted commas around what is being said ... [a] wholesale 'nudging' commitment to doubleness, or duplicity" (*Politics* 1–2). What could be more Atwoodian?

Contractual matters would seem to be the prime territory of the literary agent. Many writers feel enormous relief in handing off this aspect of their business to a professional who often has legal training, even though, of course, they retain final say over any agreements entered into. But Atwood may intervene in these discussions when they become thorny. When Anansi suggested that it might be entitled to a portion of proceeds from the American volume of essays *Writing with Intent*, Atwood e-mailed the parties concerned to make her own position clear: that "The Work" specified in the Anansi contract was not the same "Work" as the book that Carroll and Graf proposed to publish in the United States (MS COLL 335.127:1:20; 15 Oct 2004). She e-mailed Sarah McLaughlin of Anansi a few days later to explain that "I don't usually deal with contractual matters. I only did this one because I was told Phoebe and Anansi were at an impasse" (MS COLL 335.1:27:21; 18 Oct 2004). It is always clear, in dealings handled by intermediaries, that Atwood is the ultimate agent.

Even on matters of pricing, Atwood intervenes when she feels it is incumbent on her to do so. There is a fascinating correspondence with Bill Hushion of McClelland and Stewart about the pricing of the Canadian edition of *The Robber Bride*. The publisher's proposal is to list it at $28.99, but Atwood is not convinced that this would be a good decision in the Canada of 1993. Hushion had written her to argue that, given the length of the book, $28.99 is "almost under-priced" (MS COLL 335.2.6; 26 Aug. 1993). He also pointed out that it would cost less here, comparatively, than it would in Britain. Atwood faxed her reply the same day: "My concern is not about 'comparative pricing' or length, but about what the market will bear in this recession-conscious Canada. The buyer isn't going to ask, 'is it cheaper in the U.K.? but rather, 'Am I going to pay $28.99 plus G.S.T.?" As with the discussion about advertising copy, Atwood had an alternative to suggest, and notably, she and colleagues had even done some research:

> I think that if you lower the price a dollar you will sell more than enough extra copies to make up for it! I think $27.99 is a psychological threshold. On the other hand, Sarah Cooper has asked some booksellers –
>
> 1) the lower the better
>
> But
>
> 2) 26.99 is read as 25.
>
> 27 is in limbo
>
> 28 is read as $30
>
> Have you asked the booksellers? the book reps?
>
> If you stick with 28.99, better publicize the fact that it's cheaper here than anywhere else!? (MS COLL 335.2:6;26 Aug 1993)

Atwood's disposal of the comparative pricing argument is impressive; indeed, it *is* difficult to see how differential pricing could be a factor in a Canadian consumer's decision to buy the hardcover in this particular case, though usually books published both in Canada and the United States are more expensive in Canada, leading some consumers to defy copyright laws by ordering the book online from distributors outside the country.[2] She also immerses herself in the intricacies of marketing and the interpretation of price points, approaching such questions with her usual willingness to research: to go out and ask the booksellers on the front lines of selling her book. Any attempt to see "Atwood, Inc." as displacing agency from the author to a network

---

2 I am grateful to Siobhan McMenemy for pointing out this cross-border publishing situation to me.

of corporate suits would need to reckon with evidence like this. Though it is obviously true that writers are working within the confines of an increasingly corporate publishing world, so too are the agents, editors, and publishers who bring a writer's creations to a readership. In this particular network, though, Atwood is never less than actively engaged with those challenges. And the degree to which she, unlike most authors, is able to intervene in these issues is a measure of her celebrity power.

In the final event, in studying the veritable industry that surrounds Margaret Atwood and that brings the results of her creativity to the public, we do not find an author who is buffeted here and there by the forces of literary celebrity. We have, instead, an author who has been, from the beginning, an agent herself who can and does intervene in the forces that present and manage her literary celebrity. And during the months and years that she is actually engaged in working on a new book, it is clear that those decisions are not up for collective discussion or negotiation – not, that is, until she presents a draft to her editorial team for them to discuss and report on. This distinction between the larger discussion that takes place about the work as soon as one hires an agent or works with an editor, and the decisions for which an author needs to keep his or her own counsel, has been palpable in many a relationship between a writer and the marketplace. As early in the history of literary agency as 1837, Washington Irving sought to define that space, in a letter to his agent Thomas Aspinwall:

> I have noticed what you repeat of [publisher John] Murray's suggestion that I ought to write some light work in my old vein … There is a current in the mind which an author had better consult and humour than follow any suggestions or advice. It carries him on to what he can best effect and to what is most congenial to his distinction and talents. (Barnes and Barnes 326)

For Atwood, as for many other writers, that period of composition of the first full draft allows for a reduction in the interference with that "current in the mind," though, of course, composition never takes place in a social vacuum. As Larmore once jokingly admitted to Atwood, her discussion with Talese about Atwood's new novel (what would become *The Blind Assassin*) "went nowhere, of course, for narry [*sic*] a clue has either she or I been able to pick up about what you are writing – as usual!" (MS COLL 335.137.11:4; 19 Mar. 1999). This is one space that Atwood can construct wherein the give-and-take flurry of the business is quieted, shut out; when it does occasionally intrude, we sense her frustration. Perhaps it is this protected space alone with her writing that allows Atwood to be as patient as she is at other times with what she calls the "dread hand of Publication Stress."

In the hugely amusing 1984 documentary *Once in August*, Australian filmmaker Michael Rubbo's filmed sojourn with Atwood and her immediate family at their Northern Ontario cottage, there is a moment that always makes my students chuckle when they watch it, though afterward it can be difficult for us to articulate, exactly, what the source of the humour is. Rubbo is asking a doggedly patient Atwood about the process of working on a new novel. As it turns out, she tells him, he has caught her at a particularly challenging moment, because she has "three possible novels and I haven't decided which I can start, so all I can say is that I will hang around until it becomes clear to me." Rubbo probes, "You're worried about this?," whereupon Atwood fixes him with that steady, level gaze that Canadians have come to recognize, and quietly asks him, "Wouldn't you be worried about this, if it were you?" (Rubbo 55, 16). Rubbo has no answer; all we hear is a long, drawn-out "uh …" This is where students begin to chuckle sotto voce. It is a serious humour, though. When all is said and done, all negotiations completed, publicity arranged, revisions finalized, cover copy designed, the writing is the livelihood, the concern, and the abiding preoccupation of the writer. Recognizing how that work takes place amidst the many industrial relations of the publishing industry is crucial, therefore, not in order to divert our attention from authorial agency, but to create a context for it within which we may focus upon it anew.

2
"Who's the Very Best at Spellin'?": Editing Margaret Atwood

On her website, the American science fiction and fantasy writer Ursula K. Le Guin observes that there is a "good deal of misunderstanding, these days, about what editors actually do" (*Ursula K. Le Guin*). Editors tend to agree; in his preface to the third edition of his standard text on the editor's craft, *Editors on Editing*, long-time editor Gerald Gross observes that the "list of myths and erroneous assumptions" about editors "goes on and on and on" (xiii). For her part, Le Guin set out to clear up some of that misunderstanding by running a short article on the subject on her website, written by an editor she particularly enjoyed working with on her *Tales from Earthsea* and *The Other Wind*: Michael Kandel. Ironically, Kandel took advantage of the opportunity for cultural visibility that Le Guin offered him to justify the invisibility of the literary editor: "If the editor is an artist, he [*sic*] is an anonymous one. He is invisible. The whole point as well is to have the reader exclaim not, 'What a wonderfully edited book' but, rather, 'What a wonderful writer!' The editor is even more invisible than the translator." This editorial cloak of invisibility gives rise to the stereotype of the literary editor as an otherworldly devotee of language, for the very mystique and cultural capital of editing are wrapped up in its lack of public representation – in what Bourdieu would call its "interest in disinterestedness" (40); the editor's labour gains cultural respect in part because it is subsumed under the sign of the Author. Although what Kandel writes is true in some senses, in that the editor often appears to be a silent partner whose creativity is often felt everywhere in the process yet nowhere in the product except for the acknowledgments page, I see the editor as more thoroughly mediating the realms of publicity and its secretive-seeming underside, the creative process. So whereas in my previous chapter I defended literary agents against the charge that they are the venial handmaids of capital, in this chapter I offer the inverse reading of editors, reminding us that the reputation that successful literary editors garner as high-minded dedicatees to Art needs to be tempered by the realization that they are, necessarily, agents of commerce as well. And when the author with whom the editor is associated is as highly visible a literary celebrity as Margaret Atwood, some of that visibility inevitably rubs off; the editor may find him or herself becoming what James Monaco called a "paracelebrity" (4): one whose measure of cultural visibility is produced by and dependent on the celebrity with whom he or she is associated.

Even so, the ideology of disinterested invisibility continues to cling to the profession; Gerald Gross chose the occasion of publishing his third edition of *Editors on Editing* in 1993 to call for an end to the invisibility of the editor's labour. Editors, he notes, "have been expected to be unsung, faceless, nameless technicians assisting the author in the creation of the completed manuscript," yet there is no reason to mystify their labour in this way. Why, he wonders, "should the editor remain anonymous" when the contributions of the "jacket designer, graphic artist, illustrator, or photographer" are often acknowledged on book jackets or copyright pages (xvi)? Almost two decades later, the situation has not materially changed, in spite of the presence of noteworthy literary editors in every country around the globe. Darcy Cullen devotes an entire section of her introduction to her 2012 volume *Editors, Scholars, and the Social Text* to "The Invisible Editor"; even now, she argues, "the image of the manuscript editor as reclusive, voluntarily hidden from view . . . has been internalized in the profession" (7).

Although high-profile authors continue to offer lavish praise for editors' ministrations, in interviews, publication tours, and on acknowledgments pages, book production credits do not currently reflect this widely acknowledged appreciation of editorial labour.[1]

Rosemary Shipton, writing in Cullen's collection on editors, attributes this silencing of editorial labour to the forces of literary celebrity: "Editors remain a mystery, their work invisible," she argues, because several agents in the production of successful literary careers have an interest in maintaining the aura of the single, solitary author of genius: "Readers want to believe that writers are geniuses, or at least have exceptional talent. Authors naturally buy into this dream, and publishers find it advantageous to present their writers as stars" (44). Once we redefine celebrity, however, as a collaborative and industrial process, the door is opened to a more equitable representation of artistic labour.

Authors whose careers amount to global celebrity enterprises work with numerous editors attached to the various publishing houses that handle their work, and so Atwood, for one, has been associated with accomplished editors such as Ellen Seligman in Canada, Nan A. Talese and Janet Silver in the United States, and Liz Calder and Alexandra Pringle in the UK, among others. So the labour of editing, like literary celebrity itself, is best understood in such cases as a web of industrial relations. Add to this condition the growth in the amount of editing that literary agents now routinely do, as I recognized in the previous chapter, and you have a model of labour that is not characterized by a strict demarcation of specialized roles. Rather, more accurately, it is one wherein the roles of editing are shared by various cultural agents: editors at several publishing houses, agents, authors, and even, to some degree,

---

1 Educational publishers, on the other hand, such as Pearson and Nelson acknowledge the labour of developmental editors and copy editors. Thank you to Siobhan McMenemy for pointing this out.

personal or office assistants. Again, though, and as is the case with Atwood's relations with literary agents, such a collaborative field of production does not necessarily mute or reduce the author's agency; if anything, it lends it definition.

In the case of Atwood's many editors, there has been a core group of long-standing, trusted readers of her work – Seligman, Talese, Calder, Pringle, Louise Dennys and Lennie Goodings.[2] These women, along with Atwood's agent Phoebe Larmore, have, at one time or another, formed the nucleus of Atwood's editorial team as the deadline for publication of a new work looms. And in the case of each woman, her contribution to the production of a new Atwood work is varied and fluid, crossing job description boundaries. Seligman, who came to Canada in 1976, when she was hired by Jack McClelland, is both an editor and a publisher (she became editorial director for McClelland and Stewart in 1987 and publisher and vice-president of the company in 2000). Like others in the industry who combine such roles, she addresses herself to the business of publishing during office hours, and takes up the demanding task of reading manuscripts in evenings and on weekends – another symptom of the invisibility of this labour. Nan Talese's career trajectory is similar: after joining Random House as an editor, she moved to Simon and Shuster and then Houghton Mifflin in 1981 as Executive Editor and eventually Editor in Chief and Publisher. She joined Doubleday as Senior Vice President in 1988, bringing Atwood and others of her authors with her, and in 1990 she premiered her own imprint at the company, Nan A. Talese/Doubleday. Like Seligman, she combines the positions of administrator and active literary editor. Liz Calder, on the other hand, began in the publishing industry as a publicist at Gollancz but then moved to editing, becoming editorial director before moving to Jonathan Cape, where she began working

2 I thank Margaret Atwood for pointing out that Alexandra Pringle, Lennie Goodings, and Louise Dennys have been important members of her editorial team.

with Atwood. She became a founding director at Bloomsbury in the mid-1980s, and Atwood followed her there. Alexandra Pringle worked as both a literary agent and an editor before joining Bloomsbury in 1999, where she became Group Editor in Chief, working with Atwood after Liz Calder's time at Bloomsbury. Louise Dennys began her career as a bookseller, moving on to editing and from there to publishing, becoming partner in the Lester and Orpen Dennys firm before being named Executive Publisher of Knopf Canada and Vice President of Random House Canada. As for Lennie Goodings, she left Canada for Britain in the 1980s to join Virago Books, where she is now editor and publisher. She has also written a children's book. As this sketch of Atwood's key editors reveals, they have approached editorial work from a broader experience in the publishing industry, which is fairly typical of literary editors, so they bring to their work with Atwood combined expertise in branches of publishing that span the literary and the commercial.

This synthetic nature of editorial careers, and the ways in which they may be overshadowed by the other administrative titles that successful senior editors also hold, increase the cultural invisibility that is already inherent in the task of editing manuscripts for publication. For this reason, it is important to isolate what exactly the role of the literary editor typically consists of, before examining how Atwood and her editors work together. The history and role of literary agents are fairly well documented (see the previous chapter); this cannot be said of literary editors, which has implications for the ways in which the editor is perceived to be operating in relation to cultural commodities. Whereas the agent was (mis)understood, from the beginning, as an unseemly eruption of capital into the field of literary values, the editor's labour has always operated under the sign of devotion to Art, even when the editor has been involved – as Seligman, Talese, and Calder have been – in the day-to-day exigencies of running a business.

Editors of various publications have, of course, existed for centuries. Susan Bell, in her absorbing study *The Artful Edit*, maintains that "most literature, since the late 1400s, has been altered by the editorial process on its way to the public" (3), citing the changes that medieval scribes made to texts either "by accident or will" (185). Such a narrative of origins may overgeneralize what one might consider "the editorial process," though Bell is on firmer ground when she discerns the seeds of modern editorial practice in the work of fifteenth-century Venetian freelance editors, who set out to feed the growing demand for printed material in the wake of the invention of the printing press. These editors located and authenticated old manuscripts, corrected their grammar (a tricky job in an age when that grammar was slowly becoming standardized), and wrote exegeses of the manuscripts (186–7). Essentially, Bell believes, their work formed a "tacit manifesto" that editors still follow today: "be savvy enough to find good manuscripts, suave enough to navigate their ambiguities, and erudite enough to discuss them persuasively" (187). The site of that persuasive discussion may have shifted from textual exegesis to the Monday morning editorial meeting, but the skills involved are the same.

Moving to America, Gerald Gross traces the genesis of the publisher's editor as a cultural force to 1898, when Appleton's Ripley Hitchcock made dramatic revisions to the manuscript of *David Harum* by one Edward Noyes Westcott, an upstate New York banker. Other publishers had shown no interest in Westcott's book, but Hitchcock saw some potential in the manuscript. Chapter 6, he felt, was really the opening of the novel, so he moved it, relocated the previous five chapters, and made other substantial suggestions, with the result that *David Harum*, when released, became the top-selling title of 1899. As Gross comments, it isn't so much that Hitchcock performed duties that editors had not undertaken before; this time, though, "people found out what the editor had done" (11). This set the stage, Gross argues, for the "cultural mythology" of editing, which reached a climax in the 1930s with the rise of charismatic figures such as Maxwell Perkins, editor of Fitzgerald and Hemingway, who was noted both for seeking out younger writers and for meticulously editing their manuscripts. Here, for Gross, was the birth of the ideology of "the editor as savior, finding the soul of a manuscript, the editor as alchemist, turning lead into gold; the editor as seer, recognizing what others had missed" (12). Although this seems a very late development, if we compare it to the rise of the literary agent that I described in the previous chapter, this belatedness is attributable to the lack of British copyright protection until 1891; reprints of the leading English writers of the day required no textual editing on the North American end.

The fact that all three of Atwood's key editors are women is also reflective of the history of the profession. Though Gross maintains that editing has remained "one of America's least [racially] integrated professions" (18), it is one in which women – specifically, white women – have attained senior administrative roles (as the publishing credentials of Talese, Seligman, and Calder suggest). (Compare Toni Morrison's experiences as a senior editor at Random House from 1970 to 1983, during which time she edited Toni Cade Bambera, Lucille Clifton, June Jordan, and other influential African-American writers, an achievement that was seen as unprecedented in American publishing history; Wall). This is the sort of commitment that subsequent women editors, drawn from various communities, have sought to emulate: Janet Silver, who was manuscript editor on *The Handmaid's Tale* under Nan Talese's direction at Houghton Mifflin, has said that during those years, Talese sought out authors who countered the conservatism of the house's offerings; and Silver, for her part, as an editor moving up the corporate ladder, "just felt that there was a need to hear from those kinds of voices [like African-American writers Connie Porter and Carolyn Ferrell, whom she signed] and that Houghton should be supporting writers like that" (Ferrari-Adler, "Agents & Editors: A Q&A with Editor Janet Silver"). Historically, too, the mentoring of young writers has been part of the editor's job since the early days of periodical publishing in America (Colbert 346); like the discovery of writers from communities that are underrepresented in print, this mentoring of the young is a perfect example of the dovetailing of commercial, political, and artistic imperatives, since part of this mission of nurturing the next generation of writers has to do with supplying the market with fresh voices that will prove attractive to consumers.

Beyond this, the roles fulfilled by editors are notable for their number and their diversity. As a recent *National Post* series on book publishing in Canada noted, this situation is partly a result of the decrease in the number of editors at major publishing houses as those houses seek, in neoliberal fashion, to reduce their "bottom line" production costs. As a result, according to the literary agent Dean Cooke, the "workload [of editors] has increased inversely" (Medley, "Licence to Deal"), and editors are facing strong pressure to perform many tasks, to the point that the task most people would associate with the job – micro-editing manuscripts or "line editing" – is, as I have mentioned, often performed by editors during their "leisure" hours. The distinction that Dan Franklin, writing of British publishing in 1993, draws between copy editors and commissioning editors (111), therefore, seems more notional than demonstrable. Franklin sees the commissioning editors as the visible labourers (visible, that is, "at the author's side" [116] at major prize galas, or copiously thanked in acknowledgments); whereas the copy editors are the unsung heroes of editorial labour, "poorly paid, underrated by senior management, and usually grossly undervalued" (111). In the wake of the recessions of the 1980s and 1990s, and the concomitant economic "restructurings" in the publishing industry, Franklin's job distinctions have broken down. Though underpaid, unsung copyeditors are still plentiful enough, there has been a good deal of reabsorption of their labour into the job descriptions of commissioning editors (among whom Franklin includes senior editors, chief editors, and other administratively senior editors). In the United States, Lee Boudreaux, editorial director at Ecco, declares that "I've never worked with an editor who doesn't edit all weekend long, every single night" (Ferrari-Adler, "Agents & Editors: A Q&A with Four Young Editors"). Here in Canada, the situation is the same; Ellen Seligman finds that "most of her editing is confined to mornings, evenings and weekends" because of her administrative duties (Medley, "Mark of an Editor").

For the most part, though, the core duties of the publisher's editor are the following:

- "Product development": "Planning of the list ... the titles which the firm publishes" (Feather 108). Senior editors at the firm will be involved in deciding what this list will look like; editors working under them will work within that business plan.
- Recruiting authors and commissioning titles (Feather 208).
- Dealing with literary agents in acquiring those titles and in arranging contracts between the publishing house and the author.
- Working with the marketing department to promote books.
- In the case of assistant editors, dealing with the author on the details of production leading up to the publication of the book (Feather 209).
- Attending a multitude of meetings. One editor lists these: "editorial meetings, acquisitions meetings, marketing meetings, focus meetings, meetings about the jackets, meetings about the titles" (Ferrari-Adler, "Agents & Editors: A Q&A with Pat Strachan" 10).

Those are, baldly speaking, the editor's duties, but what strikes me about them is how insufficiently they describe the manifold roles of the editor and the implications of those roles. Gross feels that contemporary editors face many more demands than their predecessors did: "they must master an entire gamut of disciplines including production, marketing, negotiation, promotion, advertising, publicity, accounting, salesmanship, psychology, politics, diplomacy, and – well, editing" (34). But however much the pace and technological delivery of these roles may have intensified and diversified, I perceive elements of Gross's daunting list in the work of editors of the past. As Patricia Okker notes of nineteenth-century American editors, they were "part author, part literary critic, part entrepreneur"

(355), and this broad designation has not, to my mind, essentially changed over the intervening years.

As Okker's description suggests, a great deal of the work of editing involves mediation. Eric Chinski, vice-president and editor-in-chief at Farrar, Straus and Giroux, observes that "as an editor, you're in this funny position of both being an advocate for the house to the author and agent but also being an advocate for the author to everybody in house" (Ferrari-Adler, "Agents & Editors: A Q&A with Four Young Editors"). This sounds admirably high-minded and abstract, but on the ground, this mediation can be demanding and tense; as Gerald Gross points out, this can mean explaining to the author the limits on marketing budgets – "why," for instance, "a full-page ad in the *Times Book Review*, color illustrations, a coast-to-coast tour, or whatever is unwarranted and/or unaffordable" (8). As the respected American editor Pat Strachan puts it, "the editor's role, in part, is to translate for the writer the logic behind certain decisions on the house's part" (Ferrari-Adler, "Agents & Editors: A Q&A with Editor Pat Strachan"). But the editor must do this while continuing to convince the author that she or he is representing his or her best interests. No wonder Gross calls this bi-directional act of representation that the editor performs a "Janus-like function" (4).

Representing the author to the firm largely comes down to representing the book and its strengths. As Gross maintains in his handbook, "one of the editor's most crucial challenges is to be able to articulate, clearly and appealingly, the signal virtues of a given book" (7) – the contemporary version of fifteenth-century editorial exegesis. He maintains that this activity is central to the actions that an editor undertakes on behalf of a book: everything from arguing in favour of its publication in editorial meetings, to assisting with catalogue and jacket copy, to formulating publicity statements. That advocacy on behalf of authors sometimes involves a great deal of risk taking. Ellen Seligman recalls "fighting with the sales department to sign *In the Skin of a Lion* [Michael Ondaatje's first novel]. They were trepidacious. But it was a huge success" (Hampson). Many interviews with editors, in fact, feature at some point or other a story about a publishing success of this kind – and its inverse, the story of a gamble taken and lost.

Particularly for high-profile writers such as Atwood, part of the editor's promotional work involves representing the book and its author to a broader public. Whenever Atwood publishes a new book – or is about to – Ellen Seligman is quoted frequently in the media as to the nature and importance of the new addition to Atwood's oeuvre. For example, a month before Atwood's *The Year of the Flood* was published in September 2009, Seligman was interviewed by the *Toronto Star* about the creative spin on the traditional book tour that Atwood and her team were planning for that autumn: live performance of the novel's God's Gardeners' hymns. Seligman was quoted as saying that "the idea of this performance and gathering the public – these are public performances and very inexpensive tickets – is a way of kind of joining everybody together in this global concern, which is our world and life as we know it" (DeMara). Here Seligman, as editor–publisher, is mediating the world of the novel that is about to be released for the benefit of a readership that does not yet have access to it – the better to promote sales in the all-important autumn season to come.

As if the exigencies of representing the author to the firm, the firm to the author, and the book to the public were not demanding enough, editors also see themselves as representing that impossible-to-define constituency, the reader. As the independent publisher Richard Abel argues, "the authentic editor plays the culturally critical role of reconciling the author's raw MS with the demands/needs/expectations/capacities of both the historic tradition and the reader." That is quite a tall order. But many editors who are interviewed about their work keep coming back to this idea that they are, in editor Richard Nash's term, "proxies for the reader" (Ferrari-Adler, "Agents & Editors: A Q&A with Four Young Editors"). Gerald Gross emphasizes this role in his authoritative handbook; in carrying out detailed line editing, he says, "the editor is acting as the first truly disinterested reader" (6). The language that editors assume when they present themselves as the *ur*-Reader powerfully suggests the broadly cultural role they see themselves fulfilling, one that reaches back to the modernist romanticizing of the editor as "il miglior fabbro."

This notion of the editor as the Janus-faced agent of literary production – at once advocate of author, publisher, and reader – makes itself felt in editorial processes as editors continually seek a balance among these authorial, publishing, and readerly affiliations. For example, Ellen Seligman has described the first round of editing, for her, as "taking a journey through the book with the author" and trying to understand the workings of that manuscript from an authorial perspective before making any suggestions. "Before having that dialogue with the author," she declares, "I would never just say, 'You've got to cut 80 pages, you've got to throw out the first chapter, you've got to do this" (Medley, "Mark of an Editor"), though she acknowledges that there are editors out there who do this. What Seligman is saying is that she, personally, opens the process with an act of authorial affiliation before shifting to the other editorial personae: editor as representative of the publisher's needs, or editor as readerly surrogate. Other editors arrange and overlap those roles differently, but most combine them in some fashion. And because they do, they can never be simply representative of art or commerce alone.

Looking closely at the Atwood archives, there are many examples of this fascinating exchange, wherein author and text meet editor-as-author/publisher/reader. My purpose here is not to delve into the minute details of specific editorial revisions of Atwood's texts, though the archive would afford a textual scholar rich resources for the carrying out of such studies. Instead, I am interested in the general nature and mechanics of the exchange. I am impressed, in my reading of the archives, by the ways in which the various facets of this editing relationship are respected and reinforced. During the period when Atwood is composing a work, for instance, the editor does not have access to the manuscript; as Nan Talese describes, at this point in the process she will typically "have before me an enigmatic chart of her [Atwood's] progress on a new book" made up of a list of sections each followed by a box. The boxes that have x's drawn through them represent those chapters that Atwood has drafted so far. But this is all that Talese, like Phoebe Larmore, knows about the new work at this stage: "The subject of the book is unknown to me – it has not even been hinted at – nor will it be known until the manuscript is before me" (Nischik 289). From time to time, she will receive updates informing her of the number of manuscript pages completed – but that is all. Initial composition, then, "belongs" to the author, and the editor is no different at this stage from the reading public awaiting the next book by Margaret Atwood.

Once the manuscript is handed over, the editor's role shifts to that of publisher's representative and reader's proxy, and the ornate web of editorial relations begins to take shape. To cite just one of many examples from the archives, there is a detailed letter from Nan Talese to Margaret Atwood, just onto three pages single-spaced, containing specific queries and responses to the poems in *Morning in the Burned House* (MS COLL 335.6:2). Typically, once Atwood decides what changes are to be made in response to these editorial queries, she responds in writing, and her office assistant records those changes in a computer file. The assistant then double-checks that changes have been made to that file (there is evidence, for example, of Sarah Cooper checking, change by change, that all editorial alterations have been made to the new computer file [MS COLL 335.163:34]). It is up to the assistant to make clear which documents have had approved editorial changes made to them, so that Atwood's records are organized and everyone has an up-to-date copy of the manuscript as it exists in its current version.

As this editorial timeline suggests, the process shifts dramatically from a model of solitary authorial agency to one of editorial collaboration. Take, for example, the correspondence among Atwood, Nan Talese, and Phoebe Larmore in the archives on the subject of the constitution of the American edition combining *Murder in the Dark* and *Good Bones*, titled *Good Bones and Simple Murders*. Again, the process takes its inception from authorial agency: Atwood opens by proposing selections from the two books that should appear in the combined edition (MS COLL 200.164:1). Next, the other two weigh in, expressing their opinions regarding the shape of the volume (Talese) and the contractual restrictions involved (Larmore). Again, the forces of art and commerce intermingle, as they must in any such process.

In several senses, then, the act of editing Atwood is profoundly collaborative. In addition to the necessary participation of editors from publishing houses in several countries that I have already described, the collaboration is compounded by the scheduling of physical meetings wherein key editors, such as Seligman, Talese, and Calder, and literary agent Larmore gather to read and discuss the manuscript for the first time. In preparation for the publication of *Alias Grace*, for example, Larmore, Seligman, Talese, Marly Rusoff (at that time, working in publicity for Doubleday), and Vivienne Shuster (Atwood's British agent) met in Toronto from 13 to 23 January 1996: ten days to sequester themselves in a hotel (in the case of those coming from out of town), read through the manuscript, and discuss it first among themselves and, subsequently, with Atwood (MS COLL 335.9:4). Participants describe these meetings as exciting days of readerly pleasure combined with the intellectual exchange of editorial work; as Seligman says, "we eagerly hole up in our hotel rooms, or, in my case, at home, to read and then discuss together [the manuscript] with the author and her agent, Phoebe Larmore" (Nischik 287). Talese recalls "how with one particular novel, after I began to read, I got up and pulled a soft white blanket out of the cupboard in the Toronto hotel room in which I was staying, and settled onto the sofa, knowing I was in for a delicious treat" (Nischik 289). From the point of view of understanding editorial work, it is significant that the participants in these textual marathons draw upon the languages of both labour and pleasure, for both are powerfully engaged as the editor balances her roles as proxy for both reader and publisher.

Though the archive is full of detail about the complexities of bringing the participants together for one of these sessions, it remains understandably quiet on the subject of exactly how the give-and-take of editorial negotiation takes place, since the meetings are designed to allow for oral, face-to-face discussion of the manuscript. However, Atwood has commented in interviews that the sessions offer her a "take on what people have understood, versus what is actually on the page" (MacSkimming "The Perilous Trade Conversations" 24). She used the example of all of her trusted editorial readers thinking that the landlady character in *Alias Grace* was fat; because she had not really intended for that to be the case, she altered the text to make it abundantly clear that the character was not overweight (24).

The editing of most literary texts would not occasion this sort of international summit meeting, and its existence surely points to the importance of Atwood's new titles to the publishers involved. It is an exceptional practice, as Atwood admitted when Roy MacSkimming asked her, "Do you know of any other writers who have an editorial process resembling yours?": "No," replied Atwood. "It can only work because they all get on" ("The Perilous Trade Conversations" 24). Still, these unprecedented editing sessions are emblematic of the editing process in that they illustrate its collaborative nature. The presence at the editing summits of people involved with contractual matters and publicity as well as with editing in the strictest sense of the word makes sense, given the interrelationship of the editor's work with those other functions; as Richard Abel explains, "the editor must take a lead role in advising and guiding those responsible for executing the marketing program as to the intended audience and how it can be reached." Michael Kandel, Ursula Le Guin's editor, confirms this need for integrated labour: "The designer of the book, the artists of the jacket, the publicist, the marketing person – members of the publishing team should have the editor's input in their decision making." Indeed, how could it be otherwise, since the intelligent marketing of a book requires the input of those who are intimately acquainted with it and who are ideally situated to articulate its value?

Sometimes this collaborative exchange creates the all-important "buzz" that will place a book in an advantageous position. As former Random House editor Lee Boudreaux comments, "it's almost like an electrical pulse traveling down a wire. It starts with the author, then the agent, then the editor, and then there are a lot of telephone poles it's got to go through from there" (Ferrari-Adler, "Agents & Editors: A Q&A with Four Young Editors"). The energy the book picks up in this web of relations, even before it hits the bookstores, is crucial, and its potential complicates what we normally think of as a definite line of separation between private pre-publication labour and post-publication literary promotion.

At other times, the editor welcomes this web of industrial relations because it means that he or she is not alone in approaching the author with suggestions for revision. Boudreaux adds that "an agent who can honestly appraise the work along with you and add their voice to the chorus of why, for example, the author needs to change that title" (Ferrari-Adler, "Agents & Editors: A Q&A with Four Young Editors") is a valuable ally. So the presence of Phoebe Larmore at the Atwood editing summits makes sense in terms of editorial practice and in terms of dealing with the manuscript in its totality, as an artistic and commercial product. As Larmore herself explained in an interview, this gathering, "a bit like a pajama party," is also strategic: it allows for the creation of a "unified" editorial "voice providing feedback to Atwood, who joins the group afterward" (Turbide). Given the sheer numbers of production and promotion staff providing that feedback to Atwood in the months preceding publication, such unity is crucial; otherwise, the author would be juggling multiple, potentially conflicting bits of editorial advice.

Another reason why editors are more than happy to admit agents into their midst is that agents can assist them in one of their roles: acting as the representative of the publishing house and explaining the house's decisions to the author. Indeed, as editor Pat Strachan points out, "I'm very glad to have the agents' help. The agents know much more about publishing than the writers do, obviously. Some of them have worked at publishing houses and can explain the logic behind the publisher's decisions. They know what to ask for and what not to ask for" (Ferrari-Adler, "Agents & Editors: A Q & A with Pat Strachan"). Clearly, this applies more directly to the case of relatively inexperienced authors; by this point, a writer of Atwood's stature knows just as much as the agent does about publishers and their decisions. At any rate, this cooperation contradicts the notion that editors, as representatives of art, and literary agents, as forces of commerce, are fated to embody conflicting values.

Since seasoned authors like Atwood do know a great deal about publishing, editors will commonly reflect that they must never lose sight of the author's input. Janet Silver adds to the usual advice about editors and marketing and publicity people working together that you must "bring the author in as well. One of the things that we've all learned in publishing is that the authors know their audience very well. We want to have them participate as part of the conversation" (Ferrari-Adler, "Agents & Editors: A Q&A with Janet Silver"). Because this is so – because the publication of a book has its own ecology and web of industrial relations – the all-important relationship between an editor and an author takes place within that setting of intense collaboration. "Editing is a conversation, not a monologue" (4), argues Susan Bell in her guide *The Artful Edit*, and that conversation reaches beyond the editor–author dyad that centrally concerns her in that study. Still, it is worthwhile to disentangle this one thread – the collaboration of editor and author – from the broader literary ecosystem, since it highlights much of what I have to say about editors and their relations with the commercial and artistic realms. To begin, like authors' relations with their literary agents, the author–editor relationship often frustrates the business/friendship divide. Patricia Okker has traced this relationship throughout American literature: "Many authors and editors had relationships in which business and personal matters intertwined. Correspondence between authors and their editors, for example, frequently shifts between contract negotiations and social invitations and friendly queries about spouses and children" (360). In fact, John Feather, in his study of twenty-first-century publishing, goes further: the author–editor relationship, he argues, "can never consist entirely of impersonal business dealings" (111) – which is precisely why that relationship is so unpredictable and variable and why it is impossible to isolate its essentials.

Like any relationship, whether of a predominantly business or personal nature, there are innumerable ways the association can go right – or wrong. Dan Franklin places the bond between editor and author along a spectrum that runs between "falling in love" and "trench warfare" (113). Tales abound of productive career-long editorial partnerships and of notable disasters too. On the latter side, *The New Yorker* ran a story in 2007 titled "Rough Crossings" about Raymond Carver's relationship with his editor Gordon Lish at Alfred A. Knopf. Lish drastically cut the stories in Carver's volume *What We Talk About When We Talk About Love* – two by nearly 70 per cent, several by almost half. A distraught Carver, receiving the copy edited manuscript, complained to his editor that he was "confused, tired, paranoid, and afraid" ("Rough Crossings"). Controversy continues to swirl around this editing job, with supporters and detractors of Lish weighing in, and with Carver's widow Tess Gallagher, meanwhile, fighting Knopf for the right to publish uncut versions of the stories, but what is valuable to discern in this anecdote for my purposes here is the delicacy of the interrelationship of the personal and the commercial in the editor–author relationship. Just two days after writing his despairing letter, Carver wrote another one to Lish, in which he settled minor editing issues and signed himself "with my love" ("Rough Crossings"). Was the earlier letter a product of depression and drunkenness, or was the later letter the product of resignation to Lish's judgment or connections? It seems impossible to tell. Another editor who worked with Carver, Gary Fisketjon, observed of the Carver–Lish controversy that "an editorial relationship is a private one, and nobody can see it fully and completely" ("Rough Crossings").[3]

Needless to say, there is nothing about the Atwood editorial team that can compete for sheer angst or oddity with the Carver–Lish partnership. But the relationships that Atwood has forged with her editors also reveal the delicate balancing of the private and the public. To begin, a comfortable personal working relationship between author and editor is a must, but it must be professional enough to allow for negotiation (something that Carver and Lish's seemingly did not, or at least did not in any sustained fashion). Looking to the Atwood archives, there are many instances wherein professional debate takes place comfortably but seriously. In February 1994, for example, there was some discussion as to the likeliest title for the combined American edition of *Good Bones and Simple Murders*. Atwood faxed this title to Nan Talese as a compromise, since she was less than thrilled with the title that Talese had suggested: *Good Bones and A Little Bit of Murder*. Teasingly (but with some seriousness intermixed), Atwood wrote:

> Under no circumstances will I accept GOOD BONES AND A LITTLE BIT OF MURDER (it's the "bit" that does it to me). But there may be a compromise. Let me propose this:
>
> GOOD BONES
> and Little Murders
>
> There. Now are you happy? You won on "little" and "murders," and lost on "a, " "bit" and "of. " Seems fair to me, as there are more letters in the two winning words than in the others. (MS COLL 200.164:24)

3 Thanks to Erin Aspenlieder for bringing this example of a fraught but fascinating author-editor relationship to my attention.

It's as though Atwood is parodying the language of editorial negotiation, with her talk of how many words and letters each party to the negotiation "wins" and "loses." The jokiness neatly diffuses any tension there might be in the disagreement, but amidst the clearly comfortable joking relationship, negotiation is going on here.

At other times, the professional and personal worlds may mingle in terms of the various hands involved in the editing process. The Atwood archives contain documents in which Atwood responds, in great detail, to editing suggestions made by Ellen Seligman. On 11 January 2000, she does so for *The Blind Assassin*. This time she has drawn on the considered opinions of two other close associates whose relationships with her span the professional and the personal: her personal assistant Sarah Cooper and her daughter Jess Atwood Gibson. "We are all 3 of us in agreement," she writes to Seligman, on particular questions arising from Seligman's edits. In a less collaborative group, this might seem like gathering forces to resist the editor's suggestions, but the Atwood office has long worked in a consultative, collaborative way, so this is, simply, the way in which decisions are taken – though the author, ultimately, stands alone to make the final decision. The following exchange with Roy MacSkimming makes that point abundantly clear:

> RM: Does Ellen [Seligman] take into account the views of the British and American editors?
> MA: It doesn't matter whether Ellen takes them into account. It's whether I take them into account. Sorry to sound so megalomaniacal. ("The Perilous Trade Conversations" 24)

When MacSkimming clarifies that he "just wants to know the exact process," Atwood clarifies in turn: "I take Ellen's views into account too. I take all their views into account. And at a second meeting, I tell them yes, I agree to this, and no, I don't agree to that" (24). Again, exchange and collaboration in the context of the Atwood industry distils rather than diffuses authorial agency.

Because the editor–author relationship is an amalgamation of the personal and the professional, writers often follow their editors to the new jobs and publishing houses that they join as part of their evolving careers. In recent decades, this mobility has increased. As the *National Post*'s 2008 study of Canadian literary agencies discovered, editors are now much "more likely to jump from one publisher to the next" (Medley, "Licence to Deal"). Writing of the publishing industry in Britain at the same time, Dan Franklin attributes this mobility to the economic instability and domination of the industry by large bookselling chains during the 1980s and 1990s, a time when "editors changed jobs with increasing regularity; authors became disillusioned when their editor left, and then the next one and the next; old loyalties melted away" (118). In Canada, the *National Post* 2008 survey suggests that this editorial peripateticism is the reason why the author–agent relationship has become the primary source of consistency for authors in the last couple of decades. That stability, however, can also be achieved when an author moves with his or her editor, and in this respect Atwood's career has been fairly representative, in that she has followed some of her editors to their new houses. The Atwood archives include a file containing correspondence about Nan Talese leaving Houghton Mifflin for Doubleday in 1988 and Atwood's subsequent decision to follow her (MS COLL. 335:136.10:20). And when Liz Calder paid tribute to Atwood twenty years after they first worked together in 1980, she highlighted the issue of loyalty, first and foremost. Speaking of the period just after she left Cape and founded Bloomsbury, Calder declared, "I cannot recall a moment of greater joy in my professional life than when someone handed me a scrap of paper at the Booksellers' Conference in Eastbourne in 1988 on which was written 'We've got the Atwood'" (Nischik 292). The language is that of wooing accounts in business, but the joy that Calder describes exceeds the financial. For an author, to take this measure of risk is to offer a ringing vote of confidence for both the personal and the professional qualities that combine to make a talented editor.

Understandably, then, Calder reads this act as one of great personal loyalty and integrity. "I can think of few other authors who have remained so faithful to their editors and agents," she declares. Indeed, she sees this capacity for loyalty as a departure from the more self-aggrandizing narratives of literary celebrity; it is "in marked contrast to much of what happens in pursuit of fame and fortune in the book business" (Nischik 293). The sorts of stories Calder refers darkly to here are those of mid-career writers being wooed by new houses with larger monetary advances – the sorts of stories that move editor Chuck Adams to remark, "I just get frustrated when agents and authors go for the money … and don't think about building careers" (Ferrari-Adler, "Agents & Editors: A Q&A with Chuck Adams"). But on the other hand, do we have to read the choice to remain with one editor as one of personal loyalty and the choice to move elsewhere as evidence of unseemly and inartistic greed? After all, when Atwood followed Liz Calder to Bloomsbury and Nan Talese to Doubleday, she was also leaving production people with whom she'd no doubt enjoyed working over the years. In opting to follow an editor, a writer may be moved by generosity and indebtedness for the work that the editor has contributed to the writer's career, but practical reasons usually play a role as well. And some reasons will be so much a product of the two motives that it would be impossible to disentangle them: staying with an editor with whom you work well, and who has helped represent your books successfully, is not just a decent act but a canny one as well.

Atwood's loyalty to editors goes back a long way, though, and it cannot be reduced to any simple commercial motive. In the flurry of tributes that marked the passing of Robert Weaver, Atwood was a prominent participant; she granted an interview to Elaine Kalman Naves for her book *Robert Weaver: Godfather of Canadian Literature*, which was published at the end of Weaver's life, in which she described how he had assisted her as a young writer, as well as how they collaborated on anthologies later in her career. "Robert Weaver was a great editor," she commented at the book's launch, "for very simple reasons. He took the work seriously" (Atwood "A Fond Farewell to a CanLit Giant"). Much the same could be said of Atwood's long-standing commitment to William (Bill) Toye at Oxford University Press. Shortly after she had published *The Circle Game* in 1966, Toye phoned her out of the blue, and after consulting with him, Atwood agreed to submit the manuscript of *The Animals in That Country* to him. From that point, Oxford became the publishing home for Atwood's poetry, and Toye became a trusted editor and mentor. Toye even supplied her with the early Canadian illustrations that inspired her collages in *The Journals of Susanna Moodie*. In Roy MacSkimming's words, "Atwood remained loyal to Toye as a poet while publishing her fiction primarily with McClelland and Stewart" (*The Perilous Trade* 87).[4] Like a host of other writers, Atwood is bound to her editors by the loyalty of respect: a loyalty that cannot be uncomplicatedly parsed into the personal and the professional.

If this amalgamation of heart and head in writer–editor relationships sounds potentially volatile, it is – and it requires careful management to make those relationships work. Editors are the first to acknowledge that, no matter how close the personal friendships that evolve between themselves and the writers they work with, these are, nevertheless, business relationships. As Ellen Seligman has commented, "I think you do have to be careful, and there has to be a sort of understanding, whether it's silent or explicit, that it has nothing to do with friendship," though she acknowledges that "there's a little post-partum … a little bit of separation sadness" on the part of editor and

4 The question of genre and literary celebrity is a fascinating one to ponder in the career of Margaret Atwood; given the differential sales involved, it is unsurprising that Atwood's celebrity is more closely tied to her work in fictional genres, particularly the novel; as evidence, one might compare the publicity that attends the release of a new Atwood novel in comparison with the (increasingly rare) release of a volume of poems.

author when their intense period of collaboration comes to a close. Ever accurate, though, Seligman adds, "incidentally, not all the time, but many times" (Medley, "Mark of an Editor"). I cite Seligman's complicated musings on editorial friendships at length because their complexity should keep us from reading these relationships as dominated either by friendship or by money. By consistently celebrating successful editor–author pairings as animated by friendship, we are imprinting on this complicated relationship the mystique of the "tireless, even heroic devotion to the author" (Gross 14) that has attached itself to legendary modern editors. Conversely, reading these partnerships as invariably soiled by the economic misses out on the rich satisfactions of collaboration on artistic production: satisfactions that are also, and not only, personal.

Learning how to manage these relationships so that they, too, are not "only personal," so that they do not lose their professional edge, is the particular challenge faced by the apprentice editor. All four young editors interviewed by *Poets and Writers* had stories to tell on this score. Alexis Gargagliano, an editor at Scribner, confessed to having "the impulse to protect my authors and treat them as if they are more fragile than they actually are" (Ferrari-Adler, "Agents & Editors: A Q & A with Four Young Editors") – a quasi-parental tendency. She found that if she could have a frank discussion with the author as early as possible, it would enable her to talk about difficult issues as they came up, and she would not be left wondering how to turn this relationship from mothering to mentoring. In the last portion of the interview with these four young editors, which features unattributed reflections (undoubtedly a good idea, given their relatively new careers), one of them reflects that "despite the fact that there is a real personal connection, authors should realize that we're not their therapists, we're not their best friends in the world, etcetera. I can fix your book but I can't fix your whole life." Another discussant laughingly confided that an author once put in a call because there were not enough hangers in his hotel closet. (Ferrari-Adler, "Agents & Editors: A Q & A with Four Young Editors").

Moving from the intimacies of author–editor relations to the broader industrial picture, how are we to conceptualize these unruly relationships, compounded of personal kismet and professional skill? First of all, it is undeniable that editors, particularly those who assemble a roster of successful artists, garner a considerable measure of cultural capital. The press announcement of Ellen Seligman's election as President of PEN Canada in June 2009 referred to her as "the Maxwell Perkins of Canadian publishing" ("Literary Publisher Ellen Seligman Elected President of PEN Canada at 2009 AGM"). And indeed, with the sort of record she has assembled for seeing the promise in a manuscript, it is understandable that she would be so celebrated. Poet Patrick Lane, for instance, started a prose-writing exercise while recovering from acute alcoholism and soon found himself writing a book. The manuscript needed work, as manuscripts will, yet "only one" of the publishers his agent sent the manuscript to "showed an interest, Ellen Seligman at McClelland and Stewart" (Lane). The editing process was painstaking but revelatory to Lane, and the resulting book, *There Is a Season*, went on to win the B.C. National Award for Canadian Non-Fiction and to be nominated for the Charles Taylor Award. There are many such stories and testimonials to Seligman circulating among Canadian writers. As her *National Post* profile points out, she has edited more Giller Prize winners than any other editor and was named to the Order of Canada in 2009 (Medley, "Mark of an Editor"). Impressive cultural credentials for a worker whose labour, at least as a textual editor, remains invisible on the page. Atwood's American editor inspires similar encomiums; editor and colleague Janet Silver draws attention to Nan Talese's "reputation for excellence and quality and sticking with writers over the long term" (Ferrari-Adler, "Agents & Editors: A Q&A with Editor Janet Silver"). In the case of such high-profile partnerships of writer and editor, the cultural capital becomes a shared quantity: Seligman and Talese share the excellence of their author lists, and authors who sign with them receive a measure of it by association.

For this reason, some analysts of the publishing industry have tended to bracket off literary editors as an entirely different species. Dan Franklin specifies that his account of editing in late-twentieth-century Britain is mainly concerned with non-fiction editing, since "fiction editors tend to be a different breed from those who specialize in non-fiction. They have to work more from instinct, their skills owing more to art than science" (116).

This view of the literary editor as an intuitive high-art devotee, though, is purchased at the price of forgetting the economic. As literary agent and writer Richard Curtis sardonically notes, to place Maxwell Perkins and his like on a pedestal seals them off from the economics of book publishing: editors from "'the Good Old Days,'" he jokes, "placed literature high above crass commerce, and discussed author compensation with the same delicacy they reserved for childbearing" (Gross 31). Curtis's volley seems a response to a much-discussed manifesto by Norton editor Gerald Howard on the state of publishing today, in which he argues that it has confused "its two classic functions": the mission to civilize and the business of selling units (Gross 57–8). Howard concludes that Maxwell Perkins – that avatar of the profession – would scarcely recognize the money-driven concern that publishing has become; hailing Perkins as his lodestar, Howard titles his piece "Mistah Perkins – He Dead: Publishing Today." Historically, though, editing has always been an act of balancing art and commodity. Ann Mauger Colbert opens her entry on "Editors" for *American History Through Literature 1870–1920* by noting that in that period, editors "continued to mediate and walk a kind of balancing act between business interests and creative talent" (345). To hear Howard put his case, though, one would think that the Golden Age had irremediably passed; though he admits that Perkins and his associates did need to consult the ledgers, he tends to see evidence of this in specific popular titles they published, not in the simultaneous status of every book as both commodity and cultural artefact.

Even though that simultaneity is at the heart of this profession, new editors continue to be surprised at the extent of the commercial dealings in their day-to-day work; as Eric Chinski recalls, "I had no idea that the role of the editor was to communicate to the marketing and sales departments. I had this very dark-and-stormy night vision of the editor sitting in a room poring over manuscripts" (Ferrari-Adler, "Agents & Editors: A Q & A with Four Young Editors"). As his colleague Alexis Gargagliano observes, even after having become familiar with the artistic and commercial dimensions of the job, an editor can still, at times, identify primarily with one or another pole: "I always have to remind myself … that the people who are on the sales end also love books, and they also love to read, and they could be making more money in another industry too" (Ferrari-Adler, "Agents & Editors: A Q & A with Four Young Editors"). A third "young editor," Richard Nash, identifies more with the other end of the spectrum; he feels frustration at authors who "assume that it is everybody else's job to sell their books while they get to be pure and pristine. They don't have to get the book-publishing equivalent of dirt under their fingernails" (Ferrari-Adler, "Agents & Editors: A Q & A with Four Young Editors"). From this welter of allegiances, I conclude that editors must calibrate the relative importance of the economic and the artistic day after day; on the hot topic of literary agents auctioning manuscripts to the highest bidder, agent Lee Boudreaux maintains the fundamental nature of his aesthetic response: an agent calling and telling him that there is "interest" in a book – that is, several possible offers – is "not going to change my mind about whether I liked the book or not" (Ferrari-Adler, "Agents & Editors: A Q & A with Four Young Editors"), though to be fair, it has demonstrably influenced other editors and houses.

Even in the case of the controversial auctioning of manuscripts, editors' responses are complicated, some editors regretting years afterward that they let a big book "get away" because of lack of funds. When Pat Strachan was asked whether she had any regrets in a long and distinguished career, she reached back for one such story. In the 1970s, as a young editor with Farrar, Straus and Giroux, she happened upon a copy of Alice Munro's *Lives of Girls and Women* at a street bookstall and was enormously taken with the writing. She made inquiries and discovered that Munro had obtained an agent in the United States, Virginia Barber, and that there was a manuscript in the works. Strachan tried to talk Robert Giroux into buying the American edition of *Who Do You Think You Are?*, but Farrar, Straus and Giroux could not quite meet Norton's bid (which, at $7,500, looks quite modest by today's standards).[5] In retrospect, this was a bidding war that publishers could feel economically and artistically proud of having participated in, and only regretful for having lost. Considered this way, there is not a magic balancing spot between the commercial and the artistic in the job of literary editing; both variables are present, in various proportions as a fundamental condition of the job, and individual editors face the challenge of navigating between them in order to bring an author's work to a reader.

Sometimes editors dream of creating a sliding scale of literary and commercial values, as Janet Silver does when she, like others editors, deplores the large advances given to many books. Such advances, she argues, create undue risk and "so much distortion of the value of a particular work based on how much is paid" (Ferrari-Adler, "Agents & Editors: A Q&A with Editor Janet Silver"). She wonders if editors could take on more low-level risks, so that authors of books that are not likely to win a huge audience could be cut more slack. The disappointment of lower-than-anticipated sales would not wear on their subsequent careers the way it can today, particularly in the case of young writers entering the market for the first time. The creation of imprints within publishing houses is one way to do this; an example is the Nan A. Talese imprint for Doubleday. Predictably,

5 As it turned out, the book was transferred to Knopf, for various reasons, anyway, and was published as *The Beggar Maid* in the U.S.

though, the titles chosen for such imprints gain another form of desired capital: a reputation for the aura of high quality inherent, as Bourdieu argues, in small-scale production. So this may not address the specific needs of young, apprentice writers.

I would take the argument further: art and commerce are inextricably bound up in each other, to the point where plotting them, Bourdieu-like, on a scale of ascending and descending values does not really capture their mutual imbrication. Editing, throughout its long history, has been a wonderful lens through which to see the interwoven nature of commerce and aesthetics in the production of art. A perfect example is one of the rules that M. Lincoln Shuster, co-founder of Simon & Shuster, devised for young editors learning their craft:

> Learn to read with a pencil – not simply to note possible revisions and corrections, but to indicate both to yourself and to your colleagues ideas for promotion and advertising that may be activated many months later. Such ideas will be infinitely better if you spell them out while you are excited and inspired with the thrill of discovering the author or book. (Gross 25)

Cynics might deplore this dictate as the insidious seepage of the commercial into artistic realms, but I think it is more complicated than that. I think that Shuster is saying that every editor's act of aesthetic excitement is accompanied by a need to find the most effective way to bring that excitement to other readers – as, indeed, it is their business to do. The implied corollary of his statement is that promotional ideas that are not enlivened by aesthetic appreciation will be less successful. Far from being competing entities, as we are used to discussing them theoretically and practically, the editor's allegiances to art and business are deeply enmeshed.

Moving to the broader concerns of this study – the labour that has produced the remarkable literary celebrity of Margaret Atwood – editing has, it seems to me, a particularly key role to play, in that it occurs on the cusp of the private and public performances of authorship. Indeed, it makes any confident distinction between the two difficult to theorize. The editor is granted a privileged glimpse into the pre-publication state of a piece of writing, and she or he accompanies the author on the journey to making it the public document that it eventually becomes. As the British writer Zadie Smith wryly observed, "You need a certain head on your shoulders to edit a novel, and it's not the head of a writer in the thick of it" (108). The relative privacy of the "thick" of composition needs to be pried open, a little bit at a time. The editor, then, performs the arrival of the public and the publicity that will attend a writer's work. When Ellen Seligman paid tribute to Margaret Atwood on the occasion of the latter's sixtieth birthday, it was significant that she opened her comments by drawing attention to "the distinction between Margaret Atwood the writer and the public persona," which is a "particularly meaningful" one (Nischik 287). Seligman praised Atwood's "skill at maintaining a workable balance" between the two; poised between the private and public stages of publication, editors are ideally situated to observe that tricky nexus at work.

Susan Bell, writing passionately on editing, does a wonderful job of deconstructing the privacy–publicity, art–commerce conversation that has absorbed my attention here. She decries the way in which readers have come to signify anonymous privacy in a setting where authors have become, by contrast, public celebrities, and she challenges the very opposition:

> By defining successful writers as celebrities, for instance, our media, publishing industry, and educational system train us to view readers, in contrast, as nerds, and reading as functional – a service we offer up to the author, who appears to cook up a book by putting his brilliance in a pot and stirring. We are rarely told that it is the nerdy reader in every serious author that makes the ultimately creative decisions. (183–4)

Bell's central purpose is to argue that successful editing is the teaching of the writer to self-edit: to internalize his or her editor. What I draw from Bell's observation, though, is that the more externalized version of the editor – Ellen Seligman, Nan Talese, Janet Silver, Liz Calder – grounds literary celebrity in labour.

In the simultaneously public and private spaces of the Margaret Atwood Archives lies a testament to this grounding of celebrity in editorial labour. It is a handwritten poem, not dated but written sometime in the 1990s[6] – perhaps for an occasion, perhaps initially for Ellen Seligman's eyes alone. In its jokey camaraderie and its insistence on the razor-sharp skills of her Canadian editor, this poem captures the public intimacies of editing itself:

"Ellen Poem"

Who's the very best at spellin'
Ellen!
Who is crackerjack at smellin'
Out the typos? Ellen!
At the grammar,
She's a slammer,
To the colons she takes a hammer!
If your metaphors you mix,
You'll find yourself in a dreadful fix!
If your infinitives you've split,
Ellen will give you royal s__t!
Nothing escapes her eagle eye,
Says each author with a strangled cry.
As for her covers, they're to die for!
Who's the editor we sigh for?
Ellen! Three cheers!
Peerless amongst* her peers!
Love,
Peggy
(*shouldn't this be "among"?—Ellen)" (MS COLL 335.136.10:18).

6 It is located in the McClelland and Stewart correspondence folder for 1991-97.

3
Keeping O.W. Toad Hopping Along: The Atwood Office

Definitions of an office are numerous, so it would be well to define its minimum function, which is to direct and co-ordinate the activities of an enterprise. In an office, information is received, recorded, arranged and given out.

Alan Delgado, *The Enormous File: A Social History of the Office* (11)

No doubt the office that Alan Delgado was thinking of when he wrote his social history in 1979 was that cubicle-filled, fluorescent-lighted space that had already given rise to decades of comic treatment in *New Yorker* cartoons – the same clearing house for endless paperwork and prickly personal interaction that has inspired the British and American television series *The Office*. Still, his definition provides a productive starting point for my analysis of a much more specific "enterprise," the company that Margaret Atwood formed in order to handle the increasing complexities of her literary career. Dubbed O.W. Toad, an anagram of "Atwood," it was incorporated as a business in 1976, midway through the decade during which Atwood came to national prominence and just a handful of years before her career would assume a still broader international dimension. In her biography of Atwood, Rosemary Sullivan rightly associates the formation of the company with the growth of an industry: "In addition to an agent, she could afford an assistant who could handle all the requests and inquiries regarding her work. Indeed, students and researchers were beginning to engage in what would become the Atwood-criticism industry" (309). But academic criticism is merely the tip of the iceberg; it pales when we compare it with the international involvement in Atwood's career on the part of readers beyond academia, translators, publishers, publicists, agents, filmmakers, and many others whose work intersects with the book publishing industry. The intricacies of the day-to-day business affairs that result from this global recognition necessitated the formation of such an organization, and Atwood was typically prescient in realizing that an incorporated business was a practical and wise route to follow.

I say "prescient" because in the mid-1970s there was relatively little awareness, in a broad sense, of the importance of the step that Atwood was taking in incorporating her business as a writer. In surveys of media treatments of Atwood in Canada that I have undertaken, I find very little representation of her company and its workings in the print media for another twenty years. In the late 1990s, though, in the light of both the globalization of the cultural industries and the continued international recognition of Atwood's writings, references to her office and her assistants begin to enter the newspaper and magazine profiles (Ross 1996; Wong 1996; Stevenson 2000). And what both fascinates and disturbs me is the tenor of those mentions: the fact that Atwood has an office, with hired assistants, to help her manage her career is often looked upon askance, as though she were indulging in the most sinful of luxuries. The most biting of such commentaries is Jan Wong's interview with Atwood, first published in the *Globe and Mail* in 1996. Wong seems obsessed with the fact that Atwood has a hired assistant; among Atwood's assets gained as a result of her robust book sales, Wong lists "a rambling house in Toronto, a full-time Sarah Cooper to help her" (A6). Here she is referring to Atwood's assistant at O.W. Toad from 1993 to 2001 as though she were a pricey piece of real estate. Wong also misrepresents the nature of Cooper's labour; she opens her profile by quoting

Atwood's story about how, when she announced her career plans to her parents in high school, her mother observed that "You'd better learn how to spell," to which the cheeky teenager replied, "Others will do that for me" (A6). It's a jokey anecdote that Atwood has told before and since, about teenage insouciance and also, indirectly, about the value of editing. Wong picks up this detail later in her profile and directly associates it with Sarah Cooper, referring to her as Atwood's "devoted assistant and spelling helpmate" (A6). Then, as though calling this professional assistant a glorified spell-checker were not enough, Wong ends her profile with the observation "Her assistant arrives to whisk her away. I order lunch" (A6), implicitly likening the assistant to a member of a film celebrity's hovering retinue. As will become abundantly clear in this chapter, the labour of the office assistants at O.W. Toad does not resemble that of Wong's spell-checking, whisking-off subordinate in the least.

Even in less obviously scandal-seeking pieces, Atwood's assistants are, at the very least, represented as celebrity perks. Val Ross's piece on the launch of *Alias Grace* opens with the requests Atwood makes for fresh fruit in her hotel rooms: "These are some of the details Margaret Atwood asks her assistant, Sarah Cooper, to arrange when she goes on a book tour" (A1). Ross is making such requests sound like the spoiled demands of a hotel-room-smashing rock star rather than the healthy dietary needs of a woman on a very long and arduous book tour. By association, the O.W. Toad office, described in quasi–James Bond lingo as the "cool, subterranean Toronto office of Atwood HQ" (A1), becomes the command post from which such demands are issued: "O.W. Toad has two computers and a fax machine to send requests for bananas, carrots and good working microphones for all Atwood readings" (A6). Some journalists do make the connection between the company and the crushing workload involved in being an internationally celebrated writer. Sandra Martin, for example, muses that "to contemplate the phone calls and the invitations that must come her way every day is wearying. Will it surprise you to learn that her assistant has an assistant?" ("Atwood Interactive" R4). But for the most part, Atwood's office and assistants are invoked in envious, derogatory ways.

In this chapter, I take a close look at the *actual* working conditions of O.W. Toad, in order to represent more fairly the supportive labour that allows Margaret Atwood to continue to write while carrying on the substantial business that is her literary career. I suggest that the resentful readings of Atwood's office that persist in the media have to do with our collective reluctance to recognize writing itself as labour. Even in such a highly corporate age, we prefer to cling to our fantasies of writing as pre-industrial, cottage-style piecework that is somehow immune to the march of late capitalism.

To begin with, there is no question that what Atwood is running could, in Delgado's words, be described as an "enterprise." In the words of Sarah Cooper, "She's a little industry in herself" (Ross A1); to support her claim, Cooper cites the figure of 460 downloads a day from the company's website, owtoad.com. When she, like Phoebe Larmore, was approached on the occasion of Atwood's sixtieth birthday to write a tribute for Reingard Nischik's volume *Margaret Atwood: Works and Impact*, Cooper once again emphasized the labour-intensive nature of the Atwood "industry" by drawing on specific figures. "Just to give you a glimpse of the tip of the iceberg," she writes, "consider the fact that we get between 20 and 50 pieces of mail a day" (295). Unlike most journalistic commentators on the office, Cooper sees a logical connection between Atwood's fame and the level of secondary labour needed to carry out her job, rather than seeing the secondary labour as the luxurious fruits of that celebrity: "Being assistant to Margaret Atwood has made it really clear to me that one of the problems with being famous is that you get asked to do way more than any one person could ever actually accomplish" (295). Literary fame itself becomes a species of labour – a condition of heightened visibility that places many additional working demands upon the writer.

The assistant is the first line of contact for anyone who deals with Atwood professionally, and her duties are well summarized by Sarah Cooper: "Basically, it is my job to simplify Margaret's life so that she has time to write. Under that general category comes a whole range of activity, from research and correspondence to banking and book-keeping" (Nischik 295). This has apparently remained the core of the assistant's job, so much so that assistants who have taken over Cooper's duties, most recently Sarah Webster, have left this statement pretty much as is on the Atwood website under the heading "Frequently Asked Questions." Cooper left to pursue a successful job as a screenwriters' agent at the Saint Agency – further proof that the jobs created by the Atwood industry are, to a large degree, overlapping, like many in the book publishing industries at large. Just as many agents were editors in a previous professional life, it seems that assisting Margaret Atwood gives one a comprehensive training in all aspects of publishing. And also like the business of the literary agent, these manifold duties cannot be confidently pigeonholed as either business- or art-oriented; they are wide-ranging and disruptive of any attempt to distinguish mammon from creativity.

To be sure, dealing with the financial aspects of Atwood's empire is a major part of this job, as it is for the literary agent. In the Fisher Atwood archive, there are documents that show Sarah Cooper preparing and forwarding invoices; in one of these letters Cooper forwards an invoice from a cameraman/producer to Marly Rusoff, Doubleday's publicist, along with tapes of Atwood reading poems from *Good Bones*; presumably these tapes were to be used by Doubleday for promotional purposes (MS COLL 335: 2.1). There is also a good deal of liaison work being done with the agent; the assistant becomes used to working directly with Phoebe Larmore. In 1992, for instance, Joan Sheppard faxes reviews of *Good Bones* to Larmore for her files (MS COLL 335:1:1); she also regularly faxes bestseller lists to the agent. In addition, Sheppard passes on, by fax, messages that derive from conversations with Atwood but that she actually formulates: "I am faxing to pass on the following message from Peggy," she writes to Larmore in May 1992 (MS COL 335:1.1). Clearly, a great deal of trust and closeness develop during the course of the assistant's tenure at the Atwood office.

As this act of "passing on" messages suggests, liaison is a central part of this job; as time went on, and Atwood's literary reputation expanded across continents, there was simply more of this far-flung enterprise to organize and keep track of. This organizational work becomes particularly pressing and visible at the time of publication, when an international promotional tour needs to be orchestrated among several publishers and their publicists. A huge amount of paperwork in the Atwood archive is devoted to proposing, revising, and generally hammering out the schedules for these promotional tours. In 1993, for example, Sarah Cooper kept Phoebe Larmore up to date on Atwood's promotion schedule for *The Robber Bride* as it was regularly updated; the archive contains many copies of revised promotion schedules being faxed back and forth from the office to publishers' publicity departments. For example, Atwood faxes a letter to Marly Rusoff at Doubleday on 3 May of that year, reminding her that she needs to get these promotional events settled because her calendar is filling up quickly (MS COLL 335:2.2). One gets the sense, reading through this voluminous material, of an extremely complicated organization, one in which several appendages have to work in tandem. Most of these exchanges are handled by Sarah Cooper; she must, for instance, get all of the details of the Canadian promotional tour in place in such a way that it works with the other legs of the tour (MS COLL 335:2.6). The overall impression of the workings of the office in the months leading up to the release of a new book is that of a frenetic buzz of activity.

A few years later, in 1996, when the situation repeated itself with the run-up to the publication of *Alias Grace*, there was even more intensity in these exchanges. Indeed, as the 1990s wear on, the impression given by the archival documents relating to the scheduling of promotional events is that Atwood's career had reached a new level of complexity. In January 1996,

Cooper had the challenging task of bringing Phoebe Larmore, Vivienne Shuster (Atwood's British agent), Ellen Seligman (Canadian editor), Nan Talese (American editor), and Marly Rusoff together for one of their marathon editing sessions in Toronto. This is one of the occasions when, having not heard a thing previously about the manuscript in preparation apart from a tally of the number of pages completed, Atwood's trusted editorial team holes itself up in a hotel to read and respond to the new novel. Over several days, this detailed itinerary is revised, re-revised, and faxed repeatedly to the various participants. Bringing together these women, each of whom has an intensely demanding career, for ten days in Toronto is clearly no easy feat, but the very fact that they felt it so important to devote this time to an intensive reading of the new manuscript is evidence enough of the economic impact of Atwood's publications.

No sooner is this marathon session completed than Sarah Cooper needs to coordinate the details of the *Alias Grace* tour (MS COLL 335:9.5, 9.6). Finally, she formulates a typed version and forwards it to Atwood for her response. Though my impression, while reading in this archive, was that these promotional tours were steadily expanding in terms of ambitiousness and complexity, Cooper writes to Bill Thompson of Briarwood Writers' Alliance, a group that arranges speaking engagements for writers, to report that "Margaret's doing a very minimal tour this year, for a combination of reasons. Suffice to say that the focus of the tour is going to be the audience (not media)" (MS COLL 335:9.7; 6 May 1996). It may be that Cooper took this approach as a means of containing the demand for speaking engagements within reasonable bounds during this time; certainly, as I read through the archival materials relating to the tour, it did not strike me that this tour was anything but extremely gruelling and complicated in all of its organizational details.

During the intense and demanding weeks before the release of a new book, the assistant is also taken up with coordinating even the tiniest of details for the promotional tour. Though these duties are looked at askance by commentators such as

Jan Wong, who breezily refers to requesting "good working microphones" for readings, these are actually very important micro-managerial tasks that are often, unfortunately, not adequately taken care of by the hosts of these events. For example, in the lead-up to the ambitious multi-country tour for *The Robber Bride*, Sarah Cooper wrote to Kate Messenger from the Curtis Brown agency to ensure that Dutch translations of the novel would be available on shelves by the time Atwood was to appear in the Netherlands to read and do promotional events (MS COLL 335:2.5; 22 Dec. 1993). What could be more important than ensuring that the books are available for the audience to buy? As for the duties that Wong dismisses, Cooper herself acknowledges that she should probably not be spending her valuable time micro-managing such minutiae, but someone must; as she writes to Atwood's American publishers, someone needs to ensure that reading venues have "mic, podium, water – that stuff we should be able to take for granted but can't" (MS COLL 335:2.4; 25 Oct. 1993).

In the day-to-day operations of the business, the assistant undertakes other seemingly minute tasks that could be grouped under the heading "paperwork" but that are essential to the smooth running of the business. For example, assistants may, under order, actually do the paperwork associated with submitting work for publication. In May 1992, Joan Sheppard submitted pieces of writing on behalf of Atwood to *This Magazine* (MS COLL 335;1.2). This also extends to making up a package of selections for a new edition of a volume as, for instance, when Atwood got the rather inspired idea of combining *Murder in the Dark* and *Good Bones* in one volume for the American market. On that occasion, she wrote a note to Cooper instructing her on how to make up the package of selections, as well as directing her to copy and FedEx the final manuscript to Nan Talese and Phoebe Larmore (MS COLL 200:164.4). Proofreading is another task that, while seemingly mundane, involves a significant measure of trust on the part of the author, particularly when the manuscript in question is a poetry volume, where slips in wording can have substantial consequences. Cooper wrote to

Ellen Seligman on 6 October 1994 that Atwood "does not want to read the proofs, but does want me to" (MS COLL 335.6.4). And, accordingly, just four days later, Cooper faxed the corrected proofs to Seligman.

Even the most mundane-sounding paperwork has its role to play in managing an enormously successful literary career. Filing reviews of new publications, for instance, is key to supporting the promotional activities of the agents and publishers. For example, when *Good Bones* appeared in 1992, Atwood's assistant Joan Sheppard faxed reviews and bestseller lists to Phoebe Larmore for her files (MS COLL 335.1.1). Keeping the various branches of the "Atwood industry" apprised of the state of the business, on a day-to-day basis, is vital to its smooth operation. If the agent is up to date on the reception of new work, she can use that information to further promote the work of the writer, as well as to obtain favourable contracts for the work to come.

As Alan Delgado says of the office, it is largely in the business of handling information, and in the case of O.W. Toad, it does so most efficiently. As Sarah Cooper's estimate of twenty to fifty pieces of mail per day nicely illustrates, much of the assistant's time is consumed by the handling of requests. And those requests, as befits a global literary career, may come from any spot on the globe. To choose just one of numerous examples, in September 1995, Cooper handled a request from the Brazilian publishers, Editora Marco Zero, for interviews with Atwood to support and promote their publication of *The Robber Bride* in Brazil (MS COLL 335.2.5). On a macrocosmic scale, the organization of information is also exactly what the archive itself is designed to achieve, so the assistants at O.W. Toad are, basically, for much of their time, involved in the formation of an archive. As Val Ross noted in one of those first newspaper profiles to take notice of the Atwood office, "Atwood Industry Goes Global," "Ms. Cooper collects Atwoodiana, studies, anthologies and journals, and has 40 volumes. So far" (A6). Beyond this collection of the results of academic critical activity, the Atwood assistants are constantly engaged in a self-consciously archival project; as they handle the day-to-day correspondence, they are also, simultaneously, preserving that correspondence for regular accessions to the Atwood archive at the Fisher Library. As Diane Turbide reports in a 1996 issue of *Maclean's*, "according to her assistant, Sarah Cooper, Atwood generates so much material – manuscripts, reviews, speeches – that it is archived, annually, with the documents going to the Thomas Fisher Rare Book Library at the University of Toronto." For many writers, the archiving of their materials goes on in an atmosphere of relative privacy, and we are often not aware of the existence of those archives unless we actively seek them out, but the formation of the Atwood archive, substantial and ongoing, is itself a subject for public representation – and is regularly produced as yet more evidence of her celebrity stature.

Over the years, Atwood watches – rather bemusedly – the formation of a Margaret Atwood Society dedicated to the study of her writing. Her office interacts with this organization in order to manage information about her career. Again, it is the assistant who takes on this liaison, and it quickly becomes a two-way street, with O.W. Toad granting information to the association and the association referring some requests for information to the office. When he was president of the Atwood Society, Jerome Rosenberg would request a list of appearances that Atwood had recently made for the Society newsletter's "Atwood Update" column. When Sarah Cooper sends one such list in October 1993, she helpfully adds, "Let me know if you'd like me to send you some copies [of reviews of *The Robber Bride*] or if there's any other information you require" (MS COLL:335:190.1). Clearly, this exchange of information is beneficial to both parties; the association gains the data for its interested academic Atwood-watchers, and O.W. Toad receives some measure of publicity.

Occasionally, the Margaret Atwood Society receives requests for information about Atwood and passes them along to the Atwood office. For instance, in 2001 they received a question from a webmaster for the site dedicated to George MacDonald, the Victorian fantasy writer, about whether Atwood had made a particular, positive comment about MacDonald. Wisely, Jerome Rosenberg forwarded this to Jennifer Osti, Sarah Cooper's replacement, who referred the question to Atwood (MS COLL:335:190.2). Fact checkers also tend to contact the Society for information. Jessica Murphy from *The Atlantic* wanted to verify a detail in one of that magazine's articles about Atwood teaching a course on Canadian gothic literature at New York University, so she contacted the President of the Society, Shannon Hengen, with her question. Hengen, like Rosenberg, referred the query to Osti (MS COLL:335:190.2). Clearly, in matters involving the release of information about Atwood's career, the Margaret Atwood Society and the O.W. Toad office had a working agreement to refer all such inquiries to Atwood's office, which became, in effect, the authoritative source of information on all things Atwood.

The circulation of information that takes place in the Atwood office is frequently done in the name of protection: protecting, that is, the author from commitments that would erode her time for producing more writing, but balancing that protection off against the need to promote new work. This is a regular feature of the assistant's job, as evidenced by the documents preserved in the Fisher Library. By 1993, when Atwood published *The Robber Bride*, the O.W. Toad office had devised a ten-point scale of importance for media requests received during the promotion of a new book, to assist them in constructing their labyrinthine promotion schedules for Atwood. Sarah Cooper forwards one such request for an interview, from an American radio station, to Marly Rusoff of Doubleday, in November 1993, asking how she would rate it. Rusoff gives it a "9" on the scale; Cooper then forwards it to Atwood. In this instance, Rusoff gave this request such a high rating because this particular interview would be distributed to 350 National Public Radio stations in the United States and, so far in the promotional engagements arranged for *The Robber Bride*, no NPR interviews had been scheduled (MS COLL:335:2.4). This is a way of streamlining the many requests that flood into the office during the period when Atwood is publishing a new book; it is also a means of balancing the need for privacy with the need for promotion – the need for protection with the reality of publicity. This pressing condition of literary celebrity is managed by being shared with a group of assistants.

Even when the requester is someone to whom Atwood clearly feels some indebtedness, the need to protect her time and privacy may occasionally trump personal obligation. For example, Arnulf Conradi, Atwood's long-standing German publisher, who was one of her earliest champions in Germany, wrote to Cooper in November 1997, asking if Atwood would consider doing an essay on Toronto for the German weekly *Die Zeit*; Cooper forwarded the request to Atwood with the following check-box options: "P: May I say

> Ho, sorry, writing
> novel?
>
> ☐ y
>
> ☐ n"

to which Atwood checked "y" ((MS COLL:335:141.15:4). Conradi was not only an influential publisher in a country where Atwood, since the late 1980s, has sold very well, but also a good friend. Having Cooper as intermediary allowed Atwood to protect herself while completing the draft of the novel that would become *The Blind Assassin*. (Recall that this request from Conradi came just two months after Atwood bemoaned the way in which her autumn had been more "chopped up and attached to other folks' agendas than I'd like" – a concern that her agent, Phoebe Larmore, responded to with similar gestures of protection.)

In addition to protecting precious writing time, the office's routine allows for the protection of information itself. Alan Delgado notes that the office, besides receiving, recording, arranging, and giving out information, serves as a place "where information can be safeguarded" (11). Though I am not, by any means, suggesting that there is, in the mandate of the Atwood office, a monomaniacal drive to control information about her, there is an eminently justifiable role for the office to play in the control of information. Sometimes this has to do with a basic right, such as safety, as when the office warned an association that it had inadvertently distributed Atwood's home address; it then worked with that association to find an effective way of redressing that error (MS COLL 335:190.1). As Cooper would write in response to a request that they supply Atwood's address in order for her to be made an honorary fellow of the Modern Languages Association, "I'm afraid there are too many weird folks out there for us to be comfortable circulating the address" (MS COLL 190.2).

Regarding matters of less pressing personal security, the office also exerts control over how and where Atwood's information is released and distributed. In August 1997, for example, Jerome Rosenberg wrote the office on behalf of the Margaret Atwood Society to request a copy of a letter that Atwood had written to protest the firing of a schoolteacher in Alabama. Sarah Cooper faxed it to him but wrote on the cover sheet, "Note that Margaret doesn't want it to be printed, and also that this was only one of the issues/complaints about the teacher" (MS COLL 335:190.2). This episode illustrates one of the biggest challenges in being a public figure who is frequently called upon to support various causes: making sure of the merits of the case before voicing public support. It is a difficult task, but one that an office can assist a public figure with, by vetting causes or, as in this case, by making sure that the initial voicing of support is not endlessly reproduced if other facts come to light that place that support in a more complicated light.

Sometimes the protection offered by the office assistant is much more light-hearted than the sobering concerns with personal safety or the repercussions of public political statements that I have focused upon so far. In an article for the *National Post* in November 2000, just a few days before Atwood won the Booker Prize for *The Blind Assassin*, Mark Stevenson reported that when Atwood was asked while she was in Scotland doing a promotional tour about the negative review the book had received in the *New York Times Book Review*, she replied that she had not read it "because her assistant refused to give it to her" (B7). Atwood apparently went on to report that when she asked her assistant how bad the review was, she replied, "He's got a hard-on for you." In a ribald vein, the office assistant here plays George Henry Lewes to Atwood's George Eliot. (Lewes, Eliot's long-time companion, was known to go to some lengths to hide reviews from the sensitively self-critical Eliot.) Though the episode is light-hearted, there is a serious dimension to this kind of bureaucratic protection; insulating Atwood, however temporarily, from this extremely negative review in an influential venue allowed her to continue with her promotional tour undistracted. Clearly, as an informed and canny manager of her own affairs, Atwood would need to deal with the details of this review at some point, but the timing was not, in the view of her assistant, right. Also, this way of proceeding helps recover a sense of proportion; however important the venue, this was, after all, one review.

By this point, the job description of the office assistants at O.W. Toad sounds much more wide-ranging than even Sarah Cooper's capacious list – "from research and correspondence to banking and book-keeping" – would suggest. From protective supporter to paperwork filer, from streamliner and organizer of promotional tours to first-line receiver of requests, the assistant's role, like that of the literary agent, clearly crosses the line from commercial assistant to artistic supporter. Fittingly, Cooper did not exclude aesthetic concerns when she wrote her short commentary on being Margaret Atwood's assistant: "I believe very strongly in the value of what she does, in the value of stories, particularly those as well wrought as hers" (Nischik 295).

A stronger indication of the way in which this business position has become elaborated – and also not confined to the baldly economic – is the growing role, over time, of the Atwood assistant. This expansion of the assistant's job is apparent as one reads through the archives chronologically: by 1996 there is a discernable increase in the sheer amount of writing in documents contributed by Cooper, who truly seems, by this time, to have become the lynchpin of the O.W. Toad organization. This growing role of the assistant is, I believe, a function both of increased workload and of the trust that Atwood placed in this one particular assistant during the 1990s. Cooper herself lists "research" as one of her duties, though as the 1990s wore on, Atwood came to rely more and more on hired researchers. However, from the evidence of the archive, it seems as though Cooper was drawn into research activities at times when the need became pressing – in particular, when deadlines for submitting a draft of a new novel to Phoebe Larmore were quickly approaching. So in the couple of years leading up to the 1997 publication of one of Atwood's most intensely historical novels, *Alias Grace*, Sarah Cooper lent a hand. In a memo to Atwood on 4 October 1994, she offered three answers to research questions, having checked with Atwood's trusted friend the historian Ramsay Cook and with nineteenth-century archives (MS COLL 335:9.1). She also, around the same time, approached Dr George Poulakakis to verify the effects of opium, and was able to report back to Atwood:

> "P—
> The effects of opium, courtesy of Dr. George Poulakakis—
> Pupils contract—(NOT dilate)
> tremors
> delirium
> loss of appetite.
> S.C." (MS. COLL 335.9.1)

She also obtained for Atwood a photocopy of the song "The Rose of Tralee," which she annotated with bibliographical information. These are tiny details, to be sure, but they are exactly the sorts of tasks necessary for the writing of historical fiction, no matter how fictionalized it is in other respects.

A reader of the Atwood archives can see this transformation in the assistant's role in the way that she progresses from bureaucratic scheduling of promotional activities at the time of the release of a new book to full participation in the planning of the promotion campaign itself. According to Don Gillmor's piece for *Toronto Life* on the occasion of the publication of *Oryx and Crake*, "Atwood, Phoebe Larmore and Jennifer Osti put together a promotional blueprint for the book" (90), and this blueprint, which involved reaching out to environmental and science fiction audiences, was discussed at a marketing meeting with McClelland and Stewart's publicist Laura Cameron, with Osti in attendance.

Hand in hand with this increased participation in promotion is a greater role for the assistant in dealing directly with the media. Particularly at moments when Atwood is out of town on promotional tours, her assistants can handle the media if the need should arise. When it was announced in January 1997 that Atwood would become only the second Canadian to win the prestigious American National Arts Club's Medal of Honor for Literature, she was in the United States, on a promotional tour for *Alias Grace*. In her absence, Sarah Cooper commented that "Margaret is delighted and honoured to be getting this medal" (Renzetti 1997, C2). Even on so sensitive a subject – artistically and financially – as film adaptation, Atwood's assistant may speak to the media on her behalf. When Cate Blanchett became involved in the making of a film based on *Alias Grace* in 2001, Jen Osti spoke with the *Globe and Mail's* arts reporter Sandra Martin about the prospect: "She [Atwood]'s really happy with the choice … [Blanchett] fell in love with the story and wanted to play Grace Marks" (Martin "Blanchett to Grace Atwood Adaptation" R4).

Just as the work of the literary agent has tended to intersect, of late, with the job of the editor, so too Atwood's assistants venture, at times, into editorial work. In fact, this aspect of the position grew perceptibly during the time that Cooper filled the job. There is evidence of her hand in the proofs of *Morning in the Burned House*, checking that changes to the poetry volume had been made (MS COLL 335:163.34). On another copy, she annotates a note from editor Ellen Seligman: "Here are Ellen's 'typos.' If you'll note the answers to her queries, I'll copy before returning & make the changes on our computer copy"

(MS COLL 335:6.2). Again, such changes are particularly important to get right in the production of a volume of poetry; clearly, Cooper has already, just one year after assuming her duties in 1993, won Atwood's trust, and has become, as a result, a key part of the editing process.

In other ways, too, Cooper increasingly took on greater responsibilities. In September 1993, she forwarded a letter from Coach House Press to Phoebe Larmore; when Atwood sold a short fiction from *Good Bones* to Penguin UK for *The Penguin Book of Lesbian Short Stories,* Coach House inquired whether they should have received a portion of the proceeds, as the initial publisher of the volume in 1992. Cooper forwarded the letter to Larmore, asking her either to intervene or to advise her how to respond to them (MS COLL 335:1.1). Evidently, Cooper was trusted to handle quite sensitive matters, even those with potential legal consequences. Indeed, there is a great deal of correspondence in the Atwood archives between Sarah Cooper and Phoebe Larmore, and it is clear that the two women formed a comfortable working relationship. Larmore observes in April 1994: "Was a good conversation we had yesterday working out the last kinks in this new system of contract tranking [*sic;* Larmore presumably means contract tracking]" (MS COLL 335:2.1).

There are moments, too, where Sarah Cooper feels comfortable enough in this expanded role to offer advice on specific promotional activities. For example, in November 1993, Marly Rusoff from Doubleday proposed the idea of a contest for book clubs that adopt *The Robber Bride;* the prize would be a guest appearance by Margaret Atwood at their book club meeting. On a Post-it attached to Rusoff's letter, Cooper notes that this idea is "innovative and very possibly effective," but then adds:

> danger of over-exposure?
> --meeting itself could be great or awful
> --too much like reviewing your own book? (MS COLL 335:2.4)

This is a clever, valuable response that considers the question of the activity from a number of perspectives: the long view of the career, which often the literary agent considers ("over-exposure?"); the comfort factor for the writer ("great or awful"); and the promotional "optics" of the activity ("too much like reviewing your own book?"). This document is particularly revealing of the way in which Atwood has surrounded herself with people who, while they are trained to do specific tasks for her, as assistants, agents, or editors, are also flexible enough to work outside these strict job categories. Rather than producing confusion, this degree of job-description overlap supports the overall aim – which is to support Atwood's career – mainly because to do well in the publishing business requires a detailed knowledge of various aspects of that business. This is why assistants become agents, or editors become agents, in this highly integrated industry. Atwood shows a thorough grasp of this fact when she writes to her British agent Vivienne Shuster in August 1993,

> I am thinking of having Sarah Cooper over to England to meet everyone and explore the ropes, maybe help with the travel end … She would see Bloomsbury, Virago, Farquarson & Claudia, the British book scene … She has a background in publishing & publicity, and is quick on the uptake. (MS COLL 335:2.5)

This is incredibly clever on Atwood's part: mindful of the varied background in publishing and promotion that Cooper brings to her role as assistant, Atwood wants to put that larger vision and flexibility to greater use by making her comfortable with various parts of the international Atwood business. She knows that integration and communication among the various participants in a business that, like hers, spans several nations can only make that business operate more smoothly. And the result as far as Cooper was concerned? She gained a further understanding of the various arms of the publishing business – a valuable foundation for the position she now occupies as a screenwriter agent – and she became a recognizable feature on the Canadian literary landscape in the 1990s. Members of Canada's literary world during that decade knew that if you wanted to engage with Atwood on professional matters, you needed to work through Sarah Cooper. In a strange sense, like Ellen Seligman, she became what film critic James Monaco would call a "paracelebrity": one whose social visibility depends, to a great extent, on the celebrity with whom one has an association (4).

Researchers whom Atwood has employed to help her find and verify information have been less socially visible than her assistants. That is a peculiarity of their job; however, Atwood duly thanks them in the acknowledgments to her published works. Researchers have become a discernable presence in the Atwood office – and archives – since the writing of *Alias Grace*, the first novel that Atwood chose to set in an earlier period. There was, of course, the research that Cooper contributed to the project, but Atwood also worked with her sister Ruth Atwood, who did a great deal of the detail-heavy, time-consuming historical research for the novel. On 6 September 1995, for instance, Atwood formulates a "Ruth list" – a list of details that require historical verification:

1. York Herald? (1843)
2. Grace's pardon—does it exist? Copy? Letters about where she went? Newspaper check at the time of her release—did it get into the papers?
3. Exact date of Grace's admission to Kingston—did it get into the papers? Find out what women wore in prison 1843." (MS COLL 335.9.1)

Ruth Atwood makes regular reports back to Sarah Cooper, listing which pieces of research she will have ready and when. For some, she needs to travel to specific archives; she reported just one week later that she'd made an appointment with Dave St Onge at the Kingston Penitentiary Archives to find out what women in the prison at the time would have worn (MS COLL 335:9.1).

For Atwood's next major historical novel, *The Blind Assassin*, Atwood hired April Hall to do the same sort of intricately detailed period research. What, for instance, was on the menu of the Royal York Hotel in Toronto in 1953? When did the *Queen Mary* sail? (MS COLL 335:66.1). An entire box of manuscript papers in the Atwood Archives is devoted to "Background Research for *Blind Assassin*." In this exchange as in so much else, Sarah Cooper tends to be the conduit for information: as research questions arise, Atwood passes them along to her, and she relays them to Hall. Indeed, April Hall tends to use the salutation "Dear Sarah and Margaret" when she responds with information (MS COLL 335:66.7). Once again, I get the impression of a high degree of integration in the working life of this office, with the assistant as the lynchpin.

For *Oryx and Crake*, a novel whose research went beyond the historical, Atwood hired Surya Bhattacharya, a journalism graduate. Bhattacharya also served as researcher on *Writing with Intent*, the American edition of selected Atwood essays and occasional pieces from 1983 to 2005. In this case, the research largely involved collecting articles from current affairs dealing with biological engineering and other phenomena associated with Atwood's futuristic cautionary tale. So the research was not directed so much towards uncovering details that Atwood did not know; as she observed to Don Gillmor of *Toronto Life*, "I didn't do research as such. I knew quite a bit of it anyway" ("Anatomy of a Best-seller" 2).

One of the intriguing and effective characteristics of the Atwood research team is how integrated it is with other forms of support. As I've mentioned, Atwood's sister has, on occasion, served as a research assistant, and we find her signing a letter in 1989 as "Office Management Consultant" (MS COLL 335:190.1). On occasion, Atwood has also called upon close personal friends who have particular expertise to offer her feedback or information on verifiable details from her novels. For her historical novels, she has called on Ramsay and Eleanor Cook, a historian and a literary scholar respectively, to read them with an eye to historical accuracy. Cooper checked some of the historical details for *Alias Grace* with Ramsay Cook (MS COLL 335:9.1), and Atwood showed both him and Eleanor Cook the novel in manuscript – a rare compliment and sign of trust, given her habitual secrecy about her works in progress. "Needless to say," as she wrote to Ramsay Cook on this occasion, "I'd welcome any comments re: historical anomalies" (MS COLL 335:9.1). Both of the Cooks obliged, faxing Atwood lists of careful, minute edits, for which Atwood thanked them warmly (8 January 1996; MS COLL 335:9.1). Not surprisingly, when Atwood returned to historical fiction with *The Blind Assassin*, she once again looked to the Cooks to vet her historical detail, and again they responded most generously with a list of edits faxed to her on 8 and 9 December 1999 (MS COLL 335:65.24). The copies of their faxed letters preserved in the Fisher Atwood archives bear check marks alongside each entry; Atwood clearly took these suggestions very seriously, as she had earlier with their suggestions about the historical details of *Alias Grace*, and she made sure she addressed each and every one of them.

The research net cast by O.W. Toad can be, on occasion, a wide one. On 18 March 2006, the assistants at the office faxed a letter to Atwood's long-time German publisher, Arnulf Conradi, asking "one last research question we have re: Alias Grace" (MS COLL 335:9.2). It concerned the grandfather of a doctor named Binswanger who was a friend of Freud's: was he the paternal or maternal grandfather? Atwood needed to know so that she would know what last name to give the character. The research net widened: at Conradi's company, Berlin Verlag, Katrin Schwenk asked her colleague Carsten Sommerfeldt, who in turn called a Berlin journalist, who gave them the phone number of a Zurich psychiatrist who turned out to be in the Binswanger family (19 March 1996; MS COLL. 335:9.2). The tendrils of the research community working to assist Atwood on questions of historical accuracy are wide-reaching, transnational.

Though the proliferation of actors on the scene is undeniable, there is never any question of who is in charge. The manifold reaches of Atwood's business, extending out from the O.W. Toad office in Toronto, rather than displacing the author, reinforce the sense of Atwood herself at the hub. She is constantly looking for ways to integrate the far-flung parts of her business and to foster communication among them: whether she is planning to bring her assistant to England to bring her into contact with another branch of the business, or whether she is calling upon her considerable network of associates to contribute to the researching of a work in progress, Atwood is always thinking about ways to make the branches of her operation work coherently and collaboratively.

Moving, now, from office personnel and roles to methods, the ways in which the Atwood office operates also speak to this drive for integration, albeit with an obvious head of operations in charge: the writer. I have already alluded to the checklists that Atwood's assistants devised in order to obtain Atwood's response to particular requests. Like many of the effective practices in the office, this one took hold early in Sarah Cooper's tenure as Atwood's assistant. Since the assistant deals with the mail, she can quickly affix a checklist to a request and receive, in return, a quick response from Atwood. When Cooper forwarded the request for the National Public Radio interview regarding *The Robber Bride*, she attached the following checklist, along with the information that Marly Rusoff had rated this event a "9" on their scale of important promotional activities:

☐ morning of Dec. 6
☐ Mon. Dec. 13
☐ later in week of 13
☐ don't (MS COLL 335:2.4)

More and more, into the 1990s, assistants used this checklist form to move decisions through the office in an efficient way.

Though efficiency is a major goal of the office operations at O.W. Toad, they have not always immediately adopted the most current communications technologies. I was somewhat puzzled, in particular, by their attachment to the fax machine, long after many offices tended to downplay its use in favour of e-mailed attachments. The most intense period of fax exchange is in the early to mid-1990s: the fax machine is whizzing in the months and weeks leading up to major promotional tours. By around 1997, however, the office is beginning to communicate more through e-mail, which assumes a prominence in the months leading up to the publication of *The Blind Assassin* in 2000 (MS COLL 335:65), though faxes continue to be sent back and forth. Even at the beginning of 1997, though, Cooper wrote to Margaret Atwood Society president Sally Jacobsen that "we do not use e-mail. We do have a website, but it is managed from outside of the office" (MS COLL 335:190.2).

Why the resistance to e-mail long after most offices had adopted it as their primary means of communication? As I will explore in the next chapter, Atwood has certainly not been slow to adopt new media technologies, such as Twitter, and she has even invented one: The LongPen. Part of the answer may lie in the function of this particular communication tool: whether it is primarily convenient for members of the Atwood team, or whether it is convenient for members of the public seeking to contact and make requests of the Atwood office. Remember that during the 1980s and 1990s, the Atwood office was handling a heavy load of mail from outside, from people requesting this and that: information, assistance, encouragement, donations, interviews, help of various kinds. E-mail communication, with its ease of use, might well have increased the workload for assistants exponentially, as it has arguably increased the workload for many white-collar professionals. Editors, agents, publicists, assistants, and Atwood, though, could just as easily use fax to circulate documents: contracts, schedules and the like. So there may have been some reluctance to open up the gates to fully interactive, easy communication with a large public.

The same might be said of O.W. Toad's use of the Internet, particularly its building of an Atwood website: owtoad.com, now margaretatwood.ca. In my brief commentary on the website in my book *Literary Celebrity in Canada*, I described the design of that website, as it then appeared, as a careful balancing act between the proffering of information and the fending off of demands for appearances, book blurbs, and contributions, nicely captured in the website's graphic of Margaret Atwood's desk. (Since that time, the website has been redesigned; I discuss it more fully in the next chapter on Atwood's use of electronic technology.) Originally, the site used a photo of her writing desk, the web designer allowing visitors to click on several of the desk drawers, to find documents such as comics Atwood has drawn, covers of her books, and a selection of photographs. As I reflected, the desk graphic announces Atwood's agreement "to open some personal spaces in a controlled atmosphere, while resolutely declaring her right to keep other drawers closed" (114).

I still think that the website, even as redesigned, enacts this double gesture of invitation and deferral, but considering it as part of the O.W. Toad enterprise opens up additional insights into its workings. The website is the main way in which the Atwood office represents itself to a global audience. First and foremost, the office represents itself exactly as Alan Delgado defines the "office" in general – as a clearing house for information – and it carefully balances offers of information with clearly worded lists of the forms of information and assistance that it will not grant to readers. Editors or authors seeking a valuable blurb from Atwood for a book are warned – in verse, no less – that they "will not get any from me" (margaretatwood.ca/book_blurbs.php; 23 February 2011). As she explains in a prefatory parenthesis, "I blurb only for the dead, these days." But lest that appear unduly harsh, particularly to young writers beginning their careers, the website contains supportive advice and information for young writers in the section "Resources for Writers." So I see this material as a way of dealing with the impression some visitors to the website might get that it is there mainly to ward people off. To a degree, in all honesty, the website needs to do this; it is, after all, a device for handling the workload faced by the office's assistants, particularly in areas where they would receive multiple requests (for manuscript reading, blurbs, contributions, invitations). But to counteract that inhospitable vibe, the website performs hospitality in terms of offering an impressive number of documents (essays, occasional speeches, etc.).

Another noteworthy feature of the site is that it renders explicit the labour of the assistants. Because Sarah Cooper's contribution to the Nischik volume, *Margaret Atwood: Works and Impact*, was one of the few times that the assistant was called upon to represent her labour to a public, her successors, including Sarah Webster, retained her short statement on the website, on the "Frequently Asked Questions" page, until the website was redesigned in 2010. The current website also highlights the office, first and foremost, on this page: "O.W. Toad Office" has its own tab on the main page, and the "FAQ" section therein opens

> What is O.W. Toad?
> O.W. Toad is my office, run by my assistant, Sarah Webster. In addition to Sarah, the office has a staff of one other full-time, and two other part-time employees.

This question precedes the answering of typical requests, and that, too, is revealing. It contains specific measures of the office's labour (the number of full- and part-time workers) and replaces the former statement "we get between 20 and 50 pieces of mail a day" – a figure that would require constant updating. More important, it represents to the prospective requester the volume of work that the office faces on a daily basis and places its reluctance to provide some of those requested services in a more understandable light. Balancing hospitality with limits, promotion with privacy, the office here publicly performs its primary function.

An aspect of the website that brings a whole new approach to the question of the Atwood office is its prioritizing of ecologically sustainable practices. Under the "O.W. Toad Office" tab, one finds the "Green Policies" page, an extensive listing of information about the ways in which the *physical* office of O.W. Toad, located in Toronto, complies with environmentally responsible practices. No detail is too small: compact fluorescent bulbs, use of 100 per cent recycled and ancient-forest-friendly paper, use of Bullfrog Power (Ontario's first green electricity provider), right down to the 100 per cent recycled tissues, paper towels, and toilet tissues used by staff. One fascinating portion of this detailed page is its appeal to charities not to send multiple requests in the mail; the office requests e-mail communication where possible and warns, furthermore, that multiple paper requests will put companies out of the running for donations from Margaret Atwood. The commitment of Atwood to sustainable practices is everywhere apparent here, and her office is clearly marked as a green enterprise. Setting aside all of the good reasons for this emphasis on sustainability, it is also fascinating because it is one respect in which the very operations of Atwood Inc. perform the values that have been associated, since *Surfacing*, and as recently as *The Year of the Flood*, with the writing of Margaret Atwood. The office, in this way, becomes an extension of meanings engaged and explored by Atwood texts.

Considered in this light, is the Atwood office itself an Atwood text of sorts? In its balancing of privacy and publicity, in its commitment to writing and publishing as forms of labour that need public representation, and in its environmental protocols, the O.W. Toad office represents a range of meanings that readers of Atwood's prose, fiction, and poetry have come to consider "Atwoodian." Those who see the enterprise itself as merely celebrity indulgence betray their assumption that writing is entirely mystical inspiration and not labour. To which Margaret Atwood's company website responds with a choice quotation:

> INTERVIEWER: To what do you attribute your success?
> JOAN SUTHERLAND [CELEBRATED AUSTRALIAN COLORATURA SOPRANO]: Bloody hard work, Duckie! ("For Your Corkboard")

4
@MargaretAtwood: Interactive Media and the Management of Literary Celebrity

On 11 February 2011, the media trends site Mediabistro announced that "Margaret Atwood's Got 'Klout' on Twitter" (Dilworth). The site klout.com, which assigns scores to Twitter users for the extent of their influence in the "Twitterverse," had just classified Atwood as "a Taste Maker" on the basis of her impressive scores. As the accompanying blurb on klout.com explained, in language that recalls the keys to teenage girls' magazine surveys on popularity, "You know what you like and your audience likes it too. You know what's trending, but you do more than just follow the crowd. You have your own opinion that earns respect from your network" ("Klout Influence Summary"). In the previous chapter on the Atwood office, I queried why, in the mid-1990s, the Atwood office appeared slow to embrace technological developments in communication, preferring fax exchanges to e-mail, but it would seem that, in a little over a decade and a half, Margaret Atwood has become an interactive technology trendsetter. As she explained to an interviewer at the 2011 Tools of Change (TOC) conference in New York, she began tweeting around 2009, when her publishers were setting up a website for *The Year of the Flood*: "The people building the website said, 'You have to have a twitter feed,' and I said, 'What's that and how do I do it?" ("Margaret Atwood Interviewed at TOC 2011"). Apparently Atwood proved to be a quick study; at the time of writing, she has 311,000 Twitter followers.

Grouping various types of interactive technologies together – personal websites, new publication websites, multimedia book tour performances, Twitter, and Atwood's LongPen – this chapter examines Atwood's vigorous turn towards social media and other interactive technologies in the early years of the twenty-first century, asking what it portends for her labour as a literary celebrity. Rather than serving as simple amplifications of existing marketing technologies for the Atwood "industry," they allow her to negotiate her literary celebrity in ways that refine the sort of canny balancing between publicity and privacy, art and commerce, that I have discerned throughout Atwood's career. In analyses of her interactions with literary agents and editors and her office, O.W. Toad, I have consistently maintained that these web-like industrial interactions define rather than mystify Atwood's labour as a writer, and notwithstanding the tendency of new media to create a "noisy" online environment of exponentially burgeoning texts, the same argument obtains here. There is, more generally, ample reason to put to rest early fears that social media would turn authorship into an undifferentiated blur of textuality. Recall, for instance, Jay David Bolter writing in 1991, fifteen years before Twitter, that "as long as the printed book remains the primary medium of literature, traditional views of the author as authority and of literature as monument will remain convincing for most readers. The electronic medium, however, threatens to bring down the whole edifice at once" (153). Although Bolter was talking about an "author" more broadly as anyone who places a text into circulation, there has been a tendency to sound the alarm for literary authors in particular. Still, what happens when some of these newer technologies embraced by Atwood, most pointedly the LongPen, contrive to disembody the literary celebrity? Can my definition of authorship as an assemblage of social-industrial relations sit comfortably with a technology that replaces a ritual of social contact between authorial body, text, and reader – the book signing – with the remote-powered scratchings of a robotic hand? Can literary celebrity attach itself to technological apparatuses?

At the end of the first decade of the twenty-first century, publishers' concerns about the impact of social media coexist with their eagerness to exploit applications like Twitter as merchandising vehicles. To some extent, social media have functioned as a collective dream of recovery – a silver bullet for an industry still labouring to pull itself out of the tough years of corporate concentration and big-box merchandising (MacSkimming, *The Perilous Trade* 369–70) and significant economic recessions in 1990–1 and 2008–9. This eagerness, however, does not come unattended by the former uneasiness, for, in the words of David Marshall, "with every change in the way we communicate in our culture there is a new struggle over meaning, significance, knowledge and power" (*New Media Cultures* 1). In the 2008 *Poets and Writers* interview with four young New York editors, that struggle seems palpable, for the editors are riven by their suspicion of – and fascination with – new technologies. Initially, they seem dismissive of the Internet as a merchandising tool that is supposed to "amplify" the highly prized "word of mouth" means of advertising their wares: "I don't think anybody's quite figured out exactly how to do that … We all can see, in certain cases, our books being talked about a lot online. But what does that mean in terms of sales?" (Ferrari-Adler, "Agents & Editors: A Q&A with Four Young Editors"). One editor in the group, though, is more open to the possibilities for online marketing; she describes how she uses blogging communities as niche audiences, promoting, for example, a memoir about a Prohibition bootlegging ring to beer, whiskey, and bourbon bloggers. Even so, she acknowledges the labour-intensive nature of such targeted advertising. But the biggest debate in the conversation involves the e-book, and here the conflicting tugs of fear and fascination make themselves particularly felt:

> CHINSKY: … People who have a Kindle are actually buying more books. So on one hand, it scares the shit out of me that people are reading on Kindles and Sony Readers. But on the other hand

GARGAGLIANO: Why?
CHINSKY: For no reason other than it's different.
GARGAGLIANO: I think it's so exciting. (Ferrari-Adler, "Agents & Editors: A Q&A with Four Young Editors")

They then speculate on whether the physical book may eventually become a luxury, small-production item for the collector, "like vinyl records." Strangely, even though this interview took place in 2008, two years after the founding of Twitter, the popular microblogging tool does not figure at all in their conversation: evidence that the publishing industry has been slow to engage with new technologies – perhaps because of these sorts of internal disagreements about whether they constitute friends or foes.

With every adoption of a new medium, there is a clash between advocates and critics, and theorists have argued that there tends to be little meaningful communication between the two camps (Marien 44). But in the case of the contemporary publishing industry, those two forces sit precariously within the same industrial agents. The same editor who was "scared" by the e-book in the conversation with four young editors declared seconds later that "it doesn't mean the death of literature" (Ferrari-Adler, "Agents & Editors: A Q&A with Four Young Editors"). Part of this internal conflict has to do with the uncertain relationship between online promotion and sales; as Katie Hewitt speculated in the *Globe and Mail*, publishers tend to "err on the side of cautious optimism when it comes to social networking and book promotion ... They're keeping their enemies close and befriending social media" (F7). So on the one hand, there is anxiety over the implications of e-book technologies for the publishing business, but on the other, Twitter accounts have become appealing to publishers, because they allow them to delegate more of the labour of promoting a new book to the author. As Hewitt reports, though, publishers' practices vary widely; some are cautious, like Cory Beatty, digital marketing manager at HarperCollins, who approaches all authors with the idea of online marketing but counsels "our authors to engage at a level they are comfortable with" (F7). Compare Beth Wareham, publicity director at Workman Publishing: "Not only are all of our authors told to tweet, we hire people who teach them how to tweet" (Hewitt F7).

In the promotion of "literary fiction," there is a further consideration that complicates any such arms-wide-open embrace of social media marketing: cultural capital. In my investigations of the online marketing of writing, I have found that the promotion of literary fiction treads a wary line between traditional methods of marketing books and more explicitly promotional online campaigns. In a 2011 article for (appropriately) the *Wall Street Journal*, Joanne Kaufman investigated some of the more frankly commercial online promotions by authors; not surprisingly, most of her examples were drawn from genres that are culturally marked as more profit-driven than literary fiction. Ayelet Waldman, for instance, the author of several mysteries, promoted her book of essays on motherhood, *Bad Mother*, by giving those who preordered the volume on her website scholarship donations and copies of a novel by her husband, novelist Michael Chabon. Encouraged by her first experience of online literary marketing, she promised that online buyers who preordered her next novel would be entered into a draw for a free iPod containing music relevant to the book. (The iPods were supplied by her publisher.) Another mystery writer, Bruce DeSilva, posted a slideshow on his Facebook page showing various celebrities reading from his first novel, and Lynn Schnurnberger held the book launch for her self-described "chick lit" novel at a sex toy store, Babeland (Kaufman). Kaufman points out that genre fiction writers may also buy up novels from their publishers' backlists and then offer them at a mere one dollar to online customers who buy their new novel at full price. In spite of the *Wall Street Journal*'s avowed and long-standing support for entrepreneurs, however, it treated these examples of literary entrepreneurship as the rankest sort of hucksterism; as Kaufman reflected on Waldman's expostulation "I find the whole process of self-promotion excruciating," "Ms Waldman … frankly, seems approximately as shy as a Kardashian." The message is clear: literary entrepreneurs are dirtied by their contact with money, rendered no better than reality-television starlets of dubious talent.

For the writer of literary fiction, like Atwood, the trick is to engage with new media promotional tools while carefully guarding the high-culture atmosphere of the transaction. One way in which she accomplishes this is by consigning the profits of any such promotional activities to charities that are particularly important to her, many of them environmental or culturally nationalist. For example, she supported the independent Canadian magazine *The Walrus* by auctioning off the opportunity to have one's name used for a character in her forthcoming novel (Fortney). Since the actual profits generated do not redound to the account of either writer or publisher, Atwood is spared the sort of journalistic treatment accorded to Waldman; but at the same time, participants in an event such as Atwood's character name auction are reminded that she has a new book in the offing. Writers of literary fiction, if they are to promote their writings online, need to do so under the guise of not promoting them at all.

In addition to the taint of the marketplace, there are other drawbacks to literary marketing with the aid of electronic media – drawbacks that both publishers and authors must contrive to manage in some way. For example, as I have suggested, it may be a means of shifting more of the responsibility for promotion from the publisher to the author – always a cause of tense relations between these two. Ironically, as Katie Hewitt points out, in earlier days, authors, particularly first-time authors, found it difficult to intervene at all in the promotional plans of the publishing house. One thinks of Atwood's Joan Foster from *Lady Oracle*, alarmed at being told by the head of promotion at her new publisher (a company clearly based on McClelland and Stewart) "I thought we might do you as a female Leonard Cohen … Do you play the guitar?" (227). However, the American suspense novelist M.J. Rose, co-author of the guide *How to Publish and Promote Online*, suggests that any social media promotion mandate should include a negotiated pay rate for the authors who contribute their labour; she also called for consistent author royalties for e-books (Hewitt). Atwood echoed these concerns when she warned participants at the 2011 Tools of Change Conference, "Never eliminate your primary source"; she also pointed out that only 10 percent of writers support themselves through their writing and that lower royalties for e-books are troubling. And as for the labour involved in promoting one's works on social media, she asked: "If I'm expected to do all this other work, shouldn't I get more of the pie?" ("TOC 2011: Margaret Atwood, 'The Publishing Pie: An Author's View'").

Atwood's concerns about electronic publishing go beyond marketing and economics; she is also concerned about the potential vulnerability of the product itself. At the TOC conference, she echoed other participants' concerns about the potential for a catastrophic event such as a high-altitude electromagnetic pulse attack, a nuclear detonation high above the earth, to destroy electronic texts (Boog). Beyond this extreme doomsday scenario, there are more quotidian questions about the archiving of electronic texts; *The Times*'s columnist Erica Wagner asks "what future generations will gather from the tweets of Margaret Atwood or the e-mails of Salman Rushdie. Will they even survive?" (Column).

I draw attention to these drawbacks and concerns in order to temper the general impression that Atwood is wholeheartedly embracing electronic and social media as a novice enthusiast; in recent years, especially with the multimedia launching of her 2009 novel *The Year of the Flood*, media coverage has crowned Atwood, in the words of a *Globe and Mail* critic, Canada's "national tweeting treasure" (Nestruck). But her stance is decidedly more calculated and complicated than that; Atwood both embraces and subtly distances herself from electronic media in a way that promotes her literary renown while protecting its cultural capital. To begin with, she has engaged with Twitter in a way that far outstrips her initial need to support the promotional website for *The Year of the Flood*; she is an avid tweeter. Audiences are also occasionally surprised by her familiarity with forms of electronic texts that would seem to be distant from her interests; for instance, she easily conversed with members of the UK Guardian book club about online fantasy games, particularly those of the sword and sorcery variety that are popular among teenagers and young adults (Mullan). Also, in spite of her concerns about electronic text's vulnerability, she has recognized its environmental advantages; as she reflected to an interviewer at a Hong Kong writers' festival in 2009, "Well, that would save a few trees" (Hor-Chung Lau). The comment may sound like faint praise, but it marks a shift in her thinking since 2007, the year that Amazon launched its Kindle e-book reader in the United States; that year, asked about the phenomenon on BBC Radio 4, she dismissed it on grounds of portability, which are dubious, given the Kindle's compactness: "You can't take your computer in the bath tub … And it's very uncomfortable to have your computer in bed with you" ("Another Chapter of the E-Book"). Indeed, enthusiastic e-book readers are doing both, taking to the electronic medium in bed, bath, and beyond.

In a similarly complex fashion, Atwood is both an enthusiastic blogger, with an active wordpress site (marg09.wordpress.com), and a caustic critic of blogging. As she told Joyce Hor-Chung-Lau, "it's like everyone's blogging about how they brushed their teeth this morning." All the same, she seems aware and up to date about her *own* treatment at the hands of fellow bloggers: she opened a lecture at the University of Massachusetts in 2008 by remarking,

> I sometimes think I'm a little bit old to be doing this; we have bloggers now instead of stalkers. I remember one blogger writing on her website that with my red shawl and white hair, I looked like a Q-tip on fire. Some people may have been offended, but I recognize an artist when I hear it. (Harrison)

This complicated stance – enthusiastic participant and critic – allows Atwood to avow market forces even while disavowing them whenever they appear to compromise her cultural capital. She is, as I have argued, clear-eyed about the role of business in the publishing of books, so her comments about the online marketing of literature mobilize irony – the mode that allows for simultaneous participation and critique (Hutcheon): "The term 'relentless self-promoter' used to be an insult in publishing. Now it will be a necessity," she tartly commented in one interview (Adams, "Publish and Your Book Will Probably Perish"). And in public appearances, such as her plenary address at the 2011 TOC conference, she evinced both a fascination with new media and a cautious distancing from them. Returning from the conference, she enthused on her blog about her new contacts and lesson:

> It's a new experience for me, speaking to techfolk – they're so sharp their brains poke through their skulls like the pins in the Scarecrow of *The Wizard of Oz* – but they were kind and indulgent and showed me some new toys ... Most intriguing for me are the apps that can be used to draw, colour, and paint, and I think I will test some out, though crayons, watercolours, pencils and pens are more my usual speed. (marg09.wordpress.com)

Note how her enthusiasm is eventually displaced onto more low-tech, small-scale modes of production. Indeed, Atwood began her plenary speech to the techfolk by subtly but firmly marking her cultural distance from their "new toys": "Forgive me for not being quite as hopped up about it all as some people" ("TOC 2011: Margaret Atwood, 'The Publishing Pie'"). Among electronic publishing experts, Atwood can highlight her artistic credentials, while among literary folk, she is celebrated as a texting, tweeting, blogging pioneer: living proof of the persistence of the literary culture that is often thought to have been placed under threat by social and other electronic media.

I begin my study of the particular examples of Atwood's online activities with her professional website, margaretatwood.ca, for it was the first of her online promotional activities. In the previous chapter, I briefly examined the way in which the site, in its earlier incarnation (owtoad.com) and in its redesigned version (margaretatwood.ca), represents the labour of the

Atwood office. In this segment, I ask how the redesigned site configures and negotiates her literary celebrity. First of all, one of the main differences between this incarnation of the website and the previous version is its communication of a carefully constructed "personal" touch. Now, when one visits Atwood's website, the home page is headed by a banner that appears under the general title "Margaret Atwood": "Welcome to Margaret Atwood's website."[1] The copy for this banner is written in the first person and is accompanied by a smiling photograph, as a personal invitation and greeting from the author: "Welcome readers! I am very pleased that you are interested in my writing, and I hope this site helps you to find what you are looking for. Happy reading and best wishes!" – followed by Atwood's signature. The effect is that of personability, access, friendliness, and authenticity: key discourses in celebrity culture (Dyer, "*A Star is Born*"). The desk with the opening and closing drawers – a graphic of Atwood's own writing desk, which was prominently displayed in the earlier website – is gone, but the effect is somewhat retained by the home page's item "What's on my Desk." The periodically updated feature lists current activities ("Brand new short fiction, 'I'm Starved for You,' published under Byliner Originals"), recent promotional venues ("*Payback* documentary screened at Sundance"), and political/promotional concerns ("Try a cup of Balzac's Atwood Blend Bird Friendly Coffee!"). The latter invitation is quickly followed by an acknowledgment of the charitable destination of all funds raised; again, promotion needs to proceed unavowed, distanced from the appearance of economic gain. Note, too, the continuation of the first-person, personal address in these introductory entries on the website.

The expansion of the personal on the Atwood website is mainly apparent on its welcoming home page, but it is evident elsewhere too. The collection of photos from various periods of

1 All details about the content of the sites margaretatwood.ca, yearofthe flood.com and marg09.wordpress.com are accurate as of 18 March 2012.

Atwood's life and career that appears under the heading "Audio-Visuals" has been significantly expanded. Now interested visitors may click to view not only publicity shots and photos from Atwood's childhood and experiences in northern Quebec, but also photos of her extended family.

In my previous writing about the earlier incarnations of the website, I noted its combination of invitational and defensive modes: it both invited readers to offer (selected) information and fended off or channelled some of the many demands for other bits of information or assistance that the Atwood office routinely receives. On the new website, the juxtaposition of the invitational and the regulatory is still omnipresent. Some spaces below the new, personalized, invitational introduction to the home page, there reappears a list of things that "I, and the office, can and cannot do," offered in bold print: no book blurbs (a caution repeated at several locations on the website), no short-notice requests (of less than a week), no writing of introductions for books, no reading of unpublished manuscripts, etc. – and no written responses to invitations, saying "no, I can't do it." This "Message from Margaret Atwood and the Office" is interesting because of its shared origins: the individual writer *and* the O.W. Toad office, signalling the small industry created around her works and career. The invitational welcome to the website is narrated by and attributed to – even signed by – Atwood herself, but the regulatory measures are shared out, spread over both her and her office, thereby softening such restrictions by making them corporately shared. Invoking the office points to the heavy work burdens placed on the author and, by extension, on her employees. Besides, making sure that the regulatory function shares initial space – though at a lower, less immediate level – on the page with the personal invitation has the effect of warning visitors from the outset that the invitational does need to coexist with the regulatory: that there are things that "I, and the office *can* and *cannot* do" (my emphasis). Visitors, therefore, cannot reasonably complain that an initial invitation has masked the restrictions placed on Atwood's openness or helpfulness.

The website's FAQ page is another site where invitation and regulation must intertwine, yet the latter seemingly outweighs the former. Several of the questions seem intended to call forth a negative response: "Can you provide me with a blurb for my book?" "Can you read my manuscript and help me get published?" "Can you tell me what a particular poem / novel ending / symbol means?" Not likely. The ventriloquism calls to mind a comic stunt arranged by Atwood at a charity dinner in 1982; unable to attend the dinner, Atwood arranged to have a doll caricature of herself set up on a chair at the event, with a hidden tape recorder playing an endless loop of similarly automatic negative responses; in this case, one had to imagine that the requests were similar to the ones listed on her current FAQ page: "Oh, you're a novelist, too," followed by "Oh, I wouldn't really have time to do that right now. I'm writing my own novel" (Righton).

Atwood's website balances the seeming harshness of the FAQ page with a page devoted to novice writers, "Resources for Writers," located under the tab of the same name. This short page offers five bulleted points of advice and recommendations; there is nary a negative construction to be found. The tone is supportive, even comforting: "I often receive letters from writers looking for advice and words of wisdom. Here are a few things I can recommend for writers in Canada ... Rest assured that it takes time to build a reputation and an audience. Good luck!" She even touches on the most practical sorts of advice – for example, "try to persuade your publisher or the organizers of the reading to pay for the mailing" of announcements to your friends and various contacts. Though Atwood need not worry about postal costs at this point in her career, she does at least remember a time early on, when she did.

Yet for all the kindness displayed here, a touch of Atwoodian satire and jesting malice is not absent from the website. In her playful poem about her decision not to provide blurbs for books anymore, she exhorts writers seeking her approval to find "a writer who's youthful; / Who ... would find your new book a sweet toothful, / Or else sees no need to be truthful."

Elsewhere on the site, humour – of a less stinging sort – may leaven the negative force of the regulatory messages that Atwood feels compelled to leave for her extensive fan base. Like the personal discourse of the home page, it softens the blow. For example, in providing the expected negative response to the question, "Can you provide me with a blurb for my book?", Atwood reasons that "choosing between books is akin to choosing which of your two sisters should be your maid of honour … No matter what you do, someone is bound to have their feelings hurt." For that matter, the comics, drawn by Atwood, which she chooses to share under the "Audio-Visuals" tab, offer witty reflections on the business of marketing books, particularly the perils of being interviewed by less-than-well-informed journalists. Humorous they are, but they offer their own admonitions to members of the media doing background reading for a forthcoming interview. The comical scenes of Atwood – who is rendered short, dressed in black, with electric squiggles for hair, toting around her book on wheels, puffing and declaring "Next time I won't write such a #@! **heavy** book!" – also implicitly gloss and rationalize her eventual decision to invent and develop the LongPen signing device to lessen the rigours of book touring.

Like most promotional websites, Atwood's privileges the present over the past. On the right-hand side of each web page is a vertical ribbon listing the dates and venues of upcoming readings and other appearances. The way in which the site narrates Atwood's career reflects how her literary celebrity has been constructed over time. On the revamped site, awards are listed by decade on a page under the "Life & Times" tab. This choice to break up a by now extensive list by decade has the effect of representing the movement from primarily Canadian awards to internationally sponsored ones as well. In terms of volume, the steadily lengthening lists visually communicate a burgeoning international career. Critics of her work receive a nod under the same tab, as they did on the old website, on a page called "Works About Margaret Atwood": a one-page list of critical volumes written or edited by Canadian, English,

American, and German critics (again: a telling sign of the international extent of her renown).

In narrating a steadily expanding career, the website also graphically represents Atwood's literary celebrity as the sort of web of industrial relations that has attracted my particular interest. A quick glance at the "Contact" page, listed under the "Life & Times" tab, communicates the intricate web of interconnecting responsibilities that has formed the subject of this study. We hear not only that Atwood can be contacted via McClelland and Stewart, but also that the Larmore Agency handles film and television rights and English-language rights in Canada and the United States, whereas Vivienne Shuster of Curtis Brown handles all other English-language rights, and Betsy Robbins, also of Curtis Brown, handles translation rights. The Lavin Agency, one of the largest speakers' bureaux in North America, handles her speaking engagements there. Academics seeking permissions and the like are referred to the Thomas Fisher Rare Book Library's archivists. So the contact page enacts the many agents whose labour is intertwined with the literary work of Margaret Atwood.

The "Favourite Links" page is, like the "Contact" feature, another standby of many websites. Atwood's represents the far-flung areas in which her celebrity is increasingly felt. Whereas the earlier website presented a simple list of such links, the new site groups them under the headings "Environmental," "Literary," and "Business" – in that order. "These are organizations with which I am involved or which I support," the introductory text reads. Such a presentation depicts the spreading influence of Atwood's public persona, since she is now regularly associated in the public eye as much with environmental causes as with the cause of writers. The new "Business" link leads a user to the LongPen site: yet another realm in which Atwood's presence has been felt. The site also contains a separate, final tab, "Syngrafii," which contains information and contacts for the new company, formed out of the former LongPen organization.

As one might expect of a website constructed at the end of the first decade of the twenty-first century, margaretatwood.ca also dramatizes the integrated nature of various forms of electronic and social media. At the right of every page on the website, at the top of the current-appearances column running down the page, there are links to Atwood's presence on Twitter ("Twitter Margaret") and Facebook, to her wordpress blog, and to "The Year of the Flood" website, a multipurpose promotional site. These links' prominent placement on the site pointedly dramatizes another burgeoning arena for Atwood's literary celebrity: electronic and social media. The recent, prominent profile of Atwood as a technologically savvy author is everywhere apparent, no matter where the user navigates around the site.

Such invitations, however, bring their own regulatory discourses. The welcome page also invites readers to "Take a Look at the Official Margaret Atwood Facebook Page run by my publishers!", and the page concludes with a warning note: "Margaret Atwood has no Myspace page. The only official Facebook page is monitored by Margaret Atwood's publishers." The clarification targets impersonators who have set up shop as "Margaret Atwood" online, and the admonitory tone of the verb "monitored" is calculated to guide fans towards the all-important celebrity authenticity.

Atwood is currently in the curious situation of having, in a sense, two professional websites operating in tandem; besides margaretatwood.ca, she has set up a promotional website for her most recent novel, *The Year of the Flood* (2009). But the website seems designed to last longer than most promotional websites for new books; it is a site that has grown out of one central occasion – the publication of the novel – but that has a further, long-range design. As Atwood explains, she engaged the advertising firm of Scott Thornley and Company to help her build the website because what she had in mind went beyond the resources available to most publishers: "Well, they had their own websites, and I wanted to do some non-publishing things on mine, such as raise awareness of rare-bird vulnerability … and heighten Virtuous Coffee Consumption (Arabica, shade-grown, doesn't kill birds)" ("I Love it When Old Ladies Blog"). The publication of *The Year of the Flood*, the environmental dystopic follow-up to *Oryx and Crake*, was the perfect occasion to meld publication publicity and environmental activism.

With yearoftheflood.com, Atwood's Web practice has become more complex, though the same balancing of economic and cultural capital remains. It deals more heavily and blatantly in commodities other than books than does margaretatwood.ca. *The Year of the Flood*'s website offers themed T-shirts, tote bags, downloads of music for the God's Gardeners' hymns that appear in the book (and that were performed at the launch events), ring tones: all of this a dramatic step further into merchandising than "Atwood Inc." has gone before. However, as with the auctioning off of potential characters' names to support worthy causes, all profits generated from these commodities are painstakingly identified as going to specific causes in Canada, Britain, and the United States, and all of these causes are listed under the tab "Environmental Helpers." Furthermore, the commodities for sale are identified as environmentally friendly in themselves: T-shirts and totes are made from organic fibres, for instance. Still, having a page titled "Flood Shop" on the site represents a substantial challenge to traditional notions of cultural capital and aesthetic high-mindedness; we are not quite at the point where iPods or remaindered books are being awarded as prizes for consumers, but the T-shirt, in particular, is redolent of touristic commodification. Atwood attempts to manage this challenge to her cultural capital by reminding website visitors at every turn that funds raised by these commodities benefit not-for-profit environmental organizations.

Evidence that these forces are at play appears in the press accorded to Atwood's new publication in September 2009. Within ten days of each other, two columns appeared in the *Globe and Mail* by John Barber, taking up opposing sides of the economic/cultural capital debate over Atwood's means of promoting her new book, *The Year of the Flood*. On 2 September, in a piece devoted to Atwood's use of social media to promote the novel, the rhetoric is critical and suspicious: "Who was the brave publicist who suggested that austere Margaret Atwood not only do the usual book-signing tour for her new novel, *The Year of the Flood*, but also build it into an interactive website, Twitter it, blog it, flog it on T-shirts and turn it into a contest on YouTube? In fact, it was the novelist herself" ("She Blogs, She Flogs, She Tweets" R1). This opening gambit depends on the assumption that any such baldly promotional initiatives must be the brainchildren of commercial agents – not of the disinterested ("austere") literary icon herself. The headline picks up on Barber's negative spin: "She Blogs, She Flogs, She Tweets" explicitly parallels social media with the crassly mercenary. Ten days later, however, Barber does an extensive interview/profile with Atwood, wherein the website that he had formerly lambasted as a merchandising tool now figures as an admirable activist vehicle: "In the meantime, the author-as-activist is busy spreading hope in the same straightforward spirit as her silly/holy Gardeners. The website promoting the book, yearoftheflood.com, links to an eclectic selection of environmental causes and initiatives" ("Atwood: 'Have I Ever Eaten Maggots? Perhaps ...'" R5). No mention here of the T-shirts and ring tones. Even Atwood speaks of such fundraising gambits in terms that seemingly separate it from her pre-fundraising, "authentic" self: "When I committed to this, did I glimpse what lay before me in the way of book-tour overkill? Did I know that I'd be building an interactive website … with – so help me – T-shirts, ringtones and music downloads of it?" Moi? But she immediately provides the world of *The Year of the Flood* as a countervailing explanation for her seemingly uncharacteristic promotional activities: "But such a project would be impossible without the nature of the book itself" ("5 Countries, 35 Cities = 1 Crazy Book Tour"). What social forces encourage us to disarticulate – the economic and the idealistic – are interwoven in Atwood's practice of publicity, the better to play them off against each other.

Like Atwood's O.W. Toad website, this one integrates the various social media platforms devoted to her career. Prominently displayed on the home page of theyearoftheflood.com is the Facebook logo; visitors who click on it are taken to Atwood's

Facebook page. But this is a decidedly industrial, publisher's site. The "Info" page of the Facebook site makes that clear: "*This site is maintained by the author's international publishers. Continue to check here for updates on book tours, reviews, and news" ("Margaret Atwood"). The thicket of online platforms disseminating information and updates about Atwood's activities threatens to overwhelm in its variety, but this is more the publisher's page than Atwood's. Still, Facebook fans continue to post admiring comments, pleas for help and contact, and so forth.

A more direct-seeming link to Atwood appears in the form of her blog, marg09.wordpress.com, titled "Margaret Atwood: Year of the Flood." There, Atwood does occasionally respond to reader comments. Again, like the promotional website that spawned it, yearoftheflood.com, it seems designed both to mark a specific publishing occasion and to allow the author to blog on subjects that reach beyond that occasion. Atwood has been blogging on various appearances that she has made since the publication of the novel. She regularly also uploads audio and visual content. For example, she uploaded an audio file of her presentation on electronic media and publishing "The Publishing Pie" at the February 2011 Tools of Change in Publishing conference, along with the hand-drawn illustrations on PowerPoint slides that I discuss in the Introduction – a presentation that explicitly treats the subject of art and the marketplace.

Atwood's presence on Internet websites, therefore, is as multifaceted as her career, and it involves a similarly complex web of professional connections. From margaretatwood.ca, with its links to the Atwood office, to yearoftheflood.com, with its connections both to professional advertising and to not-for-profit environmental organizations, to marg09.wordpress.com, "Margaret Atwood" on the Web is less a single site than a network of electronic connections and interfaces. Like her literary celebrity, it is a web of industrial relations: a pie with many pieces.

Moving from Internet sites to a different "social medium" – albeit one linked at various points to those sites – the public performances that Atwood and others held as part of the tour for *Year of the Flood* marked a departure in her promotional practice. There are, in fact, compelling arguments for considering them extensions of Atwood's growing interactivity and multimedia celebrity. These performances, which spanned 112 days and seven countries, involved readings from the novel interspersed with performances of the Gods' Gardeners' hymns from the novel. The hymns were set to music by the American composer Orville Stoeber, the husband of Atwood's long-time agent Phoebe Larmore – yet another instance of the interlaced relationships in Atwood's professional life. (Stoeber was drawn into discussions with Atwood and Larmore about the hymns and wondered if they could be set to music [yearoftheflood.com].) There is a detailed blog entry on Atwood's wordpress site, as well as on the CBC's website, about the tour, containing extensive documentation of the performances, including photographs. The readings and hymns were the two constants of each performance, but the participants, both chorus and actors, at each site were different and local. This inclusion of local talent was part of Atwood's commitment to making the tour as green as possible. So at the Manchester event, for instance, two *Coronation Street* cast members performed roles, and the hymns were performed by the Manchester Lesbian and Gay Chorus, the Ordsall Acapella Singers, and the Blackburn Community Choir. In Edinburgh, as reported in *The Times*, a former Bishop of Edinburgh delivered one of Adam One's sermons, clad in a leopardskin robe. (He later commented, "It was fabulous, although I wouldn't wear this often" [Boztas]). Each performance, then, was specific to the place.

Though the performances marked, as I have suggested, a departure for Atwood in terms of her promotional practices, they are not quite as revolutionary as was claimed in the press and by Atwood's representatives. Her Canadian editor Ellen Seligman called the tour "unprecedented" (DeMara), and *Toronto Star* journalist Bruce DeMara declared that "Margaret Atwood is radically designing the concept of a standard book tour." Atwood herself called it "an unprecedented experience. And not repeatable" (V. Wagner). However, the traditional book tour has become a thing of the past, and publishers are much more likely to integrate promotion with already existing events, such as writers' festivals (Adams "Publish and Your Book Will Probably Perish"). Launches are, more and more, examples of cross-marketing rather than publisher-driven affairs; the design writer Janice Lyndsay, for example, entered into an agreement with Pittsburgh Paints to fund the launch of her book on colour, at which, of course, the company promoted its products; it also agreed to sell copies of Lindsay's book in some of its stores (Adams "Publish and Your Book Will Probably Perish"). Some literary authors are blogging in the voices of their forthcoming books' characters as a means of promotion, and others hire actors to portray those characters on linked video enactments of particular scenes (McCann). Even the idea of a performance is not entirely original; Ben Karlin assembled a comedy show in a New York theatre to promote his edited collection *Things I've Learned from Women Who've Dumped Me,* and Christopher McDougall, who wrote *Born to Run,* about running barefoot, devised a cabaret show that featured an opera singer performing an aria based on a section of the text (Kaufman). Again, the examples here are drawn from genres that are perceived to have less at stake, in terms of cultural capital, than literary fiction, and there is not the least hint that the proceeds raised benefit anyone other than the author and publisher. Atwood's coup was to bring performance promotion into the realm of literary fiction, but in order to do so without suffering a loss of critical esteem, she needed to adopt a more socially conscious, not-for-profit activist approach. None of this, of course, is to question Atwood's commitment to her causes, which is both long-standing and deeply genuine; this form of promotion, however, would simply be less viable for most writers of her cultural standing and would open them up to charges of crass commercialism. As it is, as with her blogging and tweeting, media coverage of the tour did occasionally, if subtly, generate such charges; the headline for Bruce DeMara's coverage of the planned tour in the *Toronto* Star read "Margaret Atwood Offers More Bang for the Book."

As is often the case with promotional media, one spawns another, and the same is true of Atwood's performance tour for *The Year of the Flood*. Toronto documentary filmmaker Ron Mann discovered that no one was creating a filmic record of the tour, so he undertook to do so. The result, *In the Wake of the Flood*, follows Atwood to various venues and records the striking variety of the local performances. It also documents her activist interests, showing Atwood visiting a collective vegetable garden and tweeting her followers about migratory birds. In this respect, *In the Wake of the Flood* does work that is similar to the promotional website for the novel, insisting that the promotional tour is undergirded by a disinterested, non-economic motive.

By far the most attention directed at Atwood's recent promotional activities has involved Twitter, the microblogging tool that was introduced in 2006. Participants send brief messages or tweets to their followers, who follow, in turn, the tweets of other participants. The pace of communication is rapid and cumulative as users retweet others' tweets; scholarly assessments estimate that retweets reach an average of one thousand recipients (Kwak et al.). Within eight months of its launch, Twitter had 94,000 users (Java et al.), and as of 14 September 2010, it had 175 million writing 95 million tweets per day (twitter.com). As a marketing tool, though, Twitter came to the fore somewhat belatedly. Early analysts of the application, such as Java and colleagues, who did one of the first academic studies of Twitter in 2007, listed several of its functions, none of which included marketing. However, by the next year, studies were pointing to the capacity of the new blogging tool to extend word-of-mouth advertising methods. Bernard J. Jansen and colleagues found that "microblogging is a potentially rich avenue for companies to explore as part of their overall branding strategy" (2186). Of particular interest for potential marketers is the speedy diffusion of tweets; as Kwak and colleagues report, "once retweeted, a tweet gets retweeted almost instantly on the 2nd, 3rd, and 4th hops away from the source, signifying fast diffusion of information after the 1st retweet." However, some scholars cast doubt on the efficacy of Twitter as a marketing tool; Huberman and colleagues argue that the crediting of Twitter with robust applications for "the propagation of ideas, the formation of social bonds and viral marketing … should be tempered by our findings that a link between any two people [on Twitter] does not necessarily imply an interaction between them … Most of the links … were meaningless from an interaction point of view" (8). Another roadblock to effective marketing is the "'noisy' environment" of Twitter, as described by Courtenay Honeycutt and Susan C. Herring; that is, the speed and number of tweets. It would be easy for marketers' messages to become lost in the fray.

Though the medium's utility for marketing is the subject of some controversy, there is a strong connection between Twitter usage patterns and celebrity culture – a marketing of the self, so to speak. Kwak and colleagues ranked the top 20 Twitter users (in 2009); all, they discovered, "are either celebrities (actors, musicians, politicians, show hosts, and sport stars) or news media." No authors, of course, though Viv Groskop reports in a *Daily Telegraph* article called "How to Stalk Your Favourite Author" that Twitter users of a literary bent have found the insights offered by tweets into the quotidian lives of literary celebrities appealing and even addictive: "So we know, for example, that Atwood is reading *Walt Whitman's Secret* by George Fetherling, that she has recently planted sweet peas and that she is obsessed with wind turbines." The random assortment of details large and small calls to mind the range of information about celebrities thought worthy of reportage: everything from personal likes and dislikes to photographs of them walking down a street or changing an outdoor light bulb.

Some uses of Twitter for literary marketing may appear to emphasize the book (rather than the author) as the product, but often they lead back to the authorial figure and to the lure of making contact – even of an electronic sort – with that author. For example, in 2010, Goose Lane Editions' publicity and promotions director, Corey Redekop, set up a Twitter account in the name of a character from a forthcoming novel to be published by the press, without giving any indication that the character was fictional. But eventually, the character was revealed to "be" the author. Redekop designed the plan in order to test how effective Twitter could be as a marketing device, though he admitted that it would be difficult to quantify how successful it might be (Hewitt).

The danger with a marketing scheme that returns to the figure of the author is that it may be seen as purely self-promotional. Twitter user and novelist Jojo Moyes told *The Guardian* that "it's been a huge disappointment to unfollow a couple of literary heroes who were just unutterably smug or self-promoting. If you supposedly love words, then using social media for constant self-promotion rather misses the point" (Groskop "Literary Luvvies"). The line is drawn, once again, between disinterested literariness and business, and authors can find themselves diminishing their store of cultural respect if they appear to lean too heavily on promotional tactics – or if they apply too few filters between their private ego and their Twitter-selves.

As with all such dangers, however, Margaret Atwood has shown herself adept at negotiating them very skilfully. It is instructive, in this regard, to examine how she has narrated her adoption of Twitter. In the amusing piece "I Love It When Old Ladies Blog," Atwood describes her introduction to Twitter as serendipitous. As I have mentioned, her setting up a Twitter account was a natural outgrowth of the building of the website for *The Year of the Flood*, since a Twitter link was standard on any such website by 2009. She casts the experts at Scott Thornley and Company as the canny instigators and herself as the naive but willing subject: "'You have to have a Twitter Feed on your website,' they said. 'A what?' I said, innocent as an egg unboiled … And before you could say LMAO, I was sucked into the Twittersphere like Alice down the rabbit hole." The literary reference is telling: here is a technological neophyte, we are asked to believe, whose frame of reference remains firmly planted in a highbrow literary context.

However serendipitous Atwood's descent down the Twitter-hole, she nevertheless turns up in many journalistic treatments of the growing popularity of Twitter, particularly among those in the publishing industries. Her name is often invoked at the beginning of such discussions, as though she has become a veritable object-lesson on the need for literary culture to keep up with the times. When Viv Groskop of *The Observer* summed up the major trend towards tweeting among literary figures, the first name on her list was not that of a British writer, but Atwood's ("Literary Luvvies"), and her piece on literary content on Twitter for the *Daily Telegraph* opened with Atwood's memorable line about being sucked down the rabbit hole of Twitter ("How to Stalk Your Favourite Author"). *Globe and Mail* drama critic J. Kelly Nestruck opened his review of the Theatre Passe Muraille production of "Highway 63: The Fort Mac Show," a drama about Alberta oil sands town Fort MacMurray, by citing Atwood's appreciative tweet about the show: "Told this is very funny – can't wait to see how!" Yes, Atwood has become, in the same newspaper's words, "The Tweetable Woman," and followers – in Canada and beyond – are listening.

Another feature of this attentive media coverage of Atwood's use of Twitter is its tone of surprise – surprise that a writer of Atwood's generation would take up the electronic cudgels. Within the literary world, the implicit expectation is that embracing Twitter with alacrity is something reserved for the young and technologically savvy; as Random House's digital specialist Cassandra Sadek opined, as paraphrased by her interviewer, Katie Hewitt, "first-time authors tend to be more amenable to social networking, but they are also less likely to have a following than literary powerhouses (who are more likely to hold out as conscientious objectors)." (This is probably why newer authors have inspired more baroque Twitter promotions, such as setting up an account in a character's name: it is a way of building interest in the work first and, subsequently, in the writer.) So journalists covering Atwood's tweeting and Atwood's followers have registered a surprise that is often tinged with ageism. When Atwood designed superhero costumes for two of her followers, @kidney-boy (a nephrologist) and @DrSnit (a writer and comedian), *The Guardian* referred to her "surprising talent" – and the label seems to cover both her draftswomanship and her act of tweeting (Addley). *Toronto Life* was rather nastier in linking Atwood's Twitter activity to both her age and her sex: "While we are proud of our celebrated, literary grandmother for being so with it, we hope someone will stop her from ever trying Chatroulette" (a site that allows strangers to webcam randomly, often jokingly associated with pornographic exchanges [Hudson]). Atwood is aware of such ageist and sexist responses, and in typical Atwoodian fashion, she steals a march on her critics by poking fun at their jibes: as she wrote in the *Sunday Times*, in September 2009, around the time her tweeting was just beginning to attract notice,

> My hair's gone white and suddenly everyone thinks I'm cute. It struck me the other day when I started twittering on my website. Everyone seemed to think it was extraordinary that I could master a computer. People wrote in saying: 'Oh, how adorable! Isn't it cute when an old person starts to twitter? ("Fiction's High Priestess")

Another early follower's insensitive tweet, "I love it when old ladies blog!" became the title of Atwood's narrative of how she came to use Twitter. Sometimes quotation is the best revenge.

Besides being ageist and sexist, such expressions of surprise at Atwood's taking up Twitter close off other ways of understanding "the Tweetable Woman": as an artist, to name one. *The Observer*, noting in the spring of 2010 that Atwood had taken up Twitter the previous autumn, pointed out that Atwood's use of the form had its innovative touches: "She's even coining her own, idiosyncratic abbreviations: a tweet from last week read: 'WITWCT – pronounced Witwicketd–= What Is The World Coming To? KMDWAF = Knock Me Down With A

Feather!'" (Hoby). More seriously, reviews of short-short fiction (variously called micro-fiction, flash-fiction, or nanofiction) often draw connections between the renaissance of the form and the popularity of electronic formats such as Twitter and text messaging (E. Wagner "The Goddess of Small Things"; J. Sullivan). Atwood has a long-standing interest in the short-short genre and in related inter-genres such as the prose poem, from *Murder in the Dark* (1983) to *Good Bones* (1992) to *The Tent* (2006). More recently, one of Atwood's stories, "I'm Starved for You," appeared with Byline Press, a digital publisher that specializes in short fiction; the story appeared in March 2012 as a Kindle Single, as a Quick Read at the Apple iBookstore, and as a "Nook Snap" at BarnesAndNoble.com, as well as for Chapters-Indigo's Kobo (Quill). One of her micro-fictions was selected for *Wired*'s November 2006 feature on Very Short Stories; writers were invited to use only six words to create their fictions, and Atwood's was a compact classic of anti-romantic fiction: "Longed for him. Got him. Shit" ("Very Short Stories").

Regarding the substance of Atwood's tweets, the main thing to note is that they are multi-functional. Having taken the "plunge" into Twitter as a result of promotional website design, Atwood has mobilized the form to serve many other purposes – as she has done with the promotional website that started it all. Tweets may range from updates of speaking engagements and places travelled, to retweeted articles on matters of political or environmental concern or arts-related events, to playful responses to followers' tweets. They have, on occasion, become news items in themselves, as when Atwood designed witty superhero costumes for two followers or, more seriously, when she signed and forwarded an Avaaz.org petition calling upon Canadians to protest a proposed Fox-style Sun TV news channel. The latter set loose a flurry of tweets, including an angry response from Sun Media's Ottawa bureau chief, accusing her of blocking free speech, which in turn called forth a tart response from Atwood ("Free speech does not mean under-the-carpet-deals that would force people to pay for Fox out of cable fees"). Conventional news media, such as the *Toronto Star*, then picked up the story of the Twitter debate and presented it as news ("Atwood's Petition Tweet Starts Sun TV Debate"). And when she joined the rapper K'naan to support a bill before the Canadian parliament that would send generic drugs to developing countries, the *Globe and Mail* reported this, too, as news, highlighting the celebrity factor: "And K'naan isn't the only celebrity to get behind the bill. Author Margaret Atwood also used Twitter this week to urge Canadians: 'Pls write MPs 2 help developing countries have affordable meds" (Galloway).

Atwood's tweets have also, on occasion, provided obituary writers with pithy comments on the departed: a somewhat morbid application of the medium. Her tweet on the death of novelist Paul Quarrington read "A vital force gone," a phrase picked up by the *Toronto Sun* for the title of their article on Quarrington's death ("Vital Force Gone"). Michael Posner, writing in the *Globe and Mail*, opened his obituary for Fanny Silberman, Supreme Court Justice Rosalie Abella's mother, with the quotation: "So sad: Brave & kind Fanny Silberman, model 4 'Lily' in 'The Entities' story in my book Moral Disorder, has died in Toronto. A bright star" – Atwood's tweet. Posner observed that it was probably "the most succinct eulogy" of many devoted to Silberman. Again, the forces of obituary, celebrity and succinctness come into play in the context of a new medium – as they did as early as the late 1700s, according to Elizabeth Barry, when "death and its written inscriptions" were relocated "from the monumental materiality of the tomb to the two-dimensional medium of the newspaper" (261). This shift "from epitaph to obituary" marked the rise of a form of celebrity that broadened its field (towards entertainment industries, for example) and that featured the telling of eccentric or scandalous narratives about the (dead) celebrity. In the case of Twitter, we have a form that privileges the kind of pithy expression of sentiment that is friendly to newspaper reportage and headline formats. And in the case of celebrity tweeters of celebrity deaths, that reportage has the advantage of highlighting the reflections of one noted public figure upon the life and accomplishments of another: a doubling of celebrity-interest.

Literary tweets have the force, as well, of an online literary salon, as Ceri Radford maintains: "Great living writers such as Margaret Atwood are happily ensconced on the social network Twitter, sharing thoughts and ideas in the same way they might once have done in a literary salon." The way may not be the same: eighteenth-century literary salons, one gathers, were not hotbeds of verbal concision; but the larger point about literary Twitter as a community of readers and writers holds true. "Twitter is quickly becoming the ultimate online book club," writes Viv Groskop in the *Daily Telegraph* ("How to Stalk Your Favourite Author"). Atwood's tweets, though, refrain from literary endorsement; the no-blurbs policy announced on her website is a consistent one, regardless of the medium. However, she promotes not only her own scheduled events, but also others that she participates in and hears about: everything from a gigantic book sale at Simon Fraser University in Burnaby, B.C., in support of the Salvation Army (which will distribute the books to low-income families; 23 Feb. 2011) to a London group "Culturebaby," which seeks to make the English city's extensive cultural venues and events accessible to women with young children (25 Feb. 2011).

In addition to seeing Atwood's Twitter usage as influenced by her writing of flash fiction, or seeing it as creating various cultural meanings in turn, there is also the possibility that the new medium will influence some of Atwood's most recent works. In her review of *The Year of the Flood*, Sara Dowse observes of Atwood's coinages (CorpSeCorps, HelthWyzer, pleebs, pleebrats) that "much of the language derives from our rapidly developed habits of computer abbreviations, SMS-speak and Twitter-tweet." It's a brief aside, but it is an observation I will take up in more detail in my next chapter on the ways in which the various agents and technologies involved in Margaret Atwood's literary celebrity are treated in her writing.

When Atwood began tweeting in 2009, some observers linked her alacrity in taking up new electronic media with her invention of the LongPen: a signing device that allows an author to sign a book remotely, while chatting with the book's owner through a webcam setup. Atwood dreamed up the concept in 2004, while she was touring for *Oryx and Crake*; she wondered if some such device could allow writers who found travel too rigorous to sign books from afar. She formed a company called Unotchit (you-no-touch-it) to develop the technology, which eventually became incorporated as Syngrafii, with Atwood as Chair and Acting CEO. Some technical difficulties, involving ensuring Internet connectivity, persisted, and designing the writing device proved to be extremely challenging, since it had to mimic the complex movements of a writing hand. In September 2006, however, it was launched and Atwood conducted a successful transatlantic signing from the UK to Toronto. At present, Syngrafii is exploring the use of the device for applications far beyond that of book touring, such as the provision of legally recognized signatures on documents, and the technology continues to evolve: there is presently a kiosk-style LongPen for remote book signings, and a smaller, tablet-style model for business applications.

There have been suggestions that the invention could be considered an Atwoodian text, particularly by those who are attentive to her science fiction (or speculative fiction – Atwood's preferred term); as Bill Christensen writes for Technovelgy.com, a science fiction site, "not content to merely write science fiction, she [Atwood] has created a device she calls a LongPen." He sees the invention as a realization of an imagined device from Hugo Gernsback's 1911 science fiction text, *Ralph 124c41+*. Robert McCrum, Associate Editor of *The Observer*, called it "perhaps her most innovative literary creation" but did not explain his rationale for including it among Atwood's oeuvre. That explanation appears in the most extensive study on the LongPen to date, PhebeAnn Wolframe's "Invented Interventions: Atwood's Apparatuses of Self-Extension and Celebrity Control," in which she argues that the LongPen is "one in a series of texts, both written and non-written, which deal with the theme of self-extension and celebrity control" (15). She persuasively places the device in the context of Atwood's recurring fascination with the "trope of the autonomous severed hand" as a means of articulating the separation of the writing Author from the living, breathing person who goes about her everyday life, carrying the baggage of literary celebrity that attends her successful career. But can literary celebrity attach itself to a technical apparatus? More specifically, can the body be absented – or substituted – in this technological exchange of mechanical hand for living, writing hand, traditional performer of signature, that guarantor of individuality and authenticity?

First of all, that the LongPen bears a relation to the issue of celebrity seems clear. Many accounts of the device stress its applicability to celebrity culture and its demands; an online CBC arts report on the LongPen titled "Celebrities Set to Reach for Atwood's LongPen" pointed out that "authors, sports heroes, movie stars and other celebrities" could benefit from the invention, cementing the parallel between literary renown and other forms of public visibility. The official website of the LongPen company, Syngrafii, forges the same parallel, probably because it is trying to link the original conception of the tool to its possible, wider applications: "The first application of the Network™ seamlessly linked authors and other celebrities from their preferred location to retail locations around the world" ("Syngrafii"). In some instances, the parallel between "authors and other celebrities" grew so strong that the distinctions between these manifestations of celebrity became blurred; the online technology and science magazine the *Daily Galaxy* speculated that the LongPen would be particularly effective "as a way to shield authors from crazed fans and manuscript-wielding wannabees" (Tsirbas). Such a reflection overstates the parallels between literary and other forms of celebrity, for although literary stalkers are not unknown, the frequency of the problem does not approach the level faced by entertainment celebrities. (As far as the "manuscript-wielding wannabees" are concerned, it would appear that Atwood already had an effective means of staving them off, in the form of her office and its website.) In other accounts of the applications of LongPen technology, the possibility of heightening access to celebrities is, by contrast, exactly the point; as *Computer Dealer News* reported in its 9 November 2007 edition, LongPen would allow "sick kids" to "interact with their favourite celebrities without leaving the hospital (Del Nibletto).

Indeed, the celebrity applications of LongPen appeared so compelling to some commentators that they counselled the abandonment of the literary field as a venue for LongPen altogether. As Mike Hanlon wrote for *Gizmag*, "we think Unotchit should forget the book market and go after the burgeoning distance-everything market where it is a landmark tool that will enable public figures of all types to represent themselves more effectively to the global community."

This projection – the LongPen as instrument of global celebrity capital – is troubling for the way in which it potentially reconfigures celebrity by dematerializing and delocalizing the body. As Julie Rak has argued, counting the body out of celebrity is exactly what Atwood has in mind in designing the LongPen:

> In [her] characterization of celebrity as a kind of death and alienation from which it is difficult to escape, Atwood recognizes the importance of the author's body to literary capitalism. She cannot escape this economy. But, as the LongPen shows, Atwood has tried to invent her way out of the *using up* of the body for capital. (qtd in Wolframe 14)

As PhebeAnn Wolframe concludes, building on Rak's analysis, "Atwood designed the LongPen as a way to moderate the costs of her celebrity" (25). Both of these perceptions are accurate: the LongPen, with its eerily displaced authorial ghost-hand, marks an attempt to escape the bounds of the body as a marketing tool; as Atwood has reflected, "you cannot be in five countries at the same time. But you can be in five countries at the same time with the LongPen" ("Writer Margaret Atwood Unveils 'Long-Distance' Pen"). However, what I find most significant about the LongPen, from the point of view of Atwood's literary celebrity, is the *failure* of the technology to support a celebrity–fan relationship that routes itself around the body. In this, as in the other branches of the Atwood industry, human contact is central and is, ultimately, fundamental and irreplaceable.

In response to this persistence of the body in celebrity–fan relations, Atwood and other developers of the LongPen have found it necessary to reinsert a body into this technological apparatus. In short, they have found it necessary to argue that contact with an author (or other subject) via LongPen is an intimate experience. The Syngrafii website claims, for instance, that "LongPen provides the benefits of direct, personal contact without the cost, time, security issues, and carbon footprint associated with travel" ("Syngrafii"). Elsewhere on the site, on the FAQ page, however, they modify this claim somewhat. In response to the question, "Is this the end of the publicity tour?", they point out that "for many, it's not a choice between the celebrity-in-the-flesh and the remote signing. It will be a choice between the remote signing and nothing." In interviews, Atwood has reiterated the same point; not all venues are going to attract celebrities, and so this is their one chance to obtain access to them: "Let's pretend you live in Podunk, Ohio where [author] Richard Ford is never, ever going to go. This is your chance. Not only that, you can have a private conversation with Richard Ford which is going to be somewhat longer than the one you'd have in the big, long lineup at the bookstore" (Helm). So the terms of the defence have shifted, from the LongPen as a form of personal contact, to the LongPen as the best *substitution* for personal contact that non-metropolitan subjects can hope for. Such a defence does not actually make the LongPen a "democratizing" device, as Atwood has claimed on several occasions (Reid; "The Far-Reaching Pen of Margaret Atwood"). In fact, it is the reverse; it vouchsafes access to the body of the celebrity for metropolitan fans while consigning others to a (more) mediated experience.

The LongPen, then, proposes to take the body out of commercial exchange, all the while arguing that the level of intimacy and contact remains the same. As PhebeAnn Wolframe argues, though, this produces a liminal experience: a contact with a body that is simultaneously non-embodied: "Atwood's cyborg body part, the LongPen … engenders boundary confusion … It is controlled by a 'real' person, but is made out of metal … The LongPen occupies a liminal space between fiction and non-fiction, presence and absence, and past and present" (18). Rather than exiling the body from commerce, therefore, the LongPen is *haunted* by the body, which it must variously reinvest back into the technological apparatus. When what is being sold is contact with celebrity, the body is not so easily avoided or routed around.

For the most part, participants in early LongPen signings have confirmed such a view. They are intrigued by the technological feat but are not willing to place their mediated contact with a literary celebrity on the same level as a face-to-face meeting with the star. At the 2006 London Book Fair, one fan commented that he preferred direct contact: "It's nice to have the personal touch" ("The Far-Reaching Pen of Margaret Atwood"). One might compare this preferred experience of shared physical space to the "aura" that Walter Benjamin argued is lacking in any reproduction of a work of art: "its presence in time and space, its unique existence at the place where it happens to be" (220). In the case of the LongPen, the aura is not so readily banished; when the device was first tried out publicly at the book fair, and encountered difficulties (they managed the webcam connection but the remote signing device did not work), it was the bodies in the room that apparently caused the problem. As Atwood wrote in her account of the incident in the "The Ballad of the LongPen™," "It turned out that the mystery was simple – due to the extra heat added by people crowding round, the computer system had balked." For every attempt to take the body out of capitalism, out of marketing, it would seem that the body reasserts itself in one way or another.

Whereas conservative critics of electronic technologies might see this attempted negation of the body as exactly what is wrong with those technologies, I would argue that the reverse is true. In seeking to discipline the body – or to remove it from the equation entirely – the LongPen technology is actually swimming against the current of interactive technologies. As

Andrew Barry writes in "On Interactivity," the truly interactive technology does not seek to discipline and punish the body, in a Foucauldian sense, but rather to free it:

> In comparison to the instruments and codes of discipline, the various techniques of interactivity imply a much less rigid articulation of bodies and objects, coupled with a liberal sense of the limits of permissible control. There is a degree of play and flexibility between the interactive device and the user's body. Above all, the use of interactives is not intended to regiment the body but to turn it into a source of pleasure and experiment. (178)

I suspect that some such realization – that pleasure is reduced by taking the disciplinary approach to the LongPen encounter – may be connected to Syngrafii's movement to de-emphasize the applications of the device to literary culture. The LongPen may not, ultimately, be very well suited to this particular exchange, wherein proximity between the bodies of fan and celebrity is exactly the source of the pleasure. Accordingly, Syngrafii seems poised to explore the applications of the technology to legal and business arenas, where the necessity of gaining speedy access to a legally recognized, signed document trumps the presence of the signatories in the same space. More cynically, of course, this is also, simply, a larger market. Still, bodies will continue to provide the disruptive "noise" preventing any such attempt to absent the celebrity body from fandom, as they did when they crowded around the LongPen at the London Book Fair in 2006, blocking the transmission of Atwood's transatlantic signature.

In September 2009, the month that Atwood undertook her extensive, creative multimedia tour for *The Year of the Flood, Toronto Star* reporter Vit Wagner interviewed her and brought together many of the questions about Atwood's use of electronic and social media that I have pursued here. He noted, on the one hand, her recent embrace of blogging and Twitter and her introduction, three years earlier, of the LongPen – the various ways that Atwood has found, in Wolframe's words, "to moderate the costs of her celebrity" (25). Yet he also witnessed, on the same day, a warm and exuberant personal exchange between Atwood and two young fans. As she and Wagner exited the site of their interview, L'Espresso Bar Mercurio on Bloor Street in Toronto, and proceeded to set up for the photograph that would accompany the profile in the *Star*, a young man and woman approached and recognized the celebrated writer. The young woman threw her arms around Atwood, and she and her male friend posed, at Atwood's invitation, for a photo with her. The young couple happily drifted down the street, little caring that they took away with them no documented evidence of this encounter produced by a technological apparatus – no photograph – for the camera was the property of the newspaper. Wagner wondered to himself: "Can this really be the Margaret Atwood who invented the LongPen so she could sign stacks of books for readers who are so far away they might as well be on the moon?" His answer to his own question was that Atwood devised the LongPen not because of an "aversion to personal contact" but, rather, because she needs to "conserve her energy." Though that is surely so – and my analysis does not mean to ignore or downplay the rigours of promotional tours for an author, particularly for one who has entered her seventies – I think there is another way to read this episode ... and, through it, to read Atwood's extensive experimentation with electronic and social media. The body that is so central to the formation and workings of public personalities remains crucial to Atwood's literary celebrity. The various media she deploys – websites, Twitter, Facebook, blogs, the LongPen – echo, in their interconnecting, interactive workings, her public visibility, which, after all, comprises various relationships with agents, office workers, publishers, editors, website designers, accountants, lawyers, and many others. Although electronic media may appear to mask or rebuff the bodies that are involved in literary celebrity and fandom, they can never deny them altogether. There will always be bodies disrupting the apparatus, strolling down the street, hugging, careless of cameras, breaking into pleasure.

5
"The Cloak of Visibility": Art and Industry in the Works of Margaret Atwood

In her Empson Lectures, *Negotiating with the Dead*, delivered at Cambridge in 2000, Margaret Atwood briefly drew upon a metaphor that was surely a familiar one to her English audience: the fictional wunderkind Harry Potter's cloak of invisibility. Speaking of the condition of the writer who (like Harry's creator) becomes a public persona, Atwood declared that "the nobody-writer must throw off the cloak of invisibility and put on the cloak of visibility." She immediately followed up her observation with a less predictable, distinctly non-literary source: "As Marilyn Monroe is rumored to have said, 'If you're nobody you can't be somebody unless you're somebody else" (134). Although the conditions of celebrity that are experienced by a Hollywood star operate on a broader demographic scale, as Atwood herself is the first to point out whenever she is asked about being a literary celebrity, it is fitting that, in speaking publicly about the nature of writing, Atwood should yoke them together even briefly. For the author who becomes a literary celebrity truly becomes a "somebody else" – a figure that circulates more broadly in culture. As we saw in the preceding chapter on social media, Atwood launches her argument for continuing support for the writer in a digital age by pointing out that the author could be considered a primary source, like a dead deer that feeds other life forms and enriches ecosystems – the source of many other spinoff cultural products, only some of which are her actual books. As Elaine Risley notes in *Cat's Eye*, on public occasions like a painter's retrospective, the author disturbingly resembles that decaying corpse; as she walks through the rooms in which her art is displayed, she thinks, "I can no longer control these paintings, or tell them what to mean. Whatever energy they have came out of me. I'm what's left over" (551). Decades later, another Atwoodian artist, one who has certainly placed the cloak of invisibility over her head, Iris Chase Griffen in *The Blind Assassin*, witnesses the way in which the authorship of "The Blind Assassin" launches those ongoing ripple effects in her community; her unacknowledged authorial hand physically presents the Laura Chase Memorial Prize in Creative Writing to an aspiring young writer at the local high school. Iris, too, it would seem, is what's "left over" after the act of authorship, though in her case she has further emptied herself out by denying her authorship entirely. From Atwood's perspective, though, Iris's bizarre imposture is just an exaggerated version of how every writer operates as a "primary source" of art: "The author is the name on the books," she archly observes in *Negotiating with the Dead*; "I'm the other one" (37). She might just as well have said, "I'm what's left over."

The secondary industrial life forms that depend on this enormously productive author – the agents, publishers, assistants, researchers, journalists, fans – contribute their labour to the propagation of the public figure – "the name on the books" – and in so doing, they support "the other one" in the labour of writing, either by making time available for her labour or by increasing the market for her works. In this study, my focus is on these second-order cultural workers in the Atwood "industry," but it would not be complete without examining Atwood's writings, for they, too, reflect, if complexly, upon the issues that have formed the subject of this book: the public artist's condition of social visibility, the nature of literary and other forms of celebrity, and the production and industrial mediation of art. From the very beginning of her career in the 1960s, Atwood's writings have consistently probed the social production of art, in a way that forms a fascinating conversation with her own practice as a writer whose career constitutes a full-fledged business.[1]

Beginning on the most fundamental and explicit level, Atwood's works accomplish the important cultural work of placing the labour and industry of writing into representation. In *Cat's Eye*, for example, we hear brief but telling mentions of programs that support Elaine's painting at a time when becoming established as an artist is extremely difficult for her to do. First, while looking after her young daughter, she receives a "junior grant from a government arts program" (of the sort that Margaret Atwood, as a public spokesperson for the arts in Canada, fears may be jeopardized by governments of a more neoliberal, business cast of mind ["Dealing a Blank Card"]). Soon thereafter, in the wake of divorce, Elaine also benefits from a "group show organized by the Canadian government which is attended by many people who work with the Trade Commission" (512). As narrator, Elaine offers no explicit commentary on such programs, though her clear recognition of the involvement of the Trade Commission reveals that Elaine harbours no illusions about the promotion of art by the nation for economic purposes. Still, the group show is useful to her as a struggling apprentice, and Atwood allows the uneasy coexistence of art and national promotion to remain unresolved.

As Joan Foster braces for the literary celebrity that will overtake her as the author of the publishing sensation *Lady Oracle*, she is shown receiving galley proofs (234) and advance copies of the book (235). The inclusion of such professional details

---

1 Many critics have analysed Atwood's representations of authorship; see, in particular, Ellen McWilliams's *Margaret Atwood and the Female Bildungsroman*. Fewer are analyses of the various cultural agents involved in bringing writing to an audience (Kozakewich, Nischik). The representations that I examine here are drawn mainly from fictional and non-fictional works rather than from poetry, mainly because the first two genres are more given to representations of cultural and industrial interactions.

shows how the realities of her new status as a successful "respectable" author of literature are about to break in upon her formerly clandestine operations as a writer of costume gothics. Those new conditions of authorship are very much associated with a visual regime; Joan looks at the advance copy of the book and is struck by "my picture on the back, like a real author's. Louisa K. Delacourt never got her picture on the back" (236). Joan is at the crossroads, trying desperately to keep the cloak of invisibility from falling off her shoulders as the pseudonymous "Louisa K. Delacourt" while assuming the cloak of visibility as "Joan Foster, celebrated author of Lady Oracle, looking like a lush Rossetti portrait" (9). In a comic vein, *Lady Oracle* explores the serious aesthetic question of how the writer manages to wear, in effect, two cloaks: economic and cultural capital.

In *The Blind Assassin*, Iris is the keeper of a trunkful of publishing materials that we are initially asked to believe are the remainders of her sister Laura's literary career: manuscripts, author's copies of the novel, letters to publishers "from me, of course, not from Laura, she was dead by then – and the corrected proofs. Also the hate mail, until I stopped saving it" (285). Once again, authorship is figured, as in *Cat's Eye*, as a form of residue – "what's left over" – and Iris heightens the connection between authorship and the reliquary by christening this trunk her "tiny archive" (286). The seeming detritus of a literary career, though, holds some lively hints as to the authorial rebirth that takes place in this novel when Iris's authorship of *The Blind Assassin* rises from the ashes; Iris's offhand observation that the letters to publishers are "from me, of course, not from Laura" is capable, as we learn later in the novel, of a whole other explanation. Fittingly, the sister who is the public face of authorship is dead; the silent partner, meanwhile, is the living author: another sign that, for Atwood, literary celebrity is a species of death-in-life.

Moving from simple representation of the processes of publishing to its agents and industrial workings, Atwood's writings provide a rich field for pondering industrial relations in artistic circles. In this regard, the postscript, "Historical Notes on The Handmaid's Tale," is broadly representative of her lively concern for the ways in which art is produced and mediated. Indeed, this section is entirely about the way in which all texts are mediated by those who produce and reproduce, publicize, translate, or edit them. As the symposium chair, Professor Maryann Crescent Moon reminds the audience that their keynote speaker, Professor James Darcy Pieixoto, "is the co-editor … of the manuscript under consideration today, and was instrumental in its transcription, annotation, and publication" (312). As his address proceeds, listeners (and readers) learn just how much the text known as "The Handmaid's Tale" has been altered by its two editors from Cambridge University; the chronology has been arranged, for instance, by Professor Piexoto and his co-editor, Professor Knotly Wade, for they transcribed cassette tapes that were discovered in no particular order (314). Even the title of the narrative is an editorial imposition; Pieixoto recalls that his collaborator Wade bestowed the title "The Handmaid's Tale" to the taped narrative in honour of Chaucer's *Canterbury Tales*, thereby forcing it into the procrustean bed of canonical English literary history (313). Pieixoto's bumptious jokes about "tale"/"tail" and "Underground Femaleroad"/ "Underground Frailroad" (313) increase the anxiety about textual editing as an extension of Gilead's control of women's bodies, as does the nervous arbitrariness of his warning "about passing moral judgment upon the Gildeadeans" (314).

However, the "Historical Notes on The Handmaid's Tale" offer a complicated, nuanced view of textual mediation, and while the evidence for considering the Cambridge professors' editing to be sexist and controlling is incontrovertible, Atwood places some surprisingly wise words in the mouth of the boorish Pieixoto: at one point he reflects that Gilead's "racist policies, for instance, were firmly rooted in the pre-Gilead period" (317) – a proposition that the novel repeatedly demonstrates. And for all that Pieixoto pursues issues of precise historical detail with an academic zeal bordering on the fusty (was Offred's commander Frederick R. Waterford or B. Frederick Judd?

[319]), he also movingly acknowledges the limits of historical knowledge: "We may call Eurydice forth from the world of the dead, but we cannot make her answer" (324). (Still, he ends his disquisition with a deeply problematic presentist assumption: that we cannot "decipher" the texts of the past "precisely in the clearer light of our own day" [324]). The reproduction of texts, therefore, is shown in *The Handmaid's Tale* to be a power-ridden and ego-driven but crucially important and valuable act.

If we look more closely, in Atwood's works, at the representations of the various cultural agents who undertake this fraught, crucial task of bringing texts to readers, we find that some fare better than others in her critical estimation. Those who are associated with the economic "bottom line" of the artistic industries, such as promotional managers and journalists, come in for the lion's share of Atwood's biting satire, whereas editors, those cultural agents who, as I have noted, are often romantically imagined as representing cultural rather than economic capital, tend to receive a more sympathetic treatment. Why, though, do Atwood's fictional representations of the cultural industries not conform to the more nuanced balancing of the economic and the artistic that I have found represented fully in archival evidence of her working life as a novelist?

The key lies precisely in their fictional nature and in the way in which fictionalized cultural agents come to represent, not so much the well-rounded complexity of the actual workers in the publishing industry that I have discerned in my study of "Atwood Inc.," but rather the forces arrayed against the Atwoodian artist who is seeking that more equitable balance between the economic and the artistic. The most pointed critique of blatant acquisitiveness in the publishing industry is directed towards Atwood's directors of promotion and some – but not all – publishers. In *Surfacing*, for example, the narrator, a commercial artist who paints and draws book illustrations, is restricted in her choice of colours by publishers' costs; in particular, she cannot use red, which is more costly to reproduce (54). Later in the novel, when the narrator discovers the correspondence that her father has carried on with the scholar of indigenous rock paintings, she reads in one of the scholar's articles that red is the "predominant colour" in those paintings, "due either to the fact that red ... is a sacred colour or to the relative availability of iron oxides" (103). The two passages implicitly bounce off each other, suggesting that the narrator's drawings are anything but sacred; they are, instead, products of market forces, devoid of spiritual lifeblood, and her publishers are the gatekeepers of cost-effective art.

In *Lady Oracle*, Atwood's commentary on the world of publishing is more extensive than in *Surfacing*, and it is also more nuanced, for it leaves open the possibility of varying stances within the publishing industry regarding the relation between economic and cultural motives. The first meeting of Joan, the neophyte author, with her new publishers, Morton and Sturgess (a play on Atwood's Canadian fiction publishers McClelland and Stewart), is a broadly comic scene, but it has substantial commentary to offer on the various position takings in mid-twentieth-century Canadian publishing. The owner of the firm, John Morton (widely held to be a stand-in for Jack McClelland), Doug Sturgess, a partner and head of promotion, and Colin Harper, an editor for the press, taken together, represent the marketing of the creative, but they have different stakes in the ongoing negotiations between culture and business, and Atwood differentiates their comic handling accordingly. Although Tobi Kozakewich is right to point out that, in this scene, "a collectivity of men . . . interpellate the artifact of Joan's manuscript as a work of art" (186), she tends to equate all of the agents doing the interpellating as equally sexist and culpable, from Morton and Sturgess to the fatuous Barry Finkle who interviews Joan on television. However, there are distinctions to be made among these characters – distinctions that are attributable to Atwood's analysis of the agents working in the publishing industry and their varied relations to cultural and economic forms of capital. John Morton, for example, arguably the most powerful man of the triad in an economic sense, does not receive the major portion of satirical critique. Indeed, his few comments are benign and kindly; he looks at the clearly nervous Joan "benevolently, with the tips of his fingers pressed together … 'My dear,' he said, turning to me, 'we would be most happy to publish your book" (227).

In a similar fashion, Atwood tends to extend a certain amount of sympathy to publishers in her non-fictional discussions of publishing in Canada, acknowledging the mitigating circumstances that prevent the more supportive publishers from taking a chance on some deserving writers. As early as *Survival*, in her chapter on "The Paralyzed Artist," Atwood saw the artist not so much at the mercy of unscrupulous publishers and promotional agents as constrained by a publishing industry that is, in turn, constricted by larger imperialistic forces. Speaking of the early years of her career, she noted that there were "not many publishing companies, and those few did a lot of distribution for foreign companies" (182); as a result, they were unwilling to take risks on new or experimental writers. The artist, consequently, had to "squeeze his work into shapes that were not his" (182). She did, though, acknowledge that by the time of writing *Survival*, there was a greater willingness among publishers to sign Canadian writers (192). Later, in her speech "Canadian-American Relations," delivered at Harvard in 1981, she reiterated her belief that publishers were unwilling to take on experimental – or, she adds, nationalist – writers because of their dependency on broader markets; at that time, she saw the formation of small presses by writers as the only way for them to gain some measure of control over the means of production (*Second Words* 384). Clearly, Atwood was looking back at the previous decade and its burgeoning of small presses (Scherf "A Legacy of Canadian Cultural Tradition and the Small Press"), many of which featured involvement by writers – like herself. It seems as though, for Atwood, one solution to the problem of economically constrained or exploitative publishers was to combine the functions of artist and businessperson in the person of the writer–publisher.

For all that Atwood, at various points in her career, dreamed of cutting out the "middle man," she is always mindful, in her non-fictional writings, of the economic pressures brought to bear on Canadian publishers. In her influential review of Timothy Findley's *The Wars*, for example, she noted that Clarke, Irwin, which had heretofore been mainly a textbook publisher, was "making a bid for McClelland & Stewart territory" (*Second Words* 290), for they were sending Findley (as yet a relatively unknown writer in Canada) on a cross-country tour, distributing publicity materials, and hosting a promotional dinner – all quite unusual and cost-prohibitive in the Canadian publishing world of 1977.

When it comes to narrating her own experience with publishers, Atwood's satire is similarly gentle and understanding. In at least two texts, she narrates the farcical beginnings of her own long association with Jack McClelland, whose staff lost the manuscript of her first published novel, *The Edible Woman*, for two years after she sent it to them in 1965. In her introduction to the Virago Modern Classics edition of the novel in 1981, she played up the comic elements of the mix-up but also Jack McClelland's ultimate generosity: "By this time I was marginally visible, having won an award for poetry [the Governor General's Award for Poetry, for *The Circle Game*], so the publisher took me out for lunch. 'We'll publish your book,' he said, not looking me in the eye. 'Have you read it?' I said. 'No, but I'm going to,' he said. It was probably not the first book he'd published out of sheer embarrassment" (*Second Words* 370). Fifteen years later, she retold the story to Victor-Levy Beaulieu in *Two Solicitudes*, in response to Beaulieu's comment that "I believe that in your case it was a bit strange, your first meeting with your publisher." Atwood obliges, adding more comic detail to the story of the wandering manuscript. Having read in the newspaper that she had won the Governor General's Award for Poetry, and that she had recently completed a novel, Jack McClelland wrote Atwood a letter, telling her that he wished to read this novel. When he discovered, to his dismay, that his company had had the novel in their possession for the previous two years, he telephoned: "'I want to buy you a drink.' So I met him in a little café. He drank five Bloody Marys and I drank one." Atwood finishes the story as before, concluding: "I think poor Jack McClelland published my novel out of guilt" (62). Some of the comic touches echo Atwood's fictional treatment of the publishing business in *Lady Oracle*, particularly the comedy of differential alcohol intake at Joan's first meeting with Morton, Sturgess, and Harper: "They all ordered martinis. I wanted a double Scotch, but I didn't want to be thought unladylike, not right away ... So I ordered a Grasshopper" (226). The hard-drinking, hard-bargaining world of publishing is set before us, but Atwood's recollections of her actual, farcical first meeting with McClelland are laced with a gentler, sympathetic humour. After all, McClelland developed a rapport with writers, particularly because he often put the financial well-being of the company at risk in order to promote Canadian talent; as Atwood reminisced when McClelland died in 2004, "there were other publishers but nobody was as committed to publishing Canadian literature as he was, until much later" (Stoffman). In more recent comments on the publishing world, Atwood appears to see the McClelland-style publisher as a figure of the past. In *Negotiating with the Dead*, she mourns the passing of the "Maxwell-Perkins-like publisher" who "might support a writer through two or three or four financial failures," and she decries the ascendancy of the "bottom-line bean-counters. 'We don't sell books,' one publisher said, 'we sell solutions to marketing problems'" (65). Compare McClelland's famous pronouncement: "I publish authors, not books" (Donnelly).

Atwood's comic narratives of her meeting with McClelland appear to reinstate the championing of cultural capital over its grimier cousin, economic capital, yet what they arguably also do is re-establish a balance between the two that Atwood senses is sadly lacking in the current publishing world. Clearly, McClelland was an amalgamation of the roles that Atwood isolates and satirizes in her fictional portraits of Morton, Sturgess, and Harper. McClelland was every bit a businessman, and he had a good deal of the promotional wizard about him too. He was famous for devising extravagant and unprecedented publicity stunts for his authors. To launch Sylvia Fraser's novel *The Emperor's Virgin*, in 1980, for example, McClelland hired a chariot to carry himself, Fraser, and charioteers, all clad in togas, down Toronto's Yonge Street on the Ides of March. (A mid-March blizzard made the stunt rather uncomfortable, but it certainly attracted media attention [Spadoni].) And he was known as the initiator of the Canadian cross-country publicity tour; before McClelland, authors tended to promote their books more locally, but McClelland sent writers on what Atwood herself would come to call the "McClelland & Stewart Wreck-an-Author tour" (*Second Words* 418). Knowing full well the extent of McClelland's entrepreneurial flair, then, Atwood would be the last of his authors to disavow the full complexity of his (and other publishers') roles. However, she celebrates how his necessary participation in the world of marketing coexisted with an understanding of the publishing business that exceeded the economic imperative. "I don't think publishing is what he most wanted to do," Atwood reflected on the occasion of his death. "He wanted to be Sir Galahad. Canadian publishing is the history of quixotic people" (Stoffman). In painting McClelland as the Sir Galahad of Canadian publishing, Atwood appropriately interlaces a literary with an economic narrative of McClelland's life and career.

For all that Atwood tends to hold fire on publishers in her fictional writing and, even more, in her non-fictional remembrances, the same cannot be said of her fictional treatment of promotional directors, such as the amply satirized Doug Sturgess in *Lady Oracle*. Sturgess is the source of much of the scene's satire, for his no-holds-barred pursuit of profit is matched only by his condescending sexism: "It's dynamite," he says of *Lady Oracle*. "And isn't she a great little lady? We'll have a great cover. Four-color, the works" (227). Sex and promotion go hand in hand for Sturgess; he has virtually nothing to say about the creative content of Joan's volume; he is entirely taken up with the promotional aspects of her promising career: "I thought we might do you as a sort of female Leonard Cohen ... Do you play the guitar?" he pitches, to the embarrassment of his colleagues Morton and Harper, whose motives, though economic, are rather more mixed than Sturgess's. (His suggestion also provides a gentle jab at McClelland and Stewart, Cohen's publisher for several decades. McClelland was famously conflicted about the firm's decision to publish *Beautiful Losers*; as he wrote to Cohen, "It's wild and incredible and marvellously well-written, and at the same time appalling, shocking, revolting, disgusting, sick and just maybe it's a great novel" [Solecki 102].) And even when Sturgess does turn to Joan's manuscript, in search of a title, it's clear that he sees the appropriateness of a title as a promotional question rather than a creative one: "What about this bit right here … What I mean is, here's your title … Lady Oracle. That's it, I have a nose for them. The women's movement, the occult, all of that" (227–8). Appropriateness, for Sturgess, is a matter of customer demographics, not the sort of critical interpretation that imbues even McClelland's ambivalent response to *Beautiful Losers*. "You write it," Sturgess condescendingly tells Joan, "you leave it to us to sell it" (236); thus he neatly severs the creative from the promotional.

It is intriguing that Sturgess the promotions man, not Morton the publisher, is associated with the contractual nature of Joan's commitment to Morton and Sturgess. As the publication date looms and Joan begins to lose her nerve, Sturgess's gloves come off: "Look … you've signed a contract, remember?" (235). His language takes on an aggressively mechanistic hue: "We're in production …We're revving up the engines" (235), he promises Joan, and she thinks of this particular brand of industrial activity as a species of warfare: "Sturgess' battle plan was now in full swing, and my first television show was coming up" (238). That battle plan seems to involve little in the way of ethical considerations; as he smugly confides to Joan, "he'd 'placed' the most important review … 'We made sure the book went to someone who'd like it'" (236). When Joan demurs that such a proceeding seems lacking in fairness, he laughs at her naivety. Atwood makes plentiful use of her neophyte literary heroine to expose those practices of the book trade that would indeed raise the eyebrows of an outsider.

One effect of this satirical treatment of promotional directors is to level the apparent differences between the publisher of

Joan's costume gothics (Columbine – a play on the Harlequin romance publisher) and the more upscale firm of Morton and Sturgess. The former are anonymous and unforgivingly mercenary; as she recalls of the romance novel she wrote while hiding out in Terremoto, "I got less for it than usual, partly because of the length – Columbine paid by the word – and partly because the bastards knew I needed the money" (176–7). One might expect the iron fist of publishing capitalism to relax its grip on Joan once she begins to do business with publishers of literary fiction, but in the final event, the logic of the market is similarly deterministic. "We'll worry about good," Sturgess tells Joan. "That's our business, right?" (228), but it becomes clear that, for Sturgess and his ilk, business profits constitute the only "good."

In public addresses around the time that she published *Lady Oracle*, Atwood made it very clear that she was concerned about the increasing emphasis on promotional activities in publishing houses. In "An End to Audience?", which she presented at Dalhousie University in 1980, she blamed the fragmentation of the literary reading public on the growing emphasis on popular bestsellers and their paperback rights. Because more money was being directed towards promoting these high-profile bestsellers, she argued, there was less to invest in the "middle-range serious work of fiction" (*Second Words* 351). She also had harsh words for the growth of promotional "entertainment packages" in American publishing: the integrated marketing of the book, the movie, the T-shirt, and so on (352). Yet as I showed in chapter 4, by the time she came to promote *The Year of the Flood*, she had turned to such integrated marketing practices herself, pioneering the uses of promotional gambits formerly found only in mass popular book marketing to sell "serious" literary fiction.

Although Atwood's feelings about cross-marketing have changed over the years, largely due to the way in which she can use it to raise funds for causes that are dear to her (while, of course, promoting her own books), her response to a particular promotional medium – television – has remained uniformly scathing. In *Lady Oracle*, again, the figure presiding over Joan's disastrous television appearances is, not surprisingly, Sturgess. The novel contains a farcical scene in which Joan is interviewed by the bumbling, sexist television host of "Afternoon Hot Spot," Barry Finkle. And while Joan senses that she has dealt her new career a devastating blow by admitting to the twittish Finkle that her book has been composed through automatic writing, Sturgess is thrilled at the outré factor: "It was sensational! How'd you think it up?" (240). Clearly, Sturgess's promotional prowess has involved an automatic assumption that all public utterances are calculated, performed for effect.

In reminiscences about her own career, Atwood's stories about her experiences of televisual promotions come strikingly close to the broad comedy of *Lady Oracle*; in "Travels Back," she tells the story of a disastrous television interview in which the host, a "stiff-spined man in a tight suit," dangled one of her books of poetry from his fingers and asked, "What's this … a children's book? ... I suggested that if he wanted to know what was inside it he might try reading it. He became enraged … In place of the interview they ran a feature on green noodles" (*Second Words* 111). In a later essay, titled, appropriately, "Mortification," Atwood recounts her three major professional mortifications – "Early Period," "Middle Period," and "Modern Period" – and two of the three, not surprisingly, have to do with television interviews. The first, non-televisual mortification is one that she experiences as a new novelist who has not yet achieved the level of celebrity that would warrant television coverage: instead, Atwood recounts the story of how she had to sign books in the men's sock and underwear department at the Hudson's Bay Company store in Edmonton. The other two, televisual mortifications are linked specifically to the stages in her growing literary fame. The second takes place by the "time I'd achieved a spoonful or two of notoriety" (*Moving Targets* 407); and the third and most recent takes place by the "time I was famous, insofar as writers are" (408). In the former interview, she appears immediately after representatives from the Colostomy Association of America and, as

Atwood jokes, "I knew I was doomed. No book could ever be that riveting" (407). As for the later appearance, which took place in Mexico, Atwood was confronted by the inappropriate question, "Do you consider yourself feminine?" (408). Although Atwood shares this anecdote as an example of one of her professional mortifications, in her retelling, the interviewer receives the larger share of humiliation. Atwood responds to his sexist question: "You should be asking the men in my life … Just as I would ask the women in your life if you are masculine. They'd tell me the truth" (409). Atwood has also taken to other media to tell these stories of ill treatment at the hands of television interviewers. On her website, she includes two comic strips that narrate her encounters with inane interviewers, one on radio and one on television. Of the two, the television interviewer, a giggly woman with a makeup-encrusted face, is the more clueless; she claims that Atwood's book is "depressing" and asks what its "message" is, to which an irate-looking Atwood (in her comic incarnation as a curly-haired short woman in black wearing a pointy hat) intones: "The message is: eat more prunes … It's a cautionary tale." The retort is directed at television's need to simplify large and complicated narratives into short, directed sound bites.

In several of these recollected scenarios, Atwood represents herself as, in effect, having the last laugh, launching the stinging retort that cuts through the televisual inanity. As with Sturgess's delight at Joan's performance on "Afternoon Hot Spot," these engagements of the literary celebrity with the televisual medium are capable of very different readings within the promotional industry. Atwood shows television succeeding, to a degree, in remaking the writer in the shape of its own values, for the writer does have to answer the questions, in some fashion. But the writer, as the holder of cultural capital, is represented in Atwood's stories as also winning in the midst of her defeat by the televisual medium, in that she often refuses to play the game in quite the way the interviewer would prefer. This cut-and-thrust playing of the medium – at work in many of Atwood's own famously acerbic media interviews

– resembles the complicated dance of "loser wins" that Pierre Bourdieu describes as the hallmark of cultural capital: to the extent to which the artist denies or is denied by the forces of large-scale production, she or he "wins" cultural respect. In her essay "An End to Audience," Atwood explicitly makes the connection between television talk show hosts and Bourdieu's economic capital:

> In fact, the television talk-show host – who must be, in some way at least, a representative of his society – is much more likely to approve of you if you say you're in it only for the bucks and that your biggest ambition is to sell a million copies. Watch him cross his legs and wince, though, if you say you want to make good art. (*Second Words* 341)

The television interview, then, is a battleground of literary celebrity, and one that places the writer in a particularly risky position of potentially disavowing either cultural or economic capital, when the most advantageous plan, for a writer of literary fiction, is to keep the two in constant, kinetic exchange.

Considered in this way, death, in Atwood's works, becomes the ultimate promotional stunt – the way in which the author's capital is made to speak whatever narrative secondary agents (like television interviewers) wish, without fear of an embodied author resisting or contradicting the narrative. *Lady Oracle*'s dramatic action is founded on the staged death of Joan Foster, but as an inexperienced Joan finds out, this death does not release her from her public celebrity self, which has a post-mortem life of its own: "Sales of *Lady Oracle* were booming, every necrophiliac in the country was rushing to buy a copy" (315). Elaine Risley in *Cat's Eye* mordantly considers this means of increasing her artistic value as she surveys the canvasses that are gathered together, ready to be hung in her retrospective show: "If I cut off my ear, would the market value go up? Better still, stick my head in the oven, blow out my brains. What rich art collectors like to buy, among other things, is a little vicarious craziness" (115). As Elaine senses, the surge in economic capital that attends the death of the artist is intertwined with more insubstantial forms of capital. When the Gwendolyn MacEwen-like poet Selena dies in "Isis In Darkness," the narrator sombrely reflects that "she's become newly respectable … There's a move afoot to name a parkette after her, or else a scholarship, and the academics are swarming like botflies" (*Wilderness Tips* 82). The cultural capital newly extended to the dead writer circulates elsewhere in the industrial ecosystem, a further reflection of Atwood's conceit of the writer as the primary source from which other agents feed.

It might be argued, on the contrary, that acts of memorialization such as those contemplated for Selena are a means of keeping the works of the poet alive, and there are moments when Atwood's narrators recognize the devotion implied by such acts. Iris Chase, for example, in *The Blind Assassin*, comes upon a young weeping woman dressed in black placing "a single white carnation, the stem wrapped in tinfoil" on Laura's grave. "Laura touches people," she thinks. "I do not" (192), and here one can sense, retrospectively, a brief moment of regret for the authorship that she has foresworn. But for the most part, Iris recognizes that these acts of mourning are less about the author and her works and more about the extravagant desires of the mourner. Several times she finds flowers laid on Laura's grave, but the flowers are "withered" (45), "withering" (83), as the lonely white carnation will shortly do too. What's more, such acts of mourning, however deeply felt, are made the basis of economic exploitation by others in the ecosystem; as the narrator of the fable "Resources of the Ikarians" from *The Tent* observes of the artists that her society has decided to adopt as their main attraction, "they will write or paint or sing and then they will die early, and after that we can cash in" (61).

In Atwood's works, journalists are also singled out, along with promotional people, as especially implicated in this trade in artists. In several works, she takes aim at soft-news celebrity journalism; in *Bodily Harm*, Rennie Wilford soon discovers, as a neophyte journalist, that "instead of writing about the issues, she began interviewing the people who were involved in them. Those pieces were a lot easier to sell" (64). The situation takes a further turn for the worse when Rennie is encouraged not even to write about the issues at all; her unscrupulous editor Tippy advises her to find the personal dirt about a prominent judge whom Rennie is profiling. "Look in the medicine cabinet," she advises her (67). Elaine Risley, in *Cat's Eye,* has had her medicine cabinet thoroughly ransacked by journalists in the past, so to speak, and consequently is unduly cautious, even defensive when the newspaper journalist Andrea interviews her on the occasion of her retrospective. When Andrea asks, "Do men like your work?", Elaine instantly knows that she has "been going through the back files, she's seen some of those witch-and-succubus pieces" (120–1). As Elaine realizes, the celebrity's past treatment by journalists becomes a type of unofficial curriculum vitae; it attaches itself to the celebrity and becomes, for better or often worse, part of the star text.

The treatment of the relationship between the artistic celebrity and the press in *Cat's Eye* is notably perceptive, since Elaine – like Atwood – is intensely aware, at every step, of how her forays into publicity are read in the context of all previous media representations of her career. And she is also aware, again like Atwood, of how she can either facilitate or frustrate the journalistic desires of those interviewing her. For example, when Elaine sees the final product of Andrea's interview, in the newspaper, she sees its moments of nastiness ("Elaine Risley, looking anything but formidable in a powder-blue jogging suit" [302–3]) as payback for her lack of cooperation with Andrea. As she admits to her ex-husband Jon, "It's my fault. I was rude to the interviewer" (356). The portrayal here of the celebrity journalism business accords with Joshua Gamson's study in *Claims to Fame*. There, he depicts the business as an ongoing tug of war between the celebrity's need both for privacy and for publicity and the journalist's need for more, fresh information about the celebrity – the "scoop." As Gamson observes, "the celebrity is divided up into pieces, and those pieces move between parties, are exchanged, invested, cashed in" (94), in a process that sounds exactly like Atwood's metaphor of the artist as a dead deer carved up for its meat.

Where Atwood diverges from Gamson's institutional study, however, is in seeing further motivations for the aggressiveness of celebrity journalism beyond the economic: mainly in the psychology of celebrity and fandom. In Fraser Buchanan, the unscrupulous celebrity journalist of *Lady Oracle*, she has created an embodiment of the threatening media; indeed, he does the sort of journalism that Rennie Wilford in *Bodily Harm* is loath to do. He goes beyond the medicine cabinet, in fact; Joan discovers that he's been riffling through her underwear drawer (288). His sub rosa journalism grows out of his own sense of creative failure; apparently, his magazine *Reject*, formed to publish works rejected by other magazines, failed for lack of willing contributors, though he published a great deal in it himself. And as a result, he carries an animus against literary successes like Joan: "He hated celebrities, he felt they diminished him" (291). His sense of grievance is exacerbated by his sexism; he becomes convinced that Joan has won publication by sleeping with John Morton (260, 291). All in all, Fraser Buchanan is a repulsive representative of celebrity journalism as an outgrowth of obsessive stalking; even the Royal Porcupine, the ultimate in eccentricity, pronounces him "freaky" (261).

The obvious villainy of Buchanan is nuanced, though, by the fact that other, ostensibly friendlier contacts of Joan's adopt certain traits of Buchanan's trash journalism. We hear, for example, that Arthur is using bits and pieces of newspaper critiques of Joan to nourish his own growing sense of envy and grievance: "He'd cut them out and use them to belabor me. 'It says here you're a challenge to the male ego'" (270). And we also hear, in a somewhat offhand way, that the Royal Porcupine had formerly threatened to sell examples of Joan's handwriting (290). So however external and stereotypical Fraser Buchanan's villainy seems, it is rendered more complex by Atwood's awareness that it simply crystallizes the various ways in which celebrity journalism undermines the private, quotidian lives of its subjects.

As Iris Chase's reference to the academic "bot-flies" circling around her sister Laura's reputation in *The Blind Assassin* suggests, Atwood's depiction of literary scholars is filled with the language of parasitism. As early as *The Edible Woman*, academics in Atwood are driven by a ruthless pursuit of material, not unlike the celebrity journalists who people her fictions. The graduate student Duncan describes it as being a "slave in the paper-mines" (106), searching endlessly to say something new about literature that has been plentifully discussed already by critics. Iris Chase, in *The Blind Assassin,* thinks of what such slaves would do with the contents of her trunk filled with manuscripts and letters: "Material, they'd call it – their name for loot" (286). "Scavangers" ... "jackals," she calls them (287). We see examples of letters that Iris sends to these academics who write to her seeking some of this "loot," whether letters, mementoes, or interviews, and they are masterpieces of snide satire. Iris staunchly concludes that "Laura Chase is not your 'project.' She was my sister" (287). Like other secondary cultural workers whose livelihoods depend on writers' creations, the academic is, more often than not, depicted as a predator in Atwood's writings.

So far, all of these agents of literary industry in Atwood's works cut extraordinarily nasty figures, but this is not the case with one secondary cultural worker: the editor. The most extensive fictional study of the editor–writer relationship in Atwood's fiction appears in her short story "Monopoly," from *Moral Disorder*, in which the main character, Nell, had formerly been the editor of her lover's ex-wife, Oona, who writes highly marketable "Superwoman self-help" volumes (100). The story features a catalogue of Nell's editorial duties that would fit neatly into my chapter on Atwood and editors, in that it is an amalgamation of the professional and the personal: "working wonder with not-yet-publishable material"; being on time, not charging too much, "fielding midnight calls from drunken authors with encouragement and tact" (100). The labour is gargantuan, yet it is not widely publicized; as I have noted of editors, their work becomes visible only briefly if at all, in

Acknowledgments pages. For example, Oona expresses her "gratitude in the Acknowledgments section, and then again, in pen and ink, on the title page of the copy she'd given to Nell: For invaluable Nell, the rewrite queen – the power behind the scenes" (101). It is as though Oona is determined both to acknowledge Nell's labour and to subordinate it to her own, placing it off-centre.

As I have noted of the editor–author relationship, its boundaries are hazy at times: Nell must work on deletions, revisions, edits, and wholescale reorganizations, besides sorting out the "jumble" that is Oona's mind (101). Indeed, a major problem that develops over the course of this story is the loss of distinction between Nell's editorial work and Oona's creative labour. Oona decides that she wishes to write a follow-up volume to her immensely successful new age guide *Femagician*, but when Nell points out that Oona needs to "make some preliminary decisions about goals and intentions," Oona demurs: "Couldn't Nell do that?" (102). Eventually, it becomes clear that Oona expects Nell to do the writerly labour for her: "As for the project of Oona's new book, the one Nell was to have edited or – more like it – ghost-written, it had been quietly dropped" (109). This dissolution of roles comes to inform the personal relationship that develops when Nell falls in love with Oona's ex-husband Tig. Rather than being Tig's lover, Nell comes to feel, she has been, oddly, hired by Oona to be the "governess" (113), looking after Oona and Tig's children. The dynamic is similar to that of another Atwoodian triangle, that of Lesje, Elizabeth, and Nate in *Life Before Man*; Lesje comes to feel as though she is not so much Elizabeth's rival or successor but, instead, her hired help, "a kind of governess" (193). In "Monopoly," Atwood finds the perfect metaphor for role diffuseness: literary editing.

This does not mean that exploitative editors do not exist in the Atwoodian canon; Rennie Wilford in *Bodily Harm* has to negotiate with magazine editors who demand more and more fluff pieces, and one who combines professional with sexual predation ("a man who kept suggesting that they should have drinks sometime soon"; 25). But when it comes to literary editors,

Atwood sees in the editor a cultural worker who is often able to combine the demands of the marketplace with some measure of sensitivity, as Nell does. Recalling *Lady Oracle*'s publishing triumvirate, publisher John Morton, publicist Doug Sturgess, and editor for the press Colin Harper, there is a subtle distinction between Harper and the other men. He is identified as both an editor and a poet (226), so he has allegiances both to commerce and to art. And when the other two men balk at some of Joan's more recherché metaphors, Colin Harper, alone, comes to her artistic defence: "'For instance,'" complains Sturgess, 'who's the man with the daffodils and the icicle teeth?' 'I sort of like that,' Colin said. 'It's, you know, Jungian'" (227). Harper may err on the side of fatuousness, but he is, at least, attending to the artistic rationale for some of Joan's more challenging imagery. The literary editor, in Atwood's fictions, embodies what Atwood as artist has developed over the years of her long career: the capacity to juggle aesthetic and commercial criteria without losing sight of the former or denying the latter.

For all that, it is worth pointing out, before leaving this literary survey of publishing figures in Atwood's fiction, that the one major figure she does not represent is the literary agent. There are many logical reasons for this, no doubt, among them a sense that the conflicts between publishers and authors, and the relationships between editors and writers, are more dramatically absorbing than the matter of, say, contractual negotiations. But along with this, the literary agent is the figure who, more than any other with the possible exception of artists' lawyers and accountants, protects the fiscal rights of the writer. In my analysis of literary agents, I showed how their role is actually more complex than this and how it involves – certainly in the case of Margaret Atwood and Phoebe Larmore – aesthetic considerations aplenty. But the overwhelming public understanding of the agent's role is to make money for the client, so drawing attention to this figure in the cohort of cultural workers surrounding the writer runs the risk of overexposing the commercial – a move that the literary writer who sees herself as invested in cultural capital might well avoid making.

Moving towards the larger picture, away from the cultural agents – editors, publishers, journalists, academics – depicted in Atwood's oeuvre, a survey of Atwood's writings, from the earliest to the most recent, shows how obsessed they are with the relation between economics and art. It is one of the major philosophical problems to which she returns, time and again, in her writings. The text that offers the most extensive statement on art and commerce in Atwood's oeuvre is the short story "Loulou; or the Domestic Life of the Language" from *Bluebeard's Egg*. Loulou is a potter who lives with a gaggle of young male poets, who poke fun at her and who generally take advantage of her willingness to cook and clean for them. She decides, finally, that she should go to an accountant to get her business in order, so she takes two plastic shopping bags full of receipts to him (71). He tells her that the poets are taking advantage of her by living in her house rent-free (77); he sees her as an "artist" (75), ethereal and spiritual, whereas Loulou sees herself as substantial, material – of this world. The poets, on the other hand, see Loulou as resolutely physical, commenting poetically on her body and hair. Not content to see her as material for their art, they also snidely downgrade her work as "craft" rather than "art" (68). In the end, Loulou returns to her house, unconvinced by the accountant's economic perspective on her life (which itself tends to romanticize and dematerialize her as a will-o'-the-wisp romantic artist). "Maybe it's not so bad" (81), Loulou (and the story) conclude. The story offers a dynamic portrait of an artist actively negotiating between economic and cultural capital. For Loulou, it is unacceptable that the poets live off the very artistic labour that they snobbily decry as "craft," but it is even worse to hear her life summed up in economic terms tout court. When the accountant makes his speech to Loulou about "allowing herself to be imposed upon" (77), Loulou senses that her life's complexity exceeds this economic diagnosis: "Loulou may have felt this way from time to time, but hearing the accountant say it right out in the open air disturbs her. Where would the poets go?" (77). Appropriately, Loulou chooses this moment to seduce the accountant, but the encounter is an unsatisfying one. No wonder: Loulou is unseduced by a baldly economic approach to art, and she returns to her chaotic, "mangy" (79) but preferable, Palace of Art.

So many Atwoodian characters struggle to find the uneasy balance that Loulou cobbles together. In "Isis in Darkness," the poet Selena suddenly re-enters her fellow poet Richard's life many years later. The signs of her struggles to live and write (he notes the "threadbare" sleeves of her coat) excite not pity in Richard but, rather, envy (*Wilderness Tips* 76). He has become an academic and is unhappily scrambling to gain tenure at the university, but Selena's reappearance convinces him that "he should have been living in an attic, eating bread and maggoty cheese, washing his one shirt out at night, his head incandescent with words" (76). Here we see the same naive assumption, examined by Bourdieu among others, that noble poverty authorizes artistic credibility. But the ending of the story, like that of "Loulou; or the Domestic Life of the Language," refuses such stark choices between economic and artistic success. Richard, who never leaves the academy but who exists on its margins, "clinging on by his fingernails" (79), finds a way to incorporate Selena's art within his life. After her death, he begins to write about her poetry, not "to cover his professional ass; he's going to be axed from the university anyway" (82). He does not, then, count among those opportunistic academics who jump on the bandwagon of the dead literary figure, the "botflies" that are "swarming" around the corpse/corpus of the dead writer.

"The Grave of the Famous Poet," from *Dancing Girls and Other Stories*, shows how early Atwood was considering these connections among creativity, fame, commerce, and death. It is the story of a disintegrating relationship set amid a trip to see the grave and house of a famous poet who bears many resemblances to Dylan Thomas. The narrator notes how the surrounding town's economy depends, to a considerable degree, on this connection with the dead writer: the couple's bed-and-breakfast hostess expects them to ask about the location of the grave (80), and the local stores sell his works and promote his connection with the town: "In the window, half-hidden among souvenir cups, maps and faded pennants, is a framed photograph of his face, three-quarters profile" (82). The story offers a view of art consumed – killed – by commerce; it is a view of how Loulou's world would change were she to accept the accountant's disapproving view of her relationship with the poets in "Loulou; or the Domestic Life of the Language." "The Grave of the Famous Poet" is not simply the story of the disintegration of a love affair; it is also the story of the disintegration of the relationship between art and commerce.

Commercial artists are a persistent presence in Atwood's fiction, and they, too, test the relationship between business and creativity. There is, of course, the narrator of *Surfacing*: "I'm what they call a commercial artist, or, when the job is more pretentious, an illustrator" (52). This early in her career, Atwood is keenly attuned to the gradations of cultural capital; the very term "commercial artist" brusquely brings art into the realm of the economic, in a way that may sometimes, as in this case, demand an up-market rebranding of the job. Elaine Risley, too, in *Cat's Eye*, puts her artistic skills to commercial uses after university, when she takes a job with a publishing company designing book covers, but she continues to paint at night: another uneasy act of balancing the "commercial" and "art" (443). Years later, though, she teases her ex-husband Jon for the jobs he has taken with Hollywood, doing special effects "to support his artist habit" (21). When they meet after many years, they trade barbs about "selling out" (355), but ultimately they both accept their compromises, while recognizing that they are not easily made.

In *Lady Oracle*, there seems less uneasiness, at first, about art in the service of commerce, as in the writing of gothic romances, but even here, uneasiness eventually creeps in. In some respects, the novel asks readers to take costume gothics seriously, and Joan does undertake defences of her art at various points in the novel. Yet there are several signals that she views this work as déclassé; she receives payment for her first novel along with "a request for more material. Material, they called it, as if it came by the yard" (157). And the published book arrives "in a brown-paper parcel" (157) as though it were a piece of porn.

Even in works that do not deal with art and commerce as explicitly as *Lady Oracle*, the tension between necessary earnings and artistic work informs how characters see themselves. In *Life Before Man*, there is a conflict within Nate between the lawyer he is trained to be and the artist he aspires to be. He has quit law school, which his wife Elizabeth and his mother did not approve of him doing, and now, instead, he makes wooden toys: "'Toys?' his mother said. 'Is that useful?'" (33). In an effort to bridge this perceived gap between vocation and avocation, Nate "no longer tells people he makes handmade wooden toys in his basement. He says he's in the toy business" (34). Eventually, though, as his marriage with Elizabeth breaks up and his new relationship with Lesje brings other responsibilities, he is forced to go back to law and is no longer able to make toys because of lack of time (261). The complexities of Nate's character – he is a man of sensitivity who nevertheless wishes to please everyone – are neatly captured in this capitulation to the economic and cultural desires of others.

In *Cat's Eye*, Elaine Risley manages a truce between economy and art, in part by doing what Atwood said a whole generation of mid-twentieth-century Canadian writers did: by becoming an artist-businessperson. At the same time, she does not hesitate to poke fun at her art-business persona. There are several occasions on which Elaine mediates on dress as a means of playing this role; thinking of the need for a dress to wear to the opening of her retrospective, she likens herself to fellow artists, such as musicians: "This dress is black, because black is the best thing for such occasions: a simple, sober black dress, like those of the women who play cellos in symphony orchestras. It doesn't do to outdress the clients" (56). The artist, then, is located, sartorially speaking, halfway between the straitened circumstances of many cultural workers and the opulence of wealthy patrons of the arts. The black dress of the public woman artist proclaims both good taste and subservience to her patrons: yet another midway stance between art and economics in the fiction of Margaret Atwood.

As this wide-ranging account of art and money in Atwood shows, this subject has fascinated her from her earliest to her most recent writings. It is strange, then, that many commentators were surprised at Atwood's publication of *Payback: Debt and the Shadow Side of Wealth* in 2008. From the perspective of her fictional meditations on art and business, it is entirely predictable that Atwood should write a non-fiction commentary on money, finance, and the queasy state of debt, and it is entirely logical that she should rely primarily on literary texts to construct her discussion. Indeed, the non-fiction book that she wrote just six years earlier, *Negotiating with the Dead*, is substantially about art and money: "Money is often definitive, not just in what a writer eats but in what he or she writes" (65). *Payback* is a logical outgrowth of the previous volume and attests to the validity of that claim.

In recent years, Margaret Atwood has become more explicitly interested in questions of money, capital, debt, and art; as I have shown, she has also involved herself more in business and technological concerns by exploring – and even inventing – new media. The role that new and social media play in her literary celebrity occupied the preceding chapter; here, it will be equally illuminating to ponder the role they play in her literary works.

A common challenge in Atwood's writings, particularly those written from the 1980s on, is any major shift in media and information technology. These shifts challenge the systems of cultural value that Atwood keenly observes in her fiction and non-fiction. For example, Offred in *The Handmaid's Tale* is a former librarian who specialized in transferring books to computer discs – a job motivated by concerns for economic profits: "to cut down on storage space and replacement costs" (182). As with other Atwood characters, though, Offred shows a marked reluctance to abandon earlier media: "After the books were transferred they were supposed to go to the shredder, but sometimes I took them home with me. I liked the feel of them, and the look. Luke said I had the mind of an antiquarian" (182). We find a corresponding antiquarian attachment in Jimmy from *Oryx and Crake*. Like Offred, he becomes attached to a library – in his case the one at his school, the arts-focused Martha Graham Academy. By the time of Jimmy's narrative, though, we are fully in the digital age, and the library is a throwback, there only because Martha Graham, unlike the science and technology schools, is so underfunded that it cannot afford to do what those other institutions have done: "burned their actual books and kept everything on CD-ROM" (195). Jimmy becomes entranced by the library: "the more obsolete a book was, the more eagerly Jimmy would add it to his inner collection" (195). After graduation, he gets a job at the Martha Graham library, doing almost exactly what Offred did in her earlier librarian life: "going through old books and earmarking them for destruction while deciding which should remain on earth in digital form" (241), though the activity has gained a malignant cast. Offred, at least, was transferring all of the writings onto the (then) new CD-ROM format. Jimmy, instead, is exercising a Sophie's Choice in the book world, and it is one that he finds insupportable. He eventually loses this job "because he couldn't bear to throw anything out" (241). This association of medium change with cultural loss fills these two novels, written eighteen years apart. When "The Handmaid's Tale" is discovered, for example, it exists only on "thirty tape cassettes, of the type that became obsolete sometime in the eighties or nineties with the advent of the compact disc" (313). Professors Pieixoto and Wade call upon experts with similarly obsolete knowledges in order to gain access to the tapes and their contents: "our excellent resident antiquarian technician" (313). They then proceed to transcribe the tapes: a curious reversal of the medium shift that Offred was asked to carry out as a librarian, when she transferred print to digital form. Atwood, at this point in her career, focuses mainly on the many slips and losses that could potentially occur between the lip of older media and the cup of new digital forms. Her handling of new media is dominated by the fear of cultural loss, a concern that she continues to raise in public talks about new media, such as the 2011 Tools of Change publishing conference, where she warned of the possibility, however remote, of massive losses of digital material in the wake of global disasters such as high-altitude electromagnetic pulse attacks.

In the time between the publication of her first and second MaddAddam trilogy volumes – *Oryx and Crake* (2003) and *The Year of the Flood* (2009) – there was a shift in Atwood's fictional treatment of digital media from suspicion and apocalyptic critique to even-handed awareness of their dangers and possibilities. It was only a period of six years, admittedly, but what a paradigm-shifting period it was, with the foundation of Twitter in 2006. Atwood herself, in the run-up to her publication of the second volume in the trilogy, established a more fully interactive website and, in 2009, began to tweet.

In *Oryx and Crake*, however, digital media appear consistently in a context of threat and cultural degeneration. The novel is set in a future where the computer mouse and "tail" are what Jimmy calls "things from before" (7) and where today's computers are remembered with a measure of nostalgia. Jimmy fondly remembers, for example, playing on the computer with his mother (30). But even this fuzzily warm memory is disturbed by the connections between the computer and destruction; when Jimmy' s mother leaves home, she trashes his father's computer and her own with a hammer (61–2). This becomes an early portent of her resistance work and her eventual murder by the regime.

As Jimmy grows up, he associates computers with more of this destruction; with Crake, he plays Blood and Roses, a computer game in which "Blood" represents human historical atrocities and the "Roses" are human achievements such as art, inventions, and scientific discoveries that aid humankind. "The Blood player usually won," the narrator mordantly remarks, though "winning meant you inherited a wasteland" (80). All of the sites and games that Jimmy and Crake divert themselves with lean more towards Blood than Roses. They visit sites that allow them to see violent footage of executions or assisted suicides (82–3). As if this were not enough of a deluge of the dark side of the digital, we hear that there are worse sites still, password-protected, that specialize in child porn; it is on one of these sites that Jimmy first catches sight of Oryx (90). All in all, Atwood appears to home in on the negative, exploitative, and cruel aspects of digital culture.

Indeed, Atwood connects the chronic underfunding of the arts with the growth of these new media. At Martha Graham, individual access to PC-based film editing and splicing tools renders professional filmmaking out of date, so the school changes its specializations to "Webgame Dynamics" and Image Presentation (a division of Pictorial and Plastic Arts or PicPlarts). With such a degree, students "could go into advertising, no sweat" (188): art at the service of commerce. Atwood takes full aim at the growing corporatization of the university, linking this turn away from arts and sciences to digital media.

Violence and the neglect of the arts and pure sciences: these are heavy charges to lay at the door of new media. Atwood adds to these sombre critiques a host of other, less catastrophic but equally unpleasant consequences. For example, Jimmy uses e-mail as a medium for complaint and self-aggrandizement when he corresponds with Crake (192); a common complaint lodged against online communication tools is that they allow for a misleading presentation of self. The note of inauthenticity is sounded again when Atwood describes Jimmy and Crake playing Internet chess; this ancient game of intellect is undercut by their ability to look up classic chess moves on the Internet (193). "Comfort eyefood" (209), the narrator calls such online diversions, and for Atwood, the link to intellectual junk food is all too plain.

This classic conservative critique of the digital is stepped up as the novel's plot deepens. Another bit of "comfort eyefood" that Jimmy and Crake indulge in, the online game Extinctathon (214), about extinct species, is not only environmentally insensitive but politically dangerous as well. Crake soon figures out that MaddAddam, the group that runs the game, is "after the machinery. They're after the whole system, they want to shut it down" (217). Spreading his suspicion of online media even further, he asks Jimmy not to discuss this possibility on e-mail: the CorpSeCorps, he suspects, could be running Extinctathon as a front to catch subversives (217).

In all of *Oryx and Crake*, there is only one instance of the Internet providing a platform for possible resistance to the regime, and it is mentioned only briefly and quickly overrun. As the JUVE virus rapidly spreads, Jimmy watches, horrified, as the illuminated points on a private website that show locations "still communicating via satellite" go dark. In the grander battle between Blood and Roses that Atwood depicts in *Oryx and Crake*, the online world seems to deal mainly in blood.

In a small volume published in between *Oryx and Crake* and *The Year of the Flood*, there is some evidence that Atwood is softening her line on the online. In the collection of satirical fictions *The Tent* (2006), Atwood retells the story of Chicken Little, "Chicken Little Goes Too Far." In this version, Chicken Little has metamorphosed into a prophet of environmental disaster, and he fares as well in spreading the word as his nursery rhyme original. But one thing he does do that raises the ire of rich financiers is launch "a Web site" for his group, TSIF (The Sky Is Falling). His ragtag followers ("mostly wood-chucks and muskrats, but who cares?" 70) "picketed political gatherings … blocked highways … disrupted summit conferences" (70). Eventually, Chicken Little is rubbed out ("'I eat guys like that for breakfast,' said Foxy Loxy" 71), but the formation of the website and its resulting acts of political resistance cause the powers that be to take action against him. In this witty parable, new-media-enabled grassroots organizing makes its first significant appearance in Atwood's works.

Three years later, the digital media that figure in the second instalment of Atwood's MaddAddam trilogy, *The Year of the Flood*, are distinctly more variable in their potential. No longer *only* part and parcel of the repressive regime (though they are, assuredly, that too), they are capable of being turned to progressive uses. First of all, rather than seeing print culture and computers as antagonists, as is the tendency in *Oryx and Crake* and *The Handmaid's Tale*, *The Year of the Flood* sees writing, in whatever format, as dangerous to the regime – and therefore as potentially subversive. When Ren is taken to the HelthWyzer compound to live, she sees computers and notebooks in her new school and considers them equally dangerous: "all that permanent writing that your enemies could find – you couldn't just wipe it away, not like a slate ... I wanted to run into the washroom and wash my hands, after touching the keyboards and pages" (216). There seems a greater awareness of the ways in which digital writing, too, can form a record – one that can be resuscitated in unexpected ways. This differs from some of Atwood's non-fictional or public comments about the instability and tenuousness of the digital record; it may be the product of greater knowledge about the ways in which computer records may prove surprisingly resilient, to the point of infringing on personal privacy.

The brief hint of online resistance movements in *Oryx and Crake* blossoms into an entire underground movement in *The Year of the Flood*. When Ren becomes friends with Jimmy at HelthWyzer, she remembers his mother using the computer a great deal, presumably for resistant causes, since we learn later in the novel that she "made off with a lot of crucial data" (223). And so, we also learn, her apparently vengeful act of destroying her husband's computer was politically motivated; it was a way to "disguise the extent of her data thefts" (248). When Toby gains her new identity, she cautiously begins to use a computer again, but she is aware of the ways in which to negotiate the dangers of online presence. She visits only general news sites in hopes of picking up some news of God's Gardeners, but eventually she ventures onto chat rooms associated with the MaddAddam Extinctathon game that Jimmy and Crake play in *Oryx and Crake*, where she finds bits and pieces of classified CorpSeCorps documents, among other items. But Toby's nervousness about the chat rooms is clearly warranted; later, Croze describes how Shackie's and Oates's online presence led to their pursuit by the CorpSeCorps: "I figure some creep in our chatroom was a plant" (334). Accordingly, Toby herself is eventually threatened online when the violent Painballer scowls into her Web camera and threatens to kill Mordis unless she reveals her virtual handle: "Open up and we'll let your buddy live" (281).

Indeed, the computer, in *The Year of the Flood*, has become a lively network of resistance as well as oppression. Zeb tells Tony about their hacker inside Watson-Crick, now living at HelthWyzer, clearly Crake: "His mother was Diagnostics at HelthWyzer, he'd hacked her lab sign-in code, he could run stuff through the system for us. Genius hacker" (244). In Atwood's novel, the online world resembles a large game of Spy vs. Spy, but it is clearly the site of a more complicated battle of wills than in *Oryx and Crake*. Toby is at first shocked to learn that even God's Gardeners' Adams and Eves possess a laptop. Adam One rationalizes the presence of this evil piece of technology from the ExFernal world: "It's like the Vatican's porn collection … Safe in our hands" (189). Though the Gardeners devise various pious rules for the use of the contraband computer – they only use the machine to store "crucial data" from that Fallen World, they use it with "extreme caution," and they take particular care to keep the computer out of the hands of impressionable youngsters – the fact remains that it is useful to their operations. As Toby realizes, those operations, such as their opposition to commercialism and their environmental politics, may, like Chicken Little's in Atwood's fable, attract enemies.

The new media have also become more complicated in the second MaddAddam novel in that Atwood is exploiting the broader range of digital technology, not only computers and the Internet. Cell phones, with their multiple capabilities, play a key role in *The Year of the Flood*. Sometimes criticized as the expensive playthings of mall-frequenting pleebrats, the cellphone also becomes, like the computer, potentially a lifeline as well as damning evidence. Ren finds and keeps one of the pleebrats' cellphones but is warned that it is an instrument of surveillance: "If you can see it, it can see you," the Eves warn her.

But the cellphone can also be an instrument of salvation. When she is taken back to the HelthWyzer compound by her mother, Ren hides the purple cellphone Amanda has given her in a plush tiger in her closet; this is the means, for her, of keeping some kind of link to her close friend; it parallels the diary that she also keeps secreted in her closet, inside a stuffed bear this time. Writing and digital language become paralleled rather than set at odds, as they are in conservative cultural narratives about the superiority of print (witness recent nervous discussions about the advent of Kindle and the status of the book). When Ren finds computers at her new school, her sense of danger leads her to consider notebooks and computers both as species of germs, like the rampaging viruses that bring about the Waterless Flood: "I wanted to run into the washroom and wash my hands, after touching the keyboards and pages" (216). Amanda's cellphone is another potential rogue virus; after all, were it to fall into the wrong hands, it could bring about Amanda's death; it is only Ren's mother's quick-thinking response – to text the most frequently called number on the phone with the message "Dump it!" (225) – that saves Amanda from such a fate. The phone itself becomes the means of saving Amanda from the destructive potential of the phone.

On a broader social scale, the integrated media that Atwood has begun to write about in *The Year of the Flood* had, by 2009, become the focus of debates about digital technologies and social change. Although the novel predates the uprisings in the Middle East in 2010 and 2011 – uprisings that would be attributed by some (hyperbolically) as caused by social media – Atwood does refer indirectly to the revolt against the sham Iranian elections of 2010. As Toby thinks back regarding the Happicuppa Riots, the CorpSeCorps could have spraygunned everyone: "Not that you could shut down coverage of such events completely: people used their cameraphones" (266). So, like the use of Twitter by Iranian voters, and like the torture photographs from Abu Ghraib – which were taken as trophy shots by participating soldiers and made their way onto Internet sites and

Facebook pages – digital technologies may serve the cause of resistance as well as oppression: a variegated political situation that Atwood has just begun to investigate. So we should take care not to sweep all digital technologies into Atwood's capacious social satire.

Returning to the cloak of visibility – fame – that covers the successful writer, Atwood's own writing discloses some crucial insights about the roles of economy, labour, cultural agents, and social media in literary celebrity. She uses particular cultural agents such as publishers and editors to dramatize the labyrinthine workings of money and cultural esteem in the career of a writer. As time goes on, her fictions show us artist figures who are not uniformly critical of economic considerations and who, instead, labour to articulate the artistic within the economic, and the economic within the artistic. Atwood takes her witty, mordant conceit about the writer being a primary source in the food chain, like a dead deer, and she makes of it, in fiction after fiction, a parable about the operations of systems of literary value and economy. And while acknowledging the exploitative effects that economic determinisms can have on art and on artists and not flinching from the realities of the artist as an economic entity, she moves away from the position that digital media work against creativity, towards an understanding of how those same media may serve various, even clashing, ideological masters.

The cloak of visibility, as a metaphor, itself says volumes about the literary celebrity of Margaret Atwood. It is an inverse metaphor, a reworking of that familiar image from Harry Potter: the cloak of invisibility that allows Harry to do his job of fighting the evil of He-Who-Must-Not-Be-Named. But it is inverse in another way: Cloaks, by definition, permit invisibility, but it is the nature of fame to deny, or at the very least make difficult, the achievement of invisibility or privacy that lies, somewhere, under the public fabric. In *Lady Oracle*, Joan – a lover of cloaks – confesses about her new-found fame that "I felt very visible"; whereas Iris Chase, from *The Blind Assassin*, shrugging off the cloak of fame and placing it on the shoulders of her sister Laura, admits "I've never been fond of spotlights" (512). Here, in the interstices of the cloak of visibility – the mixed condition of being both public and private, both economic labourer and mystic creator, Atwood's celebrity, in all its complexity, is to be found.

Postscript: Margaret Atwood for Mayor? Literary Celebrity in the Civic Realm

On a chilly day in the autumn of 2010, as I was part-way through the writing of this book, my then-university-student daughter Anna took me on a brief walking tour of a Toronto neighbourhood. She had a specific destination in mind. Knowing that I was working on this project, she wanted to show me some graffiti she had discovered one day while walking around the Spadina–Chinatown area: "Atwood 4 Mayor." After a few turns down side streets, we found it.

Like Atwood an energetic user of social media, Anna took a photograph with her BlackBerry and tweeted it, along with a question directed to Atwood's twitter-self: @MargaretAtwood: "If elected, will you serve?" (Ross, @_Anna_Ross_). To her delight, Atwood replied a little over an hour later, "Nooo, I'm too old … anyway I'd have to wear a suit or something" (Atwood, @MargaretAtwood). This tweet was then promptly retweeted around the twitterverse, landing on several blogs and websites. For my purposes, as I draw to the end of this study of the intricate mechanics of the literary celebrity of Margaret Atwood, this story and its associated electronic texts encourage me to think more broadly about the material effects of literary celebrity in the civic realm.

This study opened with another narrative about Atwood and public space: the controversy in the summer of 2011 about the reduction of the Toronto city library budget that drew Atwood into a conflict with Mayor Rob Ford and, more immediately, with his brother, Toronto city councillor Doug Ford. In introducing this study, I used this anecdote and, in particular, the furious response of Torontonians and other Canadians to Doug Ford's snubbing of Canada's foremost literary celebrity ("I don't even know her ...") as a measure of how Atwood's celebrity is itself a matter of public comment and concern. But in my desire to refocus the question of Atwood's literary renown away from a semiotic reading of her individual star text and towards an analysis of the industrial labour relations that manage that celebrity, I did not have the time to consider another question: Does it ever work? That is, do Atwood's interventions in the public sphere as a celebrated author have material consequences in that sphere?

The more general forms of this question have a very long literary genealogy in the English-speaking world, reaching at least back to Sir Philip Sidney's argument, in *A Defense of Poesie* (1595) that poetry is ideally situated to move readers to virtue because of its combination of history's entertainments and philosophy's ethical seriousness. More than two centuries later, his position informed Percy Bysshe Shelley's notion of the poet as an unacknowledged legislator of the world in his *Defense of Poetry* (1840). Such a grandiose claim inspired opposing viewpoints, most memorably encapsulated in W.H. Auden's lines from "In Memory of W.B. Yeats": "For poetry makes nothing happen: it survives / In the valley of its making" (36–7). But Auden's own career was a study in the belief, if sometimes wavering, in the exactly opposite standpoint.

As literary celebrity has developed from its earlier manifestations into its current industrial state, the question has been reframed. It is no longer simply about whether an artist's works have social efficacy; it is also about how much leverage the artist as public persona has in the day-to-day workings of the state. Some writers have, of course, held or sought public office; one thinks of Mario Vargas Llosa and, more notably, Vaclav Havel. But the question, as framed here, has more to do with the artist acting in a specifically artistic capacity: To what extent can this figure lay claim to social efficacy?

In the case of Margaret Atwood, her interventions into the daily workings of the state have stretched over several decades. "I make a distinction between myself as a citizen and as a writer," she told Roy MacGregor, who was interviewing her for a profile in *Maclean's* in 1979. But however necessary that distinction may have been for her own writing processes and professional peace of mind, Atwood has been a visible figure on the Canadian political scene, writing articles on violent pornography in 1983 ("Atwood on Pornography"), making a speech to the Parliamentary Committee on Free Trade in 1987, and, in the same year, writing to Ontario Premier David Peterson to deplore the building of logging roads in the environmentally sensitive Temagami region. In 1997, she donated a signed and limited edition of her poetry volume *Snake Island* to help raise funds to fight the proposed amalgamation of Toronto-area municipalities. On her sixtieth birthday, in 1999, Atwood walked the picket line to support striking *Calgary Herald* workers. Such a list does not even begin to account for her long-standing activism on behalf of PEN and Amnesty International, which crosses many a national border.

Such a list, impressive as it is, also does not settle the question of whether highly visible literary celebrities actually have some impact on politics and social policy. For that matter, it is often difficult to trace the causal links between decisions made in the political realm and social activism in general on the part of think tanks, NGOs, and various high-profile spokespeople. But in the case of Atwood's recent activism on behalf of libraries in Toronto, there appears to be an unusually clear causal paper trail. After the summer of 2011, when the Atwood–Ford brothers fracas hit national and international media outlets, the story went underground for a few months, as supporters of the libraries prepared their challenges to the proposed cuts. On 12 December the Toronto Public Library Board voted not to implement the severe cuts proposed by Ford; however, this was not the final stage of the protest. The matter still had to go to City Council, where the TPLB's vote was basically a budget submission that the council could either support or overturn (Kupferman). In January 2012, the matter came before the council along with a full slate of proposed cuts to social services such as shelters, school pools, and day cares, and the proposed Ford cuts were largely reversed. The library still was subject to cuts, but far fewer than had been proposed, and the reductions affected staff and collections but not operating hours or the viability of individual branches. While this was a muted victory for the library system, it signalled, more broadly, that Ford's power over city council was on the decline. And what is significant, from the perspective of this study, is the way in which Atwood's name remained attached to the library cuts controversy, almost half a year after the media frenzy of the summer of 2011.

Although this is a limited case, it suggests several implications for the question of literary celebrity's influence in the civic realm. Atwood has lent her name to many a cause in the several decades of her high-profile career, but this one has provided the most convincing instance of her influence on actual public policy making because, I would suggest, the issue at hand is so directly related to her perceived area of expertise: reading, books, literacy. The other factor, I suggest, is that a public official – Doug Ford – tried to deny her very visibility as well as her right to comment publicly on an issue, and this served, ironically, to cement her legitimacy.

The other, related development in the controversy (or, more accurately, in the mishandling of it by the Fords) that ensured Atwood's legitimacy was the way in which her intervention dovetailed with that of other concerned citizens. When Doug Ford denied not only Atwood's celebrity recognizability but her right to be heard ("Tell her to go run in the next election and get democratically elected and we'd be more than happy to sit down and listen to Margaret Atwood"), Atwood became the proxy of the citizenry. Many of the comments, including Atwood's own, during the controversy highlighted the right of *any* citizen to be heard, and not only those who had been chosen as elected representatives. At this point, a key intervention in celebrity–fan relations took place. No longer was Atwood seen solely as a privileged individual, as celebrities tend by definition to be; suddenly she had become both a hometown celebrity *and* a citizen: one of many rather than one out of many, as it were. In terms of celebrity phenomena, the privilege associated with celebrity status was compensated for by a discourse of shared citizenship. Back in 1979, Atwood might have had solid reasons for declaring that she makes "a distinction between myself as a citizen and as a writer," but when those roles overlapped in the summer and autumn of 2011, the citizen-writer suddenly found that she had an enthusiastic following. Atwood for mayor? Probably not. But the very fact that citizens of Toronto were moved to express the thought as a slogan opens up the possibility for celebrity agency in the civic realm.

This study maintains the need to consider celebrity agency not necessarily as that quality which rises above or resists the industrialized forms of celebrity culture but, rather, as those qualities which become evident in the exchanges among agents of that industrialized culture. Often, in discussing popular forms of celebrity culture in the entertainment industries, we see resistance to the industry cited as proof of a celebrity's legitimacy; for example, struggles of early Hollywood stars with the studio system (often against typecasting) tend to get this kind of narrative treatment. In the literary realm, similar assumptions could potentially attach themselves to a highly industrialized writer like Atwood, founder of O.W. Toad; she could all too easily be misunderstood as a compliant servant of the literary celebrity machine. As I hope this study has confirmed, nothing could be further from the truth. In her interactions with agents, publicists, assistants, researchers, Web designers, editors, and publishers, Margaret Atwood and her agency as a citizen-artist are not lost but found.

Works Cited

Abel, Richard. "The Publisher, the Editor, and the Role of Critical Rationalism." *Logos.* Wilson Web, 1999. Web. 30 Oct. 2009.

Adams, James. "Publish and Your Book Will Probably Perish." *Globe and Mail.* 7 Feb. 2009. Web. 15 Feb. 2011.

Adams, James. "Release of Atwood Novel Postponed Because of U.S. Vote." *Globe and Mail.* 26 Jan. 2008: R4. Print.

Addley, Esther. "Atwood's Superheroes Let Loose on Twitter." *Guardian.* 28 Oct. 2010. Web. 2 Feb. 2011.

"Another Chapter of the e-Book." *Irish Times.* 19 May 2007: W16. Print.

Atwood, Margaret. "5 Countries, 35 Cities = 1 Crazy Book Tour." *The Times.* 22 Aug. 2009: 22.Web. 15 Feb. 2011.

Atwood, Margaret. (@MargaretAtwood). "Nooo, I'm too old. Anyway I'd have to wear a suit or something." 6 Sept. 2010, 11:20 p.m. Tweet.

Atwood, Margaret. *The Animals in That Country.* Toronto: OUP, 1969. Print.

Atwood, Margaret. "Atwood on Pornography." *Chatelaine*. Sept. 1983: 61, 118–19. Print.

Atwood, Margaret. "The Ballad of the LongPen ™." *Guardian.* 30 Sept. 2006. Web. 14 Feb. 2011.

Atwood, Margaret. *The Blind Assassin.* Toronto: McClelland and Stewart, 2000. Print.

Atwood, Margaret. *Bluebeard's Egg*. Toronto: McClelland and Stewart, 1983. Print.

Atwood, Margaret. *Bodily Harm*. 1981. Toronto: Seal, 1982. Print.

Atwood, Margaret. *Cat's Eye*. 1988. Toronto: Seal, 1999. Print.

Atwood, Margaret. *Dancing Girls and Other Stories*. 1977. Toronto: McClelland and Stewart, 1980. Print.

Atwood, Margaret. "Dealing a Blank Card." *Globe and Mail*. 1 Nov. 2000: A15. Print.

Atwood, Margaret. *The Edible Woman*. 1969. Toronto: McClelland and Stewart, 1989. Print.

Atwood, Margaret. "Fiction's High Priestess Makes Some Sacrifices to the Green Gods." *Sunday Times*. 6 Sept. 2009. Web. 10 Feb. 2011.

Atwood, Margaret. "A Fond Farewell to a CanLit Giant." *Toronto Star*. 3 Feb. 2008: ID 12. Print.

Atwood, Margaret. *Good Bones*. Toronto: McClelland and Stewart, 1992. Print.

Atwood, Margaret. *The Handmaid's Tale*. Toronto: McClelland and Stewart, 1985. Print.

Atwood, Margaret. "I Love It When Old Ladies Blog." *Toronto Star*. 17 Apr. 2010. Web. 20 Feb. 2011.

Atwood, Margaret. Interview with Charlie Rose. 29 Jan. 2007. *The Charlie Rose Show*. 29 Jan. 2007. Television.

Atwood, Margaret. *Lady Oracle*. 1976. Toronto: Seal, 1977. Print.

Atwood, Margaret. *Life Before Man*. 1979. Toronto: Seal, 1980. Print.

Atwood, Margaret. marg09.wordpress. Web.

Atwood, Margaret. *Moral Disorder*. Toronto: McClelland and Stewart, 2006. Print.

Atwood, Margaret. *Moving Targets: Writing with Intent 1982–2004*. Toronto: Anansi, 2004. Print.

Atwood, Margaret. *Murder in the Dark*. Toronto: Coach House P, 1983. Print.

Atwood, Margaret. *Negotiating with the Dead: A Writer on Writing*. Cambridge: Cambridge UP, 2002. Print.

Atwood, Margaret. *Oryx and Crake*. Toronto: McClelland and Stewart, 2003. Print.

Atwood, Margaret. *Payback: Debt and the Shadow Side of Wealth*. Toronto: Anansi, 2008. Print.

Atwood, Margaret. *Second Words: Selected Critical Prose 1960–1982*. Toronto: Anansi, 1982. Print.

Atwood, Margaret. *Surfacing*. 1972. Toronto: PaperJacks, 1973. Print.

Atwood, Margaret. *Survival: A Thematic Guide to Canadian Literature*. Toronto: Anansi, 1972. Print.

Atwood, Margaret. "Survival, Then and Now." *Maclean's*. 1 July 1999: 54–58. Print.

Atwood, Margaret. *The Tent*. 2006. London: Bloomsbury, 2007. Print.

Atwood, Margaret. *Wilderness Tips*. Toronto: McClelland and Stewart, 1991. Print.

Atwood, Margaret. *The Year of the Flood: A Novel*. Toronto: McClelland and Stewart, 2009. Print.

Atwood, Margaret, and Victor-Lévy Beaulieu. *Two Solicitudes: Conversations*. 1996. Transl. Phyllis Aronoff and Howard Scott. Toronto: McClelland and Stewart, 1998. Print.

"Atwood's Petition Tweet Starts Sun TV Debate." *Toronto Star*. 2 Sept. 2010. Web. 13 Feb. 2011.

Auden, W.H. *Collected Shorter Poems 1927–1957*. 1966. London: Faber and Faber, 1977. Print.

Barber, John. "Atwood: 'Have I Ever Eaten Maggots? Perhaps ...'" *Globe and Mail*. 11 Sept. 2009: R1. Print.

Barber, John. "She Blogs, She Flogs, She Tweets." *Globe and Mail*. 2 Sept. 2009: R1. Print.

Barber, John. "Should Writers Run for Office, Or Is the Pen Still Mightier?" *Globe and Mail*. 5 Aug. 2011. Web. 20 Aug. 2011.

Barnes, James J., and Patience P. Barnes. "'Thomas Aspinwall: First Transatlantic Literary Agent." *Papers of the Bibliographical Society of America* 78 (1984): 321–31. Print.

Barry, Andrew. "On Interactivity." Hassan and Thomas 163–87. Print.

Barry, Elizabeth. "From Epitaph to Obituary: Death and Celebrity in Eighteenth-Century British Culture." *International Journal of Cultural Studies* 11.3 (2008): 259–275. http://dx.doi.org/10.1177/1367877908092584.

Bell, Susan. *The Artful Edit: On the Practice of Editing Yourself*. New York: W.W. Norton, 2007. Print.

Benjamin, Walter. *Illuminations*. 1968. Ed. Hannah Arendt. Transl. Harry Zohn. New York: Schocken Books, 2007.

Bolter, Jay David. *Writing Space: The Computer, Hypertext, and the History of Writing*. Hillsdale, NJ: Lawrence Erlbaum, 1991. Print.

Boog, Jason. "Could Your eBooks and Digital Writings Survive an Electromagnetic Pulse Attack?" *Galleycat.* 16 Feb. 2011. Web. 16 Feb. 2011.

Boorstin, Daniel. *The Image: A Guide to Pseudo-Events in America*. New York: Athaneum, 1971. Print.

Bourdieu, Pierre. *The Field of Cultural Production: Essays on Art and Literature.* Ed. and introd. Randal Johnson. New York: Columbia UP, 1993. Print.

Boztas, Senay. "It was the End of the World, and So the Bishop Wore Leopard-Skin." *The Times.* 31 Aug. 2009. Web. 3 Feb. 2011.

Brown, Curtis. *Contacts*. London: Cassell, 1935. Print.

"Celebrities Set to Reach for Atwood's LongPen." CBC.ca. 15 Aug. 2007. Web. 14 Feb. 2011.

Christensen, Bill. "LongPen by Unotchit: Margaret Atwood's Telautograph for Book Signing." Technovelgy.com 19 Feb. 2006. Web. 14 Feb. 2011.

Cloonan, William, and Jean-Philippe Postel. "Literary Agents and the Novel in 1996." *French Review (Deddington)* 70 (1997): 796–806. Print.

Colbert, Ann Mauger. "Editors." *American History Through Literature 1870–1920.* Ed. Tom Quirk and Gary Scharnhost. Detroit: Scribner's, 2006: 345–50. Print.

Cooke, Nathalie. *Margaret Atwood: A Biography*. Toronto: ECW P, 1998. Print.

Coombe, Rosemary. *The Cultural Life of Intellectual Properties: Authorship, Appropriation, and the Law*. Durham: Duke UP, 1998. Print.

Cullen, Darcy, ed. *Editors, Scholars, and the Social Text*. Toronto: U of Toronto P, 2012. Print.

Daubs, Katie. "World Is Watching the Fords." *Toronto Star.* 29 July 2011. Web. 30 July 2011.

deCordova, Richard. *Picture Personalities: The Emergence of the Star System in America*. Champaign: U of Illinois P, 1990. Print.

Delgado, Alan. *The Enormous File: A Social History of the Office*. London: John Murray, 1979. Print.

Del Nibletto, Paolo. "The Mighty Long Pen." *Computer Dealer News.* 9 Nov. 2007. Web. 14 Feb. 2011.

DeMara, Bruce. "Margaret Atwood Offers More Bang for the Book." *Toronto Star*. 18 Aug. 2009. Web. 20 May 2010.

Deshaye, Joel. "Celebrity and Passing in Gwendolyn MacEwen's *The T.E. Lawrence Poems*." *Journal of Commonwealth Literature* 46.3 (2011): 531–550. http://dx.doi.org/10.1177/0021989411409810.

Deshaye, Joel. "Celebrity and the Poetic Dialogue of Irving Layton and Leonard Cohen." *Studies in Canadian Literature* 34.2 (2009): 77–105. Print.

Deshaye, Joel. *Privacy's Publicity: The Era of Celebrity in Canadian Poetry* [tentative title]. Toronto: U of Toronto, P. Forthcoming. Print.

Dilworth, Dianna. "Margaret Atwood's Got 'Klout' on Twitter." *mediabistro*. 11 Feb. 2011. Web. 14 Feb. 2011.

Donnelly, Judy. "Jack McClelland and McClelland & Stewart." *Historical Perspectives on Canadian Publishing*. McMaster University. Web. 29 July 2011.

Dowse, Sara. "Tongue-in-Cheek Journey to the End of the Earth." *Sydney Morning Herald*. 10 Oct. 2009. Web. 13 Feb. 2011.

Dyer, Richard. "*A Star Is Born* and the Construction of Authenticity." Gledhill 132–40. Print.

Dyer, Richard. *Heavenly Bodies: Film Stars and Society*. 2nd ed. London: BFI Macmillan, 1986. Print.

Dyer, Richard. *Stars*. 1979. London: BFI, 1998. Print.

English, James F., and John Frow. "Literary Authorship and Celebrity Culture." *A Concise Companion to Contemporary British Fiction*. Ed. James F. English. Malden, MA: Blackwell, 2006. 39–57. Print. http://dx.doi.org/10.1002/9780470757673

"The Far-Reaching Pen of Margaret Atwood." CBC.ca. 5 Mar. 2006. Web. 14 Feb. 2011.

Feather, John. *Communicating Knowledge: Publishing in the 21st Century*. Munich: K.G. Saur, 2003. Print.

Ferrari-Adler, Jofie. "Agents & Editors: A Q&A with Agent Lynn Nesbit"." *Poets & Writers*. 1 Jan. 2008. Web. 14 Apr. 2009.

Ferrari-Adler, Jofie. "Agents & Editors: A Q&A with Agent Molly Friedrich." *Poets & Writers*. 1 Sept. 2008. Web. 14 Apr. 2009.

Ferrari-Adler, Jofie. "Agents & Editors: A Q&A with Agent Nat Sobel." *Poets & Writers*. 1 May 2008. Web. 14 Apr. 2009.

Ferrari-Adler, Jofie. "Agents & Editors: A Q&A with Editor Chuck Adams." *Poets & Writers.* 1 Nov. 2008.Web. 14 Apr. 2009.

Ferrari-Adler, Jofie. "Agents & Editors: A Q&A with Editor Janet Silver." *Poets & Writers.* 1 July 2008. Web. 14 Apr. 2009.

Ferrari-Adler, Jofie. "Agents & Editors: A Q&A with Editor Pat Strachan." *Poets & Writers.* 1 Mar. 2008. Web. 14 Apr. 2009.

Ferrari-Adler, Jofie. "Agents and Editors: A Q&A with Four Young Editors." *Poets & Writers.* 1 Mar. 2009. Web. 21 May 2010.

Fetherling, George. "Literary Agents." *Encyclopedia of Literature in Canada.* Ed. William H. New. Toronto: U of Toronto P, 2002. 668. Print.

Fortney, Valerie. "Fundraiser Offers Shot at Literary Immortality." *Calgary Herald.* 18 Oct. 2007: B9. Print.

Franklin, Dan. "The Role of the Editor." *Publishing Now.* Ed. Peter Owen. London: Peter Owen, 1993. 111–118. Print.

French, William. "Icon and Target: Atwood as Thing." *Globe and Mail.* 7 Apr. 1973: 28. Print.

Frewin, Leslie. *The Late Mrs. Dorothy Parker.* London: Macmillan, 1986. Print.

Friskney, Janet B., and Carole Gerson. "Writers and the Market for Fiction and Literature." *History of the Book in Canada 1918–1980.* Ed. Carole Gerson and Jacques Michon. Vol. 3. Toronto: U of Toronto P, 2007. 131–8. Print.

Galloway, Gloria. "Bill Has Rapper, Writer Singing the Same Tune." *Globe and Mail.* 29 Oct. 2010. Web. 13 Feb. 2011.

Gamson, Joshua. *Claims to Fame: Celebrity in Contemporary America.* Berkeley: U of California P, 1994. Print.

Gillies, Mary Ann. "A.P. Watt, Literary Agent." *Publishing Research Quarterly* 9.1 (1993): 20–33. http://dx.doi.org/10.1007/BF02680630.

Gillies, Mary Ann. *The Professional Agent in Britain, 1880–1920.* Toronto: U of Toronto P, 2007. Print.

Gillmor, Don. "Anatomy of a Best-Seller." *Toronto Life* (Sept. 2003): 86–92. Print.

Gledhill, Christine, ed. *Stardom: Industry of Desire.* London: Routledge, 1991. Print. http://dx.doi.org/10.4324/9780203400425

Goldman, Jonathan. *Modernism Is the Literature of Celebrity.* Austin: U of Texas P, 2011. Print.

Groskop, Viv. "How to Stalk Your Favourite Author." *Daily Telegraph*. 24 Apr. 2010. Web. 20 Feb. 2011.

Groskop, Viv. "Literary Luvvies Come All A-Twitter about Tweeting." *Observer*. 19 Dec. 2010. Web. 6 Feb. 2011.

Gross, Gerald C., ed. *Editors on Editing*. 1962. New York: Grove, 1993. Print.

Hampson, Sarah. "Inside the Editor's Brain." *Globe and Mail*. 17 June 2006: R3. Print.

Hanlon, Mike. "The LongPen – Landmark Distance Tool." *Gizmag*. 1 Mar. 2006. Web. 14 Feb. 2011.

Harrison, Matthew. "Atwood Captivates the FAC." *Massachusetts Daily Collegian*. University of Massachusetts–Amherst. 7 Nov. 2008. Web. 15 July 2011.

Hassan, Robert, and Julian Thomas, eds. *The New Media Theory Reader*. Maidenhead: Open UP, 2006. Print.

Helm, Richard. "Step Away From the Signing Device." *Edmonton Journal*. 22 June 2007: G11. Print.

Hepburn, James. *The Author's Empty Purse and the Rise of the Literary Agent*. London: Oxford UP, 1968. Print.

Hewitt, Katie. "The Tweet Smell of Success?" *Globe and Mail*. 24 July 2010: F7. Print.

Hoby, Hermione. "In the News: Margaret Atwood, Tweeter." *Observer*. 4 Apr. 2010. Web. 26 Feb. 2011.

Holmes, Su, and Sean Redmond, eds. *Framing Celebrity: New Directions in Celebrity Culture*. London: Routledge, 2006. Print.

Holmes, Su, and Sean Redmond, eds. *Stardom and Celebrity: A Reader*. Los Angeles: Sage, 2007. Print.

Honeycutt, Courtenay, and Susan C. Herring. "Beyond Microblogging: Conversation and Collaboration via Twitter." Proceedings of the 42nd Hawai'i International Conference on System Sciences 2000. Web. 14 Feb. 2011.

Hor-Chung Lau, Joyce. "From Margaret Atwood, a Dose of Reality." *New York Times*. 9 Apr. 2009. Web. 13 Feb. 2011.

Huberman, Bernardo A., et al. "Social Networks That Matter: Twitter under the Microscope." *arXiv*. 4 Dec. 2008. Web. 14 Feb. 2011.

Hudson, Greg. "Margaret Atwood, Honest to Blog, Is Addicted to Tweeting." *Toronto Life*. 31 Mar. 2010. Web. 21 Feb. 2011.

Huggan, Graham. *The Postcolonial Exotic: Marketing the Margins*. London: Routledge, 2001. Print. http://dx.doi.org/10.4324/9780203420102

Hutcheon, Linda. *The Politics of Postmodernism*. London: Routledge, 1989. Print. http://dx.doi.org/10.4324/9780203426050

Jaffe, Aaron. *Modernism and the Culture of Celebrity*. Cambridge: Cambridge UP, 2005. Print.

Jaffe, Aaron, and Jonathan Goldman, eds. *Modernist Star Maps: Celebrity, Modernity, Culture*. Farnham: Ashgate, 2010. Print.

Jansen, Bernard J., Mimi Zhang, Kate Sobel, et al. "Twitter Power: Tweets as Electronic Word of Mouth." *Journal of the American Society for Information Science and Technology* 60.11 (2009): 2169–2188. http://dx.doi.org/10.1002/asi.21149.

Java, Akshay et al. "Why We Twitter: Understanding Microblogging Usage and Communities." 12 Aug. 2007. Web. 14 Feb. 2011.

Kandel, Michael. "Being an Editor." *Ursula K. Le Guin*. 2006. Web. 20 Mar. 2009.

Kaufman, Joanne. "How Authors Move Their Own Merchandise." *Wall Street Journal*. 18 Jan. 2011. Web. 13 Feb. 2011.

King, Barry. "Articulating Stardom." Gledhill. 167–82. Print.

"Klout Influence Summary: Margaret Atwood." *Klout*. Web. 14 Feb. 2011.

Kozakewich, Tobi. "Having It Both Ways? Romance, Realism, and Irony in Lady Oracle's Adulterous Affairs." *Margaret Atwood: The Open Eye*. Ed. John Moss and Tobi Kozakewich. Reappraisals: Canadian Writers 30. Ottawa: U of Ottawa P, 2006. 185–93. Print.

"KPMG: Cutting Through Complexity." Web. 18 Aug. 2011.

Kupferman, Steve. "Why Last Night's Library Budget Vote Isn't Necessarily Good News." *Torontoist*. 13 Dec. 2011. Web. 8 March 2012.

Kwak, Haewoon, et al. "What Is Twitter, a Social Network or a News Media?" Proceedings of the Nineteenth International Conference on the World Wide Web 2010. 26–30 April 2010. Web. 14 Feb. 2011.

Lane, Patrick. "A New Leaf." *Bookninja Magazine*. 24 Oct. 2005. Web. 20 May 2010.

"Literary Publisher Ellen Seligman Elected President of PEN Canada at 2009 AGM." *PEN Canada*. 22 June 2009. Web. 20 May 2010.

MacDonald, Paul. "Reconceptualising Stardom." Dyer, *Stars* 175–200. Print.

MacLaren, Eli. *Dominion and Agency: Copyright and the Structuring of the Canadian Book Trade 1867–1918*. Toronto: U of Toronto P, 2011. Print.

MacSkimming, Roy. *The Perilous Trade: Book Publishing in Canada 1946–2006*. Toronto: McClelland and Stewart, 2007. Print.

MacSkimming, Roy. "The Perilous Trade Conversations Four: Margaret Atwood and Graeme Gibson." *Canadian Notes and Queries* 72 (2007): 16–26. Print.

Margaret Atwood. Official Website. Web. 22 Feb. 2011.

Margaret Atwood Archives. MS COLL 200. Thomas Fisher Rare Book Library. University of Toronto.

Margaret Atwood Archives. MS COLL 335. Thomas Fisher Rare Book Library. University of Toronto.

"Margaret Atwood Interviewed at TOC 2011." *YouTube*. 14 Feb. 2011. Web. 16 Feb. 2011.

"Margaret Atwood Tweets to Save Toronto Libraries." ctv.ca. 26 July 2011. Web. 28 July 2011.

Margaret Atwood: The Year of the Flood. Web. 15 Jan. 2011.

Marien, Michael. "New Communications Technology: A Survey of Impacts and Issues." Hassan and Thomas 41–62. Print.

Marshall, P. David. *Celebrity and Power: Fame in Contemporary Culture*. Minneapolis: U of Minnesota P, 1997. Print.

Marshall, P., ed. *New Media Cultures*. London: Arnold, 2004. Print.

Martin, Sandra. "Atwood Interactive." *Globe and Mail*. 26 Aug. 2000: R1. Print.

Martin, Sandra. "B.C. Novelist Wrote a Cult Classic and Became A Lesbian Role Model." *Globe and Mail*. 29 November 2007: S8. Print.

Martin, Sandra. "Blanchett to Grace Atwood Adaptation." *Globe and Mail*. 18 July 2001. R4. Print.

Mayer, Debbie. *Literary Agents: The Essential Guide for Writers*. 1978. Foreword by Rosellen Brown. New York: Penguin, 1998. Print.

McCaig, JoAnn. "Alice Munro's Agency: The Virginia Barber Correspondence, 1976–83." *Essays on Canadian Writing* 66 (1998): 81–102. *Canadian Periodicals Index Quarterly*. Web. 6 June 2009.

McCaig. *Reading In: Alice Munro's Archives*. Waterloo: Wilfred Laurier UP, 2002. Print.

McCann, Fiona. "Characters Breathe New Lives Online." *Irish Times*. 29 Mar. 2010. Web. 31 Jan. 2011.

McCrumm, Robert. "Go Three Days Without Water and You Don't Have Any Human Rights: An Interview with Margaret Atwood." *Observer*. 28 Nov. 2010. Web. 2 Feb. 2011.

McGill, Robert. "Negotiations with the Living Archive." *Margaret Atwood: The Open Eye*. Ed. John Moss and Tobi Kozakewich. Ottawa: U of Ottawa P, 2006. 95–106. Print.

McHaney, Thomas L. "An Early 19th Century Literary Agent: James Lawson of New York." *Papers of the Bibliographical Society of America* 64 (1970): 177–92. Print.

McWilliams, Ellen. *Margaret Atwood and the Female Bildungsroman*. Farnham: Ashgate, 2009. Print.

Medley, Mark. "Licence to Deal." *National Post*. 13 Dec. 2008. Web. 5 Mar. 2009.

Medley, Mark. "Mark of an Editor." *National Post*. 21 Feb. 2009. Web. 20 May 2010.

Mole, Tom. *Byron's Romantic Celebrity: Industrial Culture and the Hermeneutic of Intimacy*. Basingstoke: Palgrave Macmillan, 2007. Print.

Monaco, James. *Celebrity: The Media as Image Makers*. New York: Delta, 1978. Print.

Moran, Joe. *Star Authors: Literary Celebrity in America*. London: Pluto, 2000. Print.

Morra, Linda. "'Vexed by the Crassness of Commerce': Jane Rule's Struggle for Literary Integrity and Freedom of Expression." *Canadian Literature* 205 (2010): 86–106. Print.

Mount, Nick. *When Canadian Literature Moved to New York*. Toronto: U of Toronto P, 2005. Print.

Mullan, John. "Rev. of *Oryx and Crake*." *Guardian*. 28 Apr. 2007: R6. Print.

Nestruck, J. Kelly. "In Big Oil's Shadow, Love and Light." *Globe and Mail*. 12 Feb. 2011. Web. 16 Feb. 2011.

Nguyen, Linda. "Author Atwood Leads the Charge to Save Toronto." *The Ottawa Citizen*. 7 Aug. 2011. Web. 20 Aug. 2011.

Nischik, Reingard, ed. *Margaret Atwood: Works and Impact*. Rochester: Camden House, 2000. Print.

Nudell, Roslyn. "A Frail Exterior Hides the Toughness in Atwood." *Winnipeg Free Press*. 17 Oct. 1979: 35. Print.

Okker, Patricia. "Editors." *American History Through Literature 1820–1870*. Ed. Janet Gabler-Hover and Robert Sattelmeyer. Detroit: Scribner's, 2006. 355–61. Print.

Ommundsen, Wenche. "From the Altar to the Market-Place and Back Again: Understanding Literary Celebrity." Redmond and Holmes, *Stardom and Celebrity*. 244–55. Print.

Panofsky, Ruth. "'Don't Let Me Do It!': Mazo de la Roche and her Publishers." *International Journal of Canadian Studies* 11 (1995): 171–84. Print.

Parker, George L. *The Beginnings of the Book Trade in Canada*. Toronto: U of Toronto P, 1985. Print.

Peat, Don. "Atwood Fires Back at Doug Ford." *Toronto Sun*. 2 Aug. 2011. Web. 5 Aug. 2011.

Percy, Owen. "GGs and Gillers and Griffins, Oh My!" *Transplanter le Canada: Semailles / Transplanting Canada: Seedlings*. Ed. Marie Carrière and Jerry White. Edmonton: Canadian Literature Centre, 2010. 138–44. Print.

Percy, Owen. *Prize Possession: Literary Awards, The GGs, and the CanLit Nation*. Forthcoming from Wilfrid Laurier UP.

Posner, Michael. "Surviving the Nazis Helped Make Her Unstoppable." *Globe and Mail*. 5 Mar. 2010. Web. 20 Feb. 2011.

Quill, Greg. "Atwood Signs on with U.S. Digital Publisher Specializing in Short-Form Literature for Online Readers." *Toronto Star*. 7 Mar. 2012. Web. 8 Mar. 2012.

Radford, Ceri. "Dash It All – Give Jane Austen the Last Word." *Daily Telegraph*. 20 Aug. 2010. Web. 15 Feb. 2011.

Reid, Melanie. "Invention Brings Writers Closer to Far-Flung Places." *Times* 15 June 2007: H37. Print.

Rein, Irving, et al. *High Visibility: Transforming Your Personal and Professional Brand*. 2nd ed. New York: McGraw-Hill, 2006. Print.

Renzetti, Elizabeth. "Atwood Awarded Arts Medal." *Globe and Mail*. 14 Jan. 1997: C1-C2. Print.

Reynolds, Paul R. *The Middle Man: The Adventures of a Literary Agent*. New York: William Morrow, 1972. Print.

Rider, David. "Margaret Atwood Fights Library Cuts, Crashes Petition Server." *Toronto Star*. 22 July 2011. Web. 28 July 2011.

Righton, Barbara. "People." *Maclean's*. 4 Oct. 1982: 36. Print.

Roberts, Gillian. *Prizing Literature: The Celebration and Circulation of National Culture*. Toronto: U of Toronto P, 2011. Print.

Rojek, Chris. *Celebrity*. London: Reaktion, 2001. Print.

Ross, Anna. (@_Anna_Ross_). "If elected, will you serve?" 6 Sept. 2010, 10:42 p.m. Tweet.

Ross, Val. "Atwood Industry Goes Global." *Globe and Mail.* 7 Sept. 1996: A1. Print.

"Rough Crossings: The Cutting of Raymond Carver." *The New Yorker* 24 Dec. 2007. Web. 10 Sept. 2009.

Rubbo, Michael, dir. *Once in August*. NFB, 1984. Film.

Samson, Natalie. "Atwood Followers Crash TPL Petition Website." *Quill & Quire* Quillblog. 22 July 2011. Web. 28 July 2011.

Scherf, Kathleen. "A Legacy of Canadian Cultural Tradition and the Small Press: The Case of Talonbooks." *Studies in Canadian Literature* 25.1 (2000): 131–49. Print.

Smith, Zadie. *Changing My Mind: Occasional Essays*. Toronto: Hamish Hamilton, 2009. Print.

Solecki, Sam, ed. *Imagining Canadian Literature: Selected Letters of Jack McClelland*. Toronto: Key Porter, 1998. Print.

Spadoni, Carl. "Publishers' Catalogues and a Chariot on Yonge Street: Marketing Canadian Books." Historical Perspectives on Canadian Publishing. McMaster University. Web. 17 Mar. 2011.

"Starr Power: Atwood Novel on the Way." *Globe and Mail.* 12 Jan. 2008: R2. Print.

Stevenson, Mark. "Written Locally, Marketing Globally: Atwood as Product." *Globe and Mail.* 4 Nov. 2000: B7. Print.

Stoffman, Judy. "Jack McClelland, 81: A Man Who Loved Writers." *Toronto Star*. 15 June 2004. Web. 15 Aug. 2011.

Sullivan, Jane. "A Brief Look at Mini-Masterpieces." *Age* (Melbourne). 31 Oct. 2009. Web. 13 Feb. 2011.

Sullivan, Rosemary. *The Red Shoes: Margaret Atwood Starting Out*. Toronto: HarperCollins, 1998. Print.

"Syngrafii." Longpen.com. Web. 14 Feb. 2011.

"Tim Hortons & Canadian Forces Announce Opening in Afghanistan." *Tim Hortons*. 8 March 2006. Web. 12 Aug. 2011.

"TOC 2011: Margaret Atwood, 'The Publishing Pie: An Author's View.'" *Margaret Atwood: Year of the Flood*. 15 Feb. 2011. Web. 16 Feb. 2011.

Tsirbas, Christos. "The LongPen: From World-Famous Novelist to High-Tech Entrepreneur." *Daily Galaxy*. 3 Dec. 2007. Web. 14 Feb. 2011.

Turbide, Diane. "Amazing Atwood." *Maclean's* 109:30 (1996). *Canadian Points of View Reference Centre*. Web. 20 Feb. 2009.

Turner, Graeme. *Understanding Celebrity*. London: Sage, 2004. Print.

Turner, Graeme, Frances Bonner, and P. David Marshall. *Fame Games: The Production of Celebrity in Australia*. Cambridge: Cambridge UP, 2000. Print.

"The Tweetable Woman." Banner headline. *Globe and Mail*. 2 Sept. 2009: R1. Print.

Ursula K. Le Guin. Web. 20 Mar. 2009.

"Very Short Stories." *Wired* 14: 11 Nov. 2006. Web. 10 Feb. 2011.

"Vital Force Gone: Award-Winning Novelist, Screenwriter, Paul Quarrington Dead." *Toronto Sun*. 22 Jan. 2010. Web. 20 Feb. 2011.

Wagner, Erica. Column. *Times*. 20 Feb. 2010. Web. 12 Feb. 2011.

Wagner, Erica. "The Goddess of Small Things." *Times*. 31 July 2010. Web. 16 Feb. 2011.

Wagner, Erica. "Margaret Atwood: The Conversation." *Times*. 15 Aug. 2009. Web. 3 May 2010.

Wagner, Vit. "Flood and Famine and Fans with Flu." *Toronto Star*. 12 Sept. 2009. Web. 2 Feb. 2011.

Wall, Cheryl A. "Toni Morrison: Editor and Teacher." *The Cambridge Companion to Toni Morrison*. Ed. Justine Tally. Cambridge: CUP, 2000. 139–148. Print.

Wolff, Janet. *The Social Production of Art*. London: Macmillan, 1981. Print.

Wolframe, PhebeAnn. "Invented Interventions: Atwood's Apparatuses of Self-Extension and Celebrity Control." *Margaret Atwood Studies* 2.1 (2008): 13–28. Print.

Wong, Jan. "An Audience With 'A Queen.'" *Globe and Mail*. 7 Sept. 1996: A6. Print.

"Writer Margaret Atwood Unveils 'Long-Distance' Pen." Fox News. 7 Mar. 2006. Web. 14 Feb. 2011.

York, Lorraine. *Literary Celebrity in Canada*. Toronto: U of Toronto P, 2007. Print.

Index